Stockholm

Kragerø

Mem

Fraserburgh

Kungälv

Corpach

Inverness

North

Sea

Portaferry

Dun Laoghaire

EUROPE

TIC

N

Madeira Is.

SAILING

SAILING TO FREEDOM

This edition, issued in 1954, is for members of the Companion Book Club, 8 Long Acre, London WC2, from which address particulars of membership may be obtained. The book is published by arrangement with the original publishers, Phoenix House Ltd.

"A blessed companion is a book"—JERROLD

SAILING
TO FREEDOM

*

VOLDEMAR VEEDAM

AND

CARL B. WALL

THE COMPANION BOOK CLUB

LONDON

*Made and printed in Great Britain
for The Companion Book Club (Odhams Press Ltd.)
by Odhams (Watford) Limited
Watford, Herts
S.854.ZSA*

ILLUSTRATIONS

Drawing of the *Erma*   *page* 30

Maia, Nora, Aunt Juliana, Arvid and the
  four children   *facing page* 64

Receiving supplies off shore from the *John
  P. Gray*   65

The *Erma*, drying her sails   96

Ellen and Grandma F. at Norfolk   96

The *Erma* at the end of her voyage   97

★ I ★

No ONE, not even an N.K.V.D. agent, watching the *Erma's* departure from the small Swedish port of Smedslatten, could possibly have suspected that this was the beginning of a transatlantic voyage. I couldn't believe it myself. The whole thing had the air of a hastily conceived family picnic.

The *Erma* herself was but thirty-seven feet long and her decks were only about two feet above the water; she looked like a fat dumpy old lady unable to waddle across Stockholm Bay, to say nothing of the Atlantic, yet sixteen of us Estonian refugees, seven men, five women and four children, were crowded on her in an attempt to flee our Russian oppressors and escape to America.

* * *

The story really began that March evening of 1945 when Harry Paalberg and I sat by the window of his apartment, half listening to the Tallin Soviet radio's version of Shostakovich's restless *First Symphony*, and watching the transparent veil of late spring snow drift across Stockholm. It was nearly twilight. The lights of the city were beginning to wink on, and we could see the blurred red and white firefly glow of traffic moving slowly through the storm.

Yuta, Harry's three-year-old daughter, curled sleepily in his lap. From time to time, Harry rambled on with an apparently endless story about a duck and a chicken which, as far as I could see, made little sense.

From the kitchen we could hear the clatter of supper dishes and the voices of Harry's mother and his young wife, Ellen.

The last movement of the symphony faded. Harry shifted Yuta slightly in his arms and looked at his wrist watch. It was time for the Tallin news and this was what we had been waiting for. The calm voice, which we had both come to hate so bitterly, tuned in clearly. There were the usual five minutes of distorted news reports and then a sudden announcement which caused Harry and me to sit up.

"And now," said the voice primly, "there is a special message for the thousands of Baltic refugees who have fled to Sweden to escape the German oppressor. The Soviet Union is welcoming back these refugees. For those good patriots of the Baltic countries who choose to return at this time, there are excellent positions now available in government offices, in museums and universities. There are splendid opportunities within the Soviet Union's factories, on the farms, and in the fishing industries. Those who return will be welcomed and granted full citizenship in the Soviet Union. . . ."

Harry reached over with a grunt and snapped off the radio. Little Yuta stirred restlessly.

"What do you make of that, Val?" he asked me. "After months of yammering at us as fascists and war criminals, the Soviets suddenly decide we're good patriots."

"I don't like it," I said.

"Neither do I. There's something in the wind. This new line fits in with the pressure on the Swedish Foreign Office to ship us back. What I'm wondering is how long the Swedes can resist."

"It's a small country," I shrugged. "And it's close to the Soviets. Who can tell what will happen?"

8

Ellen came in with the coffee and scooped Yuta from Harry's arms.

"What's the matter with you two?" she laughed. "You look gloomier than ever."

In the soft light of the single lamp, with Yuta's blonde head close to Ellen's own golden hair, her face flushed from the warmth of the kitchen, Ellen looked sixteen rather than twenty-three. Nine years younger than Harry, she was one of the gayest, happiest creatures I had ever met. Nothing worried her. Not even the Russians.

Harry explained. "The news is bad to-night."

"It always is, isn't it?" Ellen smiled.

"Well," said Harry, "it's worse than usual to-night. The folks in Moscow have decided they want to be friends with us. They want us to go back to Estonia and be good citizens of the Soviet Union."

Ellen folded Yuta over her shoulder and headed for the bedroom.

"And what's wrong with that?" she called back. "It seems to me you're both rather difficult to please. You don't like it when they. . . ."

The rest was lost behind the bedroom door. Harry grinned at me, and picked up his coffee. Then came a sharp rap on the hallway door. Harry's head jerked fearfully. After four or five years in an occupied country, you get like that no matter how good your nerves may be normally.

Harry opened the door a few precautionary inches and then threw it wide. It was Maia Andre, his cousin, a tall, broad-shouldered young woman of twenty-seven. Maia was not one for social niceties. With a brief wave of the hand in my general direction, she turned to Harry.

"Well," she said, "if something isn't done and done

right away, we're all going to find ourselves on the way to Siberia! Look at this. It came in to-day's mail."

From the depths of her voluminous handbag, Maia produced an official-looking envelope and passed it to Harry. Mrs. Paalberg and Ellen, hearing Maia's voice, hurried back from the other rooms.

"Listen to this, all of you," Maia commanded. "Read it aloud, Harry."

Harry began in his quiet voice:

"It's from the Swedish Foreign Office and addressed to Maia. It says, 'It is the wish of this government that you make immediate preparations to return to your native country of Estonia at the earliest opportunity. Authorities of the Soviet Union have given assurance to all Baltic refugees that there will be no persecution, no reprisals against those who return voluntarily at this time. . . .'"

Harry looked up from the letter. I saw the tips of his ears redden as they always did when he was deeply disturbed.

"You say you received this to-day?" he asked Maia.

"In this afternoon's post."

Harry said, "Evidently they are sending them out alphabetically. It won't be too long before we'll be getting ours."

He turned to me.

"This is what I was afraid of, Val" he said. "Something like this. It's all part of a pattern. The formal invitation to return to the Soviet Union."

Maia took the letter from him.

"But what are we going to do?" she asked. "There must be something we can do. We certainly can't allow ourselves to be shipped back like cattle."

She stood there in the centre of the room, one hand on her hip, glaring at me as though I held the answer.

10

Maia was a woman of action. It was she, alone, who had so successfully planned and executed every detail of the escape of her mother and herself from the Nazi occupation in Estonia. After a hazardous small-boat flight across the Baltic to Finland, she had enlisted with the Finnish Army's Women's Auxiliary, the Lota. Maia definitely was not a woman to sit quietly, wringing her hands in anguish.

"What is there we can do?" I asked. "Walk across the North Sea to England? Even if we could walk on water, we are helpless without visas. About the only thing we can do is to hang on here as long as the Swedes give us refuge."

Maia wrinkled her nose.

"And then allow ourselves to be led back with a Soviet noose around our necks, I suppose?" she snorted.

I shrugged and looked at Harry. He had walked restlessly across the room and was staring again out of the window, his hands behind his back, his legs spread wide as though he were standing on the bridge of a rolling ship.

I knew only too well what return to a Soviet-occupied Estonia meant for Harry and his family. At the outbreak of war, when Soviet forces first swarmed into our country, Harry's father, Captain Rudolf Paalberg, Estonian captain and ship owner, had effectively thumbed his nose at Moscow.

He had been on the high seas with one of his company's freighters. The Russians had ordered him by wireless to set course for the nearest Soviet consulate and surrender his ship. Instead, Captain Paalberg had characteristically headed the other way. When he arrived in New York harbour, a Russian delegation attempted to board the freighter and take possession, but Captain Paalberg stuck out his chin, heaved his mighty shoulders and personally threw the delegation over the rail. Later, despite Moscow court action, he loaned the vessel to the United States Maritime Commission for use during the war. Captain Paalberg himself was still in America.

As a result the entire Paalberg family, seamen for generations, were marked by the Russians as "undesirables." One of Harry's uncles had been deported to Siberia for slave labour, and other members of the shipping firm had gradually disappeared under the Soviet "nationalization."

Harry, of course, realized fully what sort of treatment his mother, Ellen, and little Yuta would get from the U.S.S.R. After hiding for months in north Estonian forests he managed to bring his family to Sweden. But even here he was not safe. Often he had told me that he would not permit the Russians to capture him alive. He always carried a razor-sharp seaman's knife to ensure his quick death. Harry had no illusions.

I knew, too, the depth of Harry's feeling for his family. A slight and mild-mannered man, he was actually deeply emotional. But very little of this emotion ever showed on the surface; he seldom talked about himself or revealed his inner thoughts. It was only through almost constant companionship, dating back to our school days, that I had come to know him as well as I did.

Now Harry turned away from the window and faced us, his hands still behind his back.

"As Maia puts it," he said "there is little point in our staying on here. Sooner or later, the Russians will force us to return."

From the way he spoke, I knew that Harry had a

12

plan of action. I knew also that whatever it was, it would be carried through to its logical conclusion. That was Harry's way.

"So," he continued, "I think we should escape from Sweden as quickly as possible. With thousands of fugitives flooding every consulate in Stockholm, it will be impossible for us to get visas without waiting possibly for years; so we will go without visas and take our chances."

"But where?" Ellen asked. "Where will we go? And how will we get there?"

"To America," Harry answered quietly. "We will sail there in a small boat."

I drew in my breath sharply. With almost any other man, I might have suspected that this was so much idle talk, a dream put into words. But not with Harry.

"Where will you get a boat?" I asked.

"Buy it," he answered.

"With what?"

I knew that Captain Paalberg sent his family a small allowance each month from America, but the amount was limited by Swedish *valuta* regulations and it was barely enough to live on.

Harry said, "We'll find a way. It won't take too much. Here, along the coast, I've seen a dozen fishing boats in which we could easily make the trip. You know, it's not necessary to buy a liner to cross the Atlantic. A forty-foot sloop with a broad beam and marconi rig would do the trick nicely—and an auxiliary engine to see us through the calms at sea and the harbour waters in America."

I glanced quickly at Harry's mother. She was looking at him with the pride of two generations of sailors and ship owners in her piercing eyes. She nodded her decisive Roman profile. On many voyages both by sail and steam, she had accompanied her husband, and she saw nothing fantastic in the notion.

Ellen was delighted.

"It's a wonderful idea," she said. "Think of it, America! Grandfather Paalberg will be able to see Yuta for the first time."

But Maia, as usual, was practical.

"How much do you think it will cost, Harry?" she asked.

"I don't know. Perhaps four thousand kroner, perhaps five thousand. It's hard to tell until I start shopping around."

"That's a lot of money," Maia said, "but we can raise it. We'll all take jobs, work overtime, save everything we earn."

Harry said, "We should be able to raise some of the money through shares. We need a crew and at least one experienced seaman, someone who knows navigation. The larger the crew, the more money we will be able to put into the boat."

He paused to consider another angle.

"But don't approach anyone until I give the word," he warned. "Our plans must be kept secret. If the Swedish Foreign Office learns of it, they won't let us leave the country. The Soviet would raise the devil with them. And if the Russians hear of it—anything might happen. There are a good many N.K.V.D. agents prowling around Stockholm. We all know that."

"I'll keep my mouth shut," said Maia looking at me.

"And so will I," I said defensively.

*　　*　　*

I left the Paalberg apartment long before midnight in time to catch the last bus for Fridtorp, the Estonian refugee camp which had been set up six miles outside

14

the city on the pine-wooded shores of Stockholm Bay. The snow had stopped falling and the night was now cold and clear with a quarter moon riding low in the west. As the bus jolted across the quiet city toward the suburbs, I felt, for the first time in years, a surge of hope deep inside me.

At thirty-two my life had been fairly typical of the thousands of Estonians whose pattern of existence had been hopelessly shattered by the Russian-German occupations of the last four years. When the Red Army first rolled across our border in 1940, I had been twenty-eight, just beginning my career as a journalist. At the University of Tartu I had graduated in history and there is nothing more useless than a historian under Soviet occupation.

As a book-keeper in one of the Soviet nationalized garages I managed to feed my mother and myself until the Germans drove out the Russians and we had a new conqueror and a new set of rules. By the summer of 1941 we million-odd Estonians were beginning to feel that we had lost control of our own destiny for ever. We were like so many ants who had built their hill in the middle of a busy highway.

Rather than work at the job the Nazis offered me —they called it "Archives of Actual History" but it was purely propaganda for the New Order—I decided to do what so many thousands were doing—flee across the Baltic to Finland. There I hoped to get a job, a place to live—then I would return for Mother. So I ran the blockade. On a windy, moonless night, fifty of us refugees made the sixty-mile trip across the Gulf of Finland in a fast motor-boat.

Good jobs were scarce in Finland, and furthermore, there were rumours that it would not be long before the Nazis would take over there too, so I made my way to Sweden, working as a salmon fisherman along the West Finnish coast. From a friendly fishing boat skirting the Swedish coast one could easily swim ashore. The kind, matter-of-fact Swedish police patrol found swimming Estonians as commonplace as sardines.

After I managed to get a job with the Swedish Institute of Handicrafts in Stockholm, I made another secret voyage across the Baltic to Estonia for my mother. But she had changed her mind; she said she had not too long to live and she wanted to be buried in the family graveyard beside my father. She warned me that it was dangerous to stay too long, so the following night I made the return trip to Sweden. A month later the Red Army rolled back across Estonia. That was the last talk I had with my mother, the last I have even heard of her.

The return of the Russians was the beginning of a mass migration. Thirty thousand Estonians scrambled across the Baltic to Finland and Sweden. They made the hazardous voyage in motor-boats, sailing boats, rowing boats. Some even tried to fashion crude rafts. German and Russian submarines had a field day. They fired on anything that came in their gun-sights. On those stormy autumn days the pounding surf washed hundreds of bodies ashore in Sweden; old and young; men, women, and children who did not wish to become citizens of the Soviet Union.

*　　　*　　　*

Now the U.S.S.R. was stretching out its tentacles across the Baltic. We must flee again. When the bus dropped me off at Fridtorp and rumbled off into the quiet moonlit night I felt strangely exhilarated and quite sleepless.

There were some five hundred Estonian refugees

living in this summer resort settlement which the Swedes had so generously set aside for us. What would they say, I wondered, if they knew of our plan to cross the Atlantic to the New World, to a new life, to a free existence?

Only a few days before, the Soviet authorities had persuaded the Swedish Foreign Office to take a poll in Fridtorp. How many, they asked, wanted to return to Estonia and become citizens of the U.S.S.R.? They would be guaranteed safety, good jobs, a decent living. The result of the poll had been unanimous. Not one of the five hundred asked to return.

2

ON THE hot May morning when Harry took me down to Smedslatten for my first look at the *Erma,* I was, to put it mildly, not very favourably impressed. She was short and beamy. Her topsides were weatherbeaten, with the paint peeling off in scales. For a long time, I stood there, staring down at her from the dock, unable to speak.

"Well," said Harry finally, "what do you think of her, Val?"

There was considerable pride in his voice and I hated to hurt his feelings.

"You know boats and I know violins," I said. "But don't you think she's, well, a little on the short side?"

"She's thirty-six and a half feet. It's the wide beam —thirteen feet—that makes her look short to you."

"I thought you said you were going to get one at least forty feet?"

Harry shrugged.

"This was the best we could do with the money we had. She cost us forty-five hundred kroner."

"Forty-five hundred kroner!"

It was impossible to keep the dismay out of my voice. "Why, that's fantastic. That's all the money we have. Forty-five hundred kroner for a leaky old rowing boat!"

Harry reddened.

"She's not a leaky old rowing boat, Val. She's a damned good seaworthy sloop—or she will be when we get her in shape. Take a look!"

He hopped down from the dock on to the *Erma's*

18

foredeck. It was a good hop since the deck was barely three feet above the water and the dock had obviously been built to accommodate boats of a respectable size.

Harry leaned over the side and rapped hard against the planking.

"Hear that?" he asked. "She's sound, let me tell you. White oak from stem to stern. She may need a little paint, but underneath she's solid. Solid as she can be."

My attention wandered from the planking to the water. It seemed incredibly close. Amidships there was less than two feet of freeboard. I thought of the Atlantic swells.

"Doesn't she lie pretty low in the water?" I asked. "Look, you can actually reach over the side and touch it—the same as you can in a rowing boat."

Harry laughed.

"That's all right, Val. She rides the waves. On top of them, like a duck."

I peered over the side and remembered having read somewhere of a lead keel weighing several tons.

"I suppose it's the keel that keeps her from capsizing in a storm?" I said.

"Well, not exactly," Harry answered. "The broad beam takes care of that. Of course, she must be properly handled in a storm."

"Do you mean there is no keel? Why, I thought all ocean-going sailing craft had tremendous lead keels."

"You're thinking of racing yachts," said Harry. "The principle is different here. The *Erma* has a keel, of course, but it's an oaken one of about twelve inches."

"Then what's to prevent her from tipping over in a storm?" I asked.

"The broad beam," said Harry patiently.

19

I looked up at the naked mast. It seemed out of all proportion. Like a duck with a three-foot neck.

"She's marconi-rigged," Harry said, following my glance. "That means a single, triangular mainsail. Makes for fairly easy handling in any kind of weather."

"It looks top-heavy to me," I said, "but then you know about these things and I don't. Where's the engine? That's something I might be able to understand."

"That," said Harry, "is one of the things we still have to buy."

"Do you mean," I asked, "that you paid forty-five hundred kroner for this—without an engine?"

Harry nodded.

"We had to, Val. Good boats are scarce these days. I hope to pick up a second-hand diesel. We can install it ourselves."

A few strides brought us to the centre of the boat. Harry threw open two small doors and slid back a wooden hatch cover.

"This," said Harry proudly, "is the main cabin."

I followed him down four short steps into a dank compartment about nine feet wide, seven feet long and five feet high. We stood there for a moment, crouching like two hunch-backs.

"You didn't buy this from a dwarf, did you?" I asked, looking at the narrow bunks on either side.

Harry ignored me.

"It's snug," he said, "and watertight. Do you notice how that skylight is reinforced with steel wire?"

I looked down instead. The floorboards were actually afloat. My feet were already wet. I had decided not to be too critical but now I was honestly stunned.

"Good God, Harry!" I said, "this thing must leak like a sieve."

"Naturally," said Harry. "She's in the water for the first time in years and the wood has to take up. Another week or so and she'll be tight as a drum."

He lay down on one of the wooden bunks and stretched out.

"How do you like this?" he smiled up at me. "Pretty comfortable, eh? And there's another cabin forward just like this. Built to sleep four."

I did some amateur calculating. Since our talk in Harry's apartment, an entire new family had been added. There was now Arvid Kuun and his wife, Nora. To say nothing of their three offspring whose names I did not yet know. That made twelve!

Harry, without too much effort, was reading my mind.

"The four youngsters won't take up much room," he said. "They're babies really. Small."

I didn't say anything. I was wondering where I was supposed to sleep.

"At sea," Harry continued, "at least two of us will always be on watch. Of course, we will have to make some alterations. For example, a few more boards alongside these will make double bunks."

Weary of crouching, I stretched out on the other bunk and stared up at the dirty, cracked skylight.

"As I've said before, Harry," I began, "I suppose you know what you're doing, but it seems to me that twelve is——"

"Arvid is a good seaman," said Harry. "He holds a master's certificate and knows navigation. We need a man like that. Need him badly."

"But wouldn't it be possible," I asked, "to find a navigator with a small family? Maybe, a single navigator?"

"Possibly," said Harry, "but Arvid is an old friend

of mine. He was a harbour pilot, one of the finest seamen in Estonia. Besides, it was Arvid who found this boat and persuaded the owner to sell her to us."

Persuaded, I said to myself, can hardly be the right word.

"How old is she?" I asked after a few moments of silence.

"Who?"

"Erma."

There was another lengthy silence and then Harry said:

"I don't know exactly, Val. It's rather difficult to tell. Arvid says the owner himself didn't know. She's what the Swedes call a *koster*. Arvid says she was originally built for mail service along the coast. Then, for a long time, she was a sort of family pleasure boat. She has old-fashioned lines but she's seaworthy, Val. Damned seaworthy."

I waited a minute and then I said:

"I was wondering how old she was."

"Oh, I don't know," Harry mumbled. "Maybe fifty years. Maybe sixty. But her age doesn't make any difference, Val. She's sound. That's what counts."

I looked up. Through that skylight even the cloudless sky looked grey. I wondered absently how many centuries it had been since the skylight was last cleaned.

"You see," Harry continued persuasively, "a good boat is like a good wife, Val. You don't want to let appearances fool you. She hasn't been painted in the last few years because she's been hauled out. The important thing is that she is fundamentally sound."

"Beauty," I said, "is only skin deep."

Harry ignored the sarcasm.

"That's right," he agreed enthusiastically. "As I say,

a good boat is like a good wife; after she gets past a certain age it's not her looks that count but how sound she is."

On the deck above we heard a sudden thump and then the sound of light footsteps. Harry sat up in his bunk.

"That must be Arvid. He's been looking all over Stockholm for a second-hand engine and said he would come out this morning if he got the chance. Hope he's found it. Come on."

Arvid Kuun greeted us with a wide grin. He was a wiry man of thirty-seven with good shoulders, a deeply tanned face and the whitest teeth I have ever seen. On top of his black hair he wore a seaman's cap. I liked him at once.

"Well, what do you think of her?" he asked, with a wave that swept the *Erma's* decks.

"Fine," I lied, "fine."

He looked at me quizzically.

"She's sound," I said.

We both laughed and he clapped me lightly on the shoulder.

"Good boy," he said. "Harry tells me you've never been to sea before. This should be quite an experience."

I laughed again because I could think of nothing to say. Quite an experience, indeed!

Arvid turned to Harry.

"I've found just the engine for us. An 8-h.p. semi-diesel."

Harry's eyes lighted.

"Good going, Arvid!"

"Two thousand kroner."

The smile on Harry's face was replaced by a bleak, frozen look.

"Two thousand kroner! Why, that's impossible, Arvid. It might as well be two hundred thousand kroner! Don't you realize we're broke? Stony broke."

Arvid sat down on the roof of the forward cabin and took a much-folded slip of paper from his trousers pocket.

"I've been working things out, Harry," he said. "We're going to need a lot more capital."

Despite himself, Harry smiled.

"You're a regular genius, Arvid."

"I mean," Arvid continued, "that we're going to need a good deal more than we can ever hope to raise with the present set-up. We're working now just as hard as we can. Maia is carrying two jobs, Nora is making wallets, purses, all sorts of fine leather work. Val here is working days at the Institute and nights at odd jobs. But even with everyone working day and night, it will be months before we can save enough to fit out the *Erma*. And by that time it may be too late. Time is working against us—not only with the Russians but with the weather, too."

Harry nodded soberly.

"If only the Swedes would relax their *valuta* regulations," he said, "and let my father send us more money from America."

Arvid consulted his sheet of paper.

"The way I figure it," he said, "it will take at least two hundred kroner for caulking and paint. Three hundred for a second-hand compass and sextant. Four hundred for water tanks. At least another hundred for a wheel to replace that tiller. A hundred for manila rope—if we can find it. Two thousand for the engine, to say nothing of diesel oil—if we can get it."

Harry groaned.

24

"And then," Arvid continued relentlessly, "there's the matter of stores. We will need plenty of canned milk for the children, potatoes, tinned beef . . ."

"I know," Harry broke in despondently, "I go over that list every night in my sleep. As I say, I've been hoping the *valuta* regulations will be lifted."

"But there's another way to raise the money," said Arvid. "The only way that I can see."

Harry lifted his head.

"How is that?"

"Take more people with us," Arvid said triumphantly. "Increase our crew."

This time I joined Harry in the groan.

"But we already have twelve in a boat that was built for four," I said.

"This isn't exactly a luxury cruise," said Arvid pointedly.

"No," said Harry, "but the thing's impossible. Where are we going to put more people? It's been hard enough trying to figure out space for twelve."

Arvid swung himself lightly off the roof.

"Look here," he said, "I have it all planned. Suppose we take just two more? That will make fourteen. In the cabins we can build shelves alongside the regular bunks. In the main cabin we can put Harry, Ellen, Yuta, Harry's mother, Maia, and her mother—what's her name again?"

"Mrs. Altenbrun," I said. "And she has *arthritis*."

"The sea voyage may help her," Arvid said cheerfully. "I've heard of some remarkable cures due to sea voyages."

"Not for arthritis," I said.

But Arvid was back to the main subject.

"That will make six in the main cabin. Three in each bunk. Now, for the forward cabin, there will be

25

the Kuun family. There are only five of us and we will do very nicely."

He looked at me speculatively. I waited somewhat tensely. It seemed certain I was not going to be a cabin passenger.

"I know about the man who must always be on watch," I said.

Arvid grinned.

"There's going to be a bunk for you, too, Val. That's the best part of the plan." He turned to Harry. "We'll certainly need a shelter for the engine, Harry."

Harry nodded sagely. So that was it. I was going to sleep with the engine. An exotic bedfellow.

"So," Arvid concluded triumphantly, "the idea occurred to me why not build a third cabin in the cockpit?"

He took a few steps along the deck to a point just behind the main cabin.

"We'll put the engine in here," he explained, "and over the engine we'll build sort of a booby hatch—a compartment with doors and a sliding cover. On either side of the engine there will be room for a little bunk —perhaps five or six feet long."

"Snug," I said.

"It's a good idea," said Harry. "We'll be able to keep the engine dry in any kind of weather."

The bunks, I took it, were purely incidental.

"You see," Arvid continued enthusiastically, "the two boys I have in mind happen to be bachelors. Men without families."

"That's a good thing," I said. "Otherwise the engine might be a little crowded."

"You have two men in mind?" asked Harry.

"I have," said Arvid. "Two men with money. At least a thousand kroner each. Good men, too, for a trip like this. One of them is a fine mechanic. He was a pilot in the Estonian Air Force and flew with the Norwegians against the Germans."

"What are their names?" Harry asked.

"The Reinholm brothers. Paul and Lembit. I believe you know Paul, Harry. He said he sailed with you years ago in the *Tormilind*."

The *Tormilind*, or *Stormbird* had been a four-masted barquentine in which Harry first sailed under his father's command.

"Of course I remember," said Harry. "He sailed with us to South America for a load of greenwood. But that was a hundred years ago. I understood he had been killed by the Nazis."

"No. Both he and Lembit have been working here in Stockholm for the last few months."

Harry's objections obviously had faded fast.

"Paul would make a good addition to any crew," he said. "He's an excellent seaman."

"So would Lembit," I said. "He has a thousand kroner."

"And that," said Arvid with a grin, "should give him a master's ticket."

He looked up suddenly and his face became grim. A small, middle-aged man in a brown suit stood on the dock directly above us. He wore a battered felt hat, pulled low over his eyes. The reflected sunlight from the water glittered on the thick lenses of his spectacles. I wondered how long he had been standing there. We had heard nothing. He had evidently walked very quietly on the wooden planking. He watched us for a few minutes and opened his mouth as though to say something, but thought better of it and scuttled off toward the shore. I glanced at Harry. Was he thinking the same thing? N.K.V.D., maybe third or fourth class but still secret police smelling around?

"I don't like it," Harry said soberly. "He may make trouble for us with the Swedes and stop us before we even get started. We'll probably need some sort of clearance papers."

Arvid looked after the little man until he disappeared.

"Well," he said with a shrug, "there's no sense worrying about it. Let's get to work."

* 3 *

THE REFITTING (or rebuilding) of the *Erma* was done in a well-protected, densely wooded cove in Smedslatten, forty-five minutes by suburban tram-car from Stockholm. Very little breeze penetrated the half-moon peninsula of pines, and the mean temperature of the *Erma's* decks in those weeks was about that of the average oven.

Harry, Arvid, Paul and Lembit worked in their shorts and by early July they looked as though they had already been across the Atlantic—and back. The Reinholm brothers were good workmen. Paul, the aviator, was a tall, blond, dashing fellow with the restless grey-blue eyes of an adventurer. He could do anything; he was a mechanic, an improviser, a man of action, a good fellow to have around, but impatient and moody. Lembit, his younger brother, was a quiet young man with a dry sense of humour. Usually he worked silently, almost grimly, but occasionally his reserve gave way to fits of boyish exuberance. He was an accomplished linguist and a good mathematician. An attractive boy—I felt I was going to like him.

By this time, with the summer slipping by so swiftly, all four men had been forced to quit their regular jobs in Stockholm and were now working around the clock on the *Erma*. Through the long days of the Scandinavian summer they laboured for sixteen hours at a stretch, pausing only to munch a sandwich or take a quick, cooling dip.

Since Harry had decided it would be better for me to keep drawing regular weekly pay from the Institute,

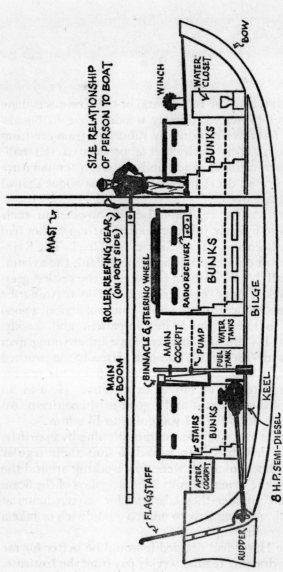

The *Erma*: overall length 36' 6".

I went out to Smedslatten only in the evenings and at week-ends.

A lot had been done but the old lady was still far from ready. Her thirsty topsides had soaked up coat after coat of grey paint. The after cabin had been built in the middle of the long cockpit and cut it into two shorter ones, the steering cockpit forward and the after cockpit abaft it. This after cabin that Arvid had designed was a masterpiece of Lilliputian architecture. By cutting a hole in the floor for the engine, he had extended the cabin space down to the bilge which he covered with floor boards. The superstructure was four feet wide and three feet long and rose about eighteen inches above the deck level.

The primary purpose of the after cabin, as Arvid had pointed out, was to shelter the engine which would extend under the cockpit. The sleeping accommodation for Paul, Lembit, and myself consisted of two shelves, cunningly built beneath deck level on either side of the engine space. These were pressed tight against the *Erma's* frames and were approximately five feet long and two feet wide. Since the three of us were six-footers, I could see that the business of going to bed was going to be something of a trick.

Entrance to this spacious cabin was achieved by pushing back a slide on the roof and opening two small doors which faced the stern—and bending yourself almost double. Ventilation, very incidentally, was provided by two small windows in the forward end, opening on to the cockpit. Without these, I suppose, the engine might have suffocated.

From a shipyard in Smedslatten, Harry and Arvid had bought a second-hand steering wheel. It was a beautiful thing of dark mahogany with a brass hub and six graceful spokes. This had been set in place just forward of the after cabin in a two-foot masonite box and was hooked up with the tiller by half-inch wire rope. The tiller was still in place for emergency use in case anything went wrong with the wheel.

The compass, set in a weather-stained brass binnacle, was fastened to the top of the box directly behind the wheel. To look at the compass the helmsman was obliged to squint backwards over his shoulder. This unorthodox and highly inconvenient arrangement was necessitated by the cramped space between the main and after cabins.

"It's something like looking backwards to see where you're going," Arvid said, "but we'll get used to it after a while. We'll have to."

The semi-diesel had not yet been installed. We had given the owner a substantial down payment and were making regular weekly contributions, but the engine was still some five hundred kroner away. Our calculations had been upset by the high cost of the water and fuel tanks which came to more than six hundred kroner instead of the estimated four hundred.

*   *   *

One Sunday morning, toward the middle of July, Harry asked me to bring his mother, Ellen, Maia, and Mrs. Altenbrun to Smedslatten for their first look at the *Erma*. The ladies packed lunch boxes. For a time we enjoyed a pleasant outing but soon Harry brought out the notebook in which he had all our expenses carefully itemized and stared at it gloomily.

"Unless a miracle happens," he said, "we won't get going before Christmas. We still need nearly five hundred kroner for the engine. We must have money for diesel oil, food and a sextant, a radio receiver set to get the time signals, and an auto battery for our running lights. Everything costs about twice as much as we had figured."

He flipped the notebook shut.

"And our time," he continued, "is getting short. The voyage will take at least fifty or sixty days and here it is the middle of July. The finest sailing weather is slipping by."

This was the chance I had been waiting for.

"I have a good friend," I began.

Harry sighed.

"We can't possibly take anyone else," he groaned.

Arvid grinned.

"There's always room for one more, Harry," he said. "And besides, what else can we do? Who is he, Val?"

"Heino Luts," I answered. "I knew him well in Tallin. He is studying pharmacy at the University of Stockholm."

"That's interesting," said Arvid. "But how many kroner does he have?"

"I believe he could raise five hundred," I said. "Maybe more. He's a good worker."

Harry looked doubtful.

"And he's not large," I added. "About five feet eight. He won't take up too much room."

Harry turned to Arvid.

"What do you think?"

Arvid shrugged.

"Why not? We can use the five hundred."

"All right," Harry agreed, "but tell him five hundred is the minimum."

Then Paul grinned at Harry.

"I've got a friend, too," he said. "He would give his right arm to come with us. I know he could scrape up at least five hundred, perhaps a thousand."

Harry gestured helplessly.

"I'm sorry, Paul, but it's absolutely impossible. The *Erma* was built for four. We already have fifteen."

"He's a good man," Paul argued. "A law student, once an Army officer. . . ."

Harry shook his head.

"Sorry, but we just can't do it."

"Wait a minute, Harry," Arvid interrupted. "We might as well be overloaded with sixteen as fifteen. Why can't they double up? Two to each bunk while the fifth man is on watch. Very simple."

"Nothing to it," I said. "The fifth man can sleep on deck while the other four exhaust themselves doubling up."

As usual, I was ignored.

"The thing I'm worried about," Harry pointed out, "is the matter of supplies for sixteen people for fifty or sixty days."

"How are we going to get the engine?" Arvid countered. "If an additional man can raise a thousand kroner, it will solve everything. As you yourself say, if we don't do something to speed things up, it'll be Christmas before we get under way."

Harry gave up.

"All right," he said, "we'll take the whole Estonian colony. We can tie them to the mast or tow them on a raft. Paul, what's your friend's name?"

"Rommy. You'll like him."

"Perhaps. Tell him we need a thousand kroner right away; to-morrow, if possible." Then Harry turned to me. "Tell your friend, too."

Toward late afternoon the rain stopped falling and the womenfolk came out of the main cabin for a thorough inspection of the *Erma*. Harry's mother moved about spryly, even accomplishing the feat of getting into the after cabin—and getting out again.

34

"How are we going to do the cooking?" she asked. "There's no galley."

"I thought we'd get small stoves for each cabin," Harry answered, "and cook our meals separately."

"That's about the only way," Grandma Paalberg agreed.

I foresaw a diet of canned sardines for the after cabin.

"In fact," said Harry, "I think it might be a good idea if each cabin stocked its own larder and had its own system of rationing."

"Rugged individualism," I put in.

"Perhaps," Harry smiled, "but it would simplify the purchasing and the cooking."

Mrs. Altenbrun whispered something to Maia. Maia whispered to Ellen. Ellen turned and said a few words to Grandma P. in a very low voice.

"I'll ask about it later," Harry's mother said aloud. There was an embarrassed silence.

"Has our friend from the N.K.V.D. been around lately?" I asked, more to break the hiatus than anything else.

"No," Arvid answered, "but the Marine Police have been asking a few questions. They seem to be a little curious about all this activity. My guess is that the Foreign Office has been prodded by our friends, the Russians."

"Will there be trouble about exit permits?" Maia asked. "As political refugees, we are not supposed to leave the country. How are we going to get around that?"

"We are not really going to leave the country," said Arvid innocently. "We are just going on a little cruise."

He took out his wallet and produced a small card.

35

"This shows," he said, "that I am now a full-fledged member of the Swedish Cruising Club and that my auxiliary yacht *Erma* is properly registered and equipped for cruises along the coast. In other words, I am a yachtsman and you are my guests."

"Wonderful!" said Maia. "So that's the way we get out of Sweden and away from the Marine Police?"

"It's a good idea," Harry said a little glumly, "for everything but the Russian patrols. We'll have to take our chances there."

"If we only had a machine gun," said Paul longingly. "Just one machine gun on the bow."

"That's a good notion," smiled Arvid, "but it's against the regulations of my club. We're neutral, you know."

"What *do* we say if we're stopped by a Russian patrol?" Ellen asked.

Harry thought for a minute, then answered with a sudden grin, "I guess the best thing to say would be 'Hello'." He threw an arm over Ellen's shoulder. "But there's nothing really to worry about. I'm just being a gloomy old man."

* * *

Then a few minutes later Harry's mother, who had been sitting with the others on the cabin roof, called to him. As he walked towards her, I noticed that Maia and Mrs. Altenbrun moved away. There was a brief discussion and then Harry rejoined us. He looked slightly bewildered and very unhappy.

I had a feeling that there was bad news.

"What's the matter, Harry?" Arvid asked. "You look as though you had spotted a Russian submarine."

"We've made a very bad miscalculation," Harry

36

answered, slumping down on the roof of the after cabin.

Everyone stopped work and looked anxiously in his direction.

"What now?" Paul asked.

"The toilet!" Harry announced. "There is no toilet!"

"Good grief, man!" said Arvid indignantly. "We can't have everything."

"No," said Harry sadly, "but I'm afraid some of the women feel that it's a necessity. It seems to be the one thing they're worried about."

"Why not pails?" suggested Lembit helpfully. "You can get good pails quite cheaply."

Harry looked at him reproachfully.

"It's easy to tell," he said, "that you've never been to sea in a small boat."

"Harry's right," put in Arvid, who had evidently reconsidered the matter in a more chivalrous light. "It must be something solid and substantial that won't jump all over the deck."

He took an envelope and pencil from his pocket.

"How about this, Harry?" he asked, sketching rapidly. "In the front end of the fore cabin we'll put up a plywood partition. A little opening to one side. Like this. The water closet. So. And a small hand-pump—we should be able to pick up a good one second-hand—right here."

He looked up beaming.

"But it will cut down on your floor space," Harry protested.

"Only about two feet," Arvid replied.

"The world's smallest water closet," laughed Paul.

37

4

FINALLY, in spite of all obstacles, the day came when we were actually ready to sail. After filling our two water tanks with a ton of fresh water the night before, we had intended to get under way in the early morning but there were a hundred and one delays.

Mrs. Altenbrun, a tall handsome woman who had been bedridden for several weeks with a bad attack of arthritis, had to be driven to the dock in a car after she had failed in a heroic effort to hobble to the tram. Aimi, Arvid's ten-year-old daughter, awake all the preceding night with toothache, waited in line for nearly three hours in a dentist's office. Diesel oil, which had been promised to us for weeks, was not delivered. In the late afternoon, Harry and Arvid had taken two ten-gallon cans and made a tour of the Smedslatten waterfront. By buying two gallons here and two there, they finally succeeded in filling the cans.

At five in the afternoon, we carried Mrs. Altenbrun aboard—no feather load—and deposited her safely in one of the main cabin bunks. At six Nora Kuun, loaded with suitcases and bundles, hove into sight, followed by the three little Kuuns. Arvid took time out from the furious last-minute preparations for a hurried introduction.

"My wife, Nora," he announced with a wave of his hand; "Aimi, Inga, and Ulla."

The three youngsters, ten, seven, and three, curtsied solemnly. Aimi and Inga were dark, slender, with hazel eyes that stared at us unblinkingly. Ulla, blue-eyed, chubby and blonde, regarded the toes of her white shoes. All three carried dolls, toys, and books.

Nora, a slender woman with a vivacious Slavic face, smilingly acknowledged the mass introduction and led her charges down the makeshift gangplank to the *Erma's* deck. They were greeted with a whoop by Ellen and Yuta and led to the fore cabin. Almost instantly the four children came bouncing up to begin an endless race around the deck. I waited breathlessly for the first one to fall overboard but neither Harry nor Arvid appeared particularly worried.

Heino Luts, my friend, had come with me. I noticed the women eyeing him with approval, and indeed, he was a handsome fellow, slender, meticulously dressed, with grey eyes and a shock of curly blond hair. He spoke little but had a charming manner. Even Maia's mother—already we had begun to call her Aunt Juliana—and Grandma Paalberg, were impressed with him.

It was nearly seven before the last member of our crew came aboard, Paul's friend, Rommy, the ex-Army officer. (We never mention his last name. He is on the proscribed list in Estonia, and we do not want to endanger his family.) I looked at him curiously, wondering how long he and Paul would remain friends because they were both such positive personalities. Rommy was nearly six feet tall and obviously a splendid athlete. He carried himself with military rigour and spoke crisply in a booming voice. His laughter sounded like a deep bronze bell. A capable man, I guessed, quick in an emergency. As a matter of fact we were a rather impressive crew.

Now it was time to cast off. The sun was low and red on the horizon. On the stern of the *Erma* hung the Swedish flag, and at the top of the mast, the triangular white pennant of the *Svenska Kruiser Klub* drooped lifelessly in the dead calm. I saw Harry and Arvid standing together in the cockpit. Harry called to Paul, "Better start warming her up."

Paul sprang to the after cabin. I watched curiously as he threw back the masonite motor cover and removed a small blowlamp from a bracket alongside the engine. This was the first time I had seen the semi-diesel close up. It was a strange-looking lump of metal and quite unlike any other engine of my experience. Its single cylinder sprouted upward mushroom-like from the base to a height of about ten inches.

To my amazement, Paul, after a good deal of priming, lighted the blowlamp and applied the blue, hissing flame to this cylinder.

"Something wrong?" I asked. I knew that the engine had been salvaged from a wrecked fishing boat and had lain for months at the bottom of Stockholm Bay, so I thought the use of the blowlamp was an emergency operation of some sort.

Paul laughed.

"Hell, no," he said. "This is the way we get the old girl warmed up. She has no electric ignition system like a gas engine so we have to produce the spark by heat."

I watched completely fascinated, as he swept the flame over every inch of the cylinder.

"Do you mean," I asked, "that you *always* have to start her like this?"

"That's right. It takes about fifteen minutes with the blowlamp to get the air in the cylinder hot enough to produce combustion by cranking."

"Suppose you want to start her in a hurry?"

"It's the same story whether you're in a hurry or not."

"And we paid two thousand kroner for *this*?" I asked.

"It's a good engine." Paul was immediately on the defensive. Evidently this lump of iron was already his pet. "Once she's started she runs very nicely," he added. "And she uses very little diesel oil."

He extinguished the blowlamp. Getting down on his hands and knees he began creeping through a foot-wide passage to the left of the engine box, in order to reach the crank which was mounted on the fly-wheel at the rear. The actual spinning of the crank called for acrobatic dexterity. With only twenty-three inches of headroom, Paul was obliged to turn the crank from a nearly prone positon. Since the wheel itself was about twenty inches in diameter, the manœuvre called for a good right arm.

I grunted with him as he spun the wheel again and again. At last there was a feeble explosion, and then another, stronger and quite deafening in the narrow cabin, Paul, his clothing spotted with the grease and oil of the bilge, wriggled feet-first out of the tiny passageway. He made a few adjustments to the jet controlling the oil flow and grinned triumphantly.

"There she is," he said, "purring like a kitten."

To me it sounded more like the laboured breathing of an elephant in the throes of bronchitis. Paul stuck his head out of the cabin.

"All ready in the engine-room, Captain!" he yelled.

I jumped to the dock with Lembit and Heino to throw off the docking lines. Everyone was on deck now, even Mrs. Altenbrun. The children had stopped their racing and were sitting, strangely quiet. In the cockpit, Arvid took a firm grasp of the wheel. Harry called to Paul, "Let her go!"

Paul threw in the clutch, the breathing of the semi-diesel deepened to a steadier 'put-put,' and we began to move slowly away from the dock through the calm, sunset-red waters. The friendly cove of Smedslatten faded into the mist as we began the tricky passage through the hundreds of small, rocky islands of Stockholm's archipelago. Ahead, indistinct in the suffused light of the fading sun, we could see the thin spire of Klara Church and the shadowy bulk of the City Hall.

As we worked our way slowly through the darkening islands there was little talking on board the *Erma*. Harry and Arvid bent over the coastal charts, which they had spread on the main cabin roof, plotting the course which would take us through this labyrinth of islands to the Baltic. The rest of us stood silently watching the lights of the friendly city wink and disappear. The long twilight gave way to darkness; Harry switched on our running light.

"Better put the children to bed," he called softly to Ellen.

The four youngsters came trooping sleepily over the deck to the cockpit to kiss Arvid and Harry good night. I wondered how long they would remember this first, strange evening at sea.

Through most of the night, until we had safely cleared the tortuous channels, both Harry and Arvid stayed in the cockpit, using a flashlight to check our course on the chart against the maze of navigation lights and bell buoys.

It was after midnight when I went below and crawled into my two-by-five bunk with Heino. He was snoring more or less peacefully with his knees drawn up to his chin. I straightened him out and climbed in beside him. As I dropped off to sleep I could feel his knees returning to their former position and I knew that by morning I would undoubtedly be on the floor.

I awoke at six to the smell of coffee perking on the stove. As I had suspected, I was on the floor with my head resting against the motor box.

"You tumbled out not fifteen minutes ago," grinned Heino, who was preparing breakfast. "Never saw such a sound sleeper."

I got to my feet stiffly. Every muscle seemed to ache. I made up my mind that after this I would beat Heino to bed. But the coffee and Swedish hard bread tasted good. Bright sunlight streamed through the open companion slide. The tiny cabin seemed cheerful and amazingly quiet. Apparently the engine had stopped.

"We hit the open sea early this morning," Heino explained, "and we've been under sail ever since. There's a light south-easterly and Arvid says we're averaging a good four knots."

Despite the fact that he had only recently kneed me out of the bunk, I decided Heino was a good breakfast companion. He had the knack of talking cheerfully—and not talking too much. He also made excellent coffee.

I had met Heino more than a year before in the refugee camp at Fridtorp. Like most of the other Estonian young men he had fled from the German occupation to escape Nazi military conscription. The Russians had come into our country just as Heino was finishing high school, but he wanted to become a pharmacist. So after escaping to Finland, he made his way to Stockholm, and alternately worked on odd jobs and studied at the university.

He was now twenty-four and the ruling passion of his life was to continue his study of pharmacy in the United States. Heino was unfailingly good-natured. He had an impish sense of humour, a wry, realistic philosophy, and a deep hatred of Fascism and Com-

43

munism. A good many of Heino's relatives had been deported by the Russians, but he seldom talked about that any more.

"We're heading southward along the coast," he told me now as we cleaned up the breakfast dishes, "and Harry says we're going to put in at Mem to consider the possibility of entering the Gota Canal. We should get there before dark to-night."

Mem was a small coast town about a hundred miles south of Stockholm. We were making good time.

Going on deck, I saw that we were running about two miles offshore. In the early morning sun, the mainland was a cool, shadowy green. I took a deep breath. My aches were vanishing. For the first time in months, I felt happy or, at least, something more than empty.

Arvid was at the wheel in the cockpit. Paul and Lembit squatted on the opposite side. No one else was in sight. Arvid greeted me with a smile.

"How did you sleep?"

"Fine," I answered and was astonished to find that I meant it.

The surface of the sea was smooth and there was only a slightly perceptible roll. The mainsail was fairly close-hauled and we were quartering the wind which came in off our port bow.

"The old lady is doing beautifully," Arvid said proudly. "Four knots isn't too bad in a light breeze like this."

Paul told me that the semi-diesel had developed a slight cough during the night, possibly due to dirty fuel oil.

"If we could only get some clean stuff," he said, "she would run like a charm."

I had my doubts, but decided to agree with him.

44

I knew he was proud of the way the little engine had brought us through to the sea.

It was nearly dusk when we tied up alongside a small fishing boat in Mem harbour. A grizzled, weather-beaten fisherman regarded us curiously as we fastened our mooring lines.

"Going far?" he asked.

Arvid, who spoke better Swedish than the rest of us, answered:

"Southward, just for a short cruise."

The old man grinned at Arvid's accent.

"You're from Estonia?"

Arvid nodded. The fisherman watched us silently for a while.

"You say you're going to head on south from here?" he asked after a time.

"That's right," Arvid said. "We might go down as far as Karlskrona and then come back."

The seaman regarded Arvid for a moment and then said very deliberately:

"It's none of my business, but if I were you I wouldn't cruise much farther south than Karlskrona. A fisherman stopped by here just this morning and told me that there have been a good many boats down there sunk lately without a trace. Since the Russians took over the island of Bornholm, a few months ago, there's been a lot of trouble. Torpedo boats. Submarines. At night they fire on anything that moves."

He stared gloomily to the south and continued:

"In fact, if anyone was thinking of beating around to the west coast, I think the best way to go might be to slip into the Gota Canal right here at Mem. I know that's what I'd do if I had a boatload of kids and women to worry about. Right into the canal, I'd head. There's

45

no Russian patrols there—at least not yet—and it's a safe passage all the way through."

As he stepped below, he gave us a broad grin and I knew that we hadn't fooled him for a second. Harry and Arvid held a hasty conference over their charts. The Gota Canal cut across Sweden for some two hundred miles, connecting lakes and waterways to the west coast.

"The question is," said Harry, "should we take the chance of being stopped by the Swedes or the Russians? If we go through the canal, our passage is certain to arouse curiosity. We know that the Russians have been watching the *Erma*. Probably they have already asked the Swedish Foreign Office to keep an eye on us and to stop us from leaving the country."

"Do you think the Swedes really would?" Paul asked.

"Certainly, if the Russians forced them to," I said. "Look at what happened to Captain Mannapso. He's an Estonian like ourselves—I knew him quite well in Fridtorp. He bought a boat, organized a crew, and planned to sail to England. The Soviet consulate probably got word of it and protested to the Swedish Foreign Office. Anyway, Mannapso was arrested in Gothenburg harbour before he could get under way. And the Captain and his whole crew were jailed for weeks."

"What happened to their boat?" Lembit asked.

"I'm not sure," I answered, "but it was probably confiscated or taken into custody by the Marine Police. At any rate, Mannapso and his men are still here in Sweden. They never tried it again."

Arvid said slowly:

"It seems the odds are against us either way."

He pointed with a brown forefinger to a spot on the

46

chart. The passage between Bornholm and Sandhammaren at the southern tip of Sweden looked very narrow indeed. Suppose we ran into contrary winds? Or a storm which might drive us into Russian waters? It seemed certain we would at least encounter Soviet patrol boats or submarines.

Harry looked toward Ellen, who sat with little Yuta watching us from the main cabin roof.

"I'm for taking our chances with the Swedes," our captain said finally. "A prison in Sweden might not be very pleasant but it's certainly better than citizenship in the U.S.S.R."

He called to Ellen:

"How about getting the children below? They seem to be turning into night owls!" And then to Paul, "We'll stay here for the night and see if we can get the engine running in the morning. You might see what you can do with that jet in the meanwhile!"

In the fore cabin we could hear Nora's low, throaty voice as she sang to the children. I realized with something of a shock that her song was an ancient Russian lullaby, and then I remembered that Nora had been born in Russia and had spent her childhood in Moscow. I wondered vaguely what the Kremlin would say about Nora's night song. Treason, no doubt. And then I went below. Heino was already in bed and snoring.

5

> *Ay-ouch-nem! Ay-ouch-nem!*
> Let us pull, lads, pull once more.
> *Ay-ouch-nem! Ay-ouch-nem!*
> Let us pull, lads, pull once more.
> See the birches drawing nigh.
> Soon those birch trees we'll go by.
> *Ai da da ai da*
> *Ai da da ai da*
> *Ay-ouch-nem! Ay-ouch-nem!*

FOR PERHAPS the twentieth time in the past hour, Lembit's clear tenor rose and fell in the nostalgic melody of the "Volga Boat Song." He had a good voice, but Rommy and I were getting a little tired of it. We were also getting a little tired of pulling fat *Erma* through the Gota Canal.

Seven days had passed since our departure from Smedslatten. Less than fifteen minutes after entering the canal at Mem, the engine had coughed, spat and died. Lembit had taken it apart and chinked great nuggets of carbon from the cylinder, but, despite hours with the blowlamp, the engine refused to turn over.

So, for the past five days, with lines secured to the *Erma's* bow, we had been hauling her down the canal. The old lady weighed at least seven tons and pulling her was not exactly child's play. In the past six days we had made less than two hundred miles. New York seemed a long way off.

The mainsail and jib were spread, but in those six days not a breath of wind had struck them. With her white sails drooping from the towering thirty-three-

48

foot mast, *Erma* slid reluctantly and soundlessly through the birch forests, the hilly meadows and the golden, freshly-cropped wheatfields—like some great stuffed duck.

At Motala, on Lake Vatter, we bought a new oil pump. But even with this the engine coughed and sputtered, barely turning the propeller. On reaching the western shore of the lake, with one, last agonized snort it collapsed completely. Since then it had been *Ay-ouch-nem!*

The late afternoon was calm and hot. The broad, tanned back of Rommy, tugging at the rope in front of me, was beady with sweat.

"I wish you'd lay off that damned Russky song," he bellowed to Lembit. "It makes me think we're headed for the salt mines. It's bad enough pulling this confounded thing without that infernal *Ay-ouch-nem!*"

Lembit obligingly lowered his voice and began humming the tune to himself. The children, who had been sunning themselves on the forward cabin roof, instantly protested.

"More, Uncle Lembit, more!" they demanded, and then began singing shrilly, *"Ay-ouch-nem! Ay-ouch-nem!"*

"Actually," I pointed out somewhat academically to Rommy, "the *Erma* weighs more than seven tons. That's net. But when you add the weight of the thirteen passengers, it's a lot more."

"Of course it is," grumbled Rommy. "Why don't they get out and walk? The exercise would do them good."

"It might attract too much attention," I explained. "When we pass through these small settlements, Harry wants everyone below deck."

"I have a feeling that we're going to pull this old

49

hulk to the very end of the canal and then be tapped on the shoulder by a policeman," Rommy said. "How can we help attracting attention? Every hamlet we pass through, the kids follow us and yell, 'Get a horse! Get a horse!' If you ask me, there's no better way of attracting attention than pulling a sailing boat through a canal. We must look like idiots." He pulled thoughtfully for a moment. "Do you know what I've been wondering? What happens on this so-called open sea when the wind doesn't blow?"

"Why, we pull her, of course," Lembit told him. "About the same as you're doing right now—only you tie the rope around your waist and swim."

"Swim!"

"Breast stroke, that's best," Lembit continued in a matter-of-fact voice. "You get more power that way. Didn't Harry ever tell you about the time the *Tormilind* was becalmed a hundred miles off the coast of Africa? They waited two days for the wind to come up and then they had to tow her in. It took fifty sailors and three days and three nights. Even then, if a sea horse hadn't turned up...."

Rommy whirled around but, luckily, Lembit was out of reach.

I looked up to see Heino lazily grinning at us from the after cabin roof. A glance at my wrist watch gave a clue to his good humour.

"Hey!" I yelled, releasing the tow-line, "we've worked ten minutes overtime."

Paul, Heino, and Harry leaped over the side to pick up the lines before *Erma* lost her momentum. Getting her under way, once she had stopped, was the hardest part of the job. It was like picking up a fat lady.

"You seemed to be having such a good time," said Paul, "that we hated to break it up."

His hands and face were smeared with oil from the hot-pot. Paul regarded the engine's failure as a personal affront and spent every spare minute working on it. By this time, I thought, he must be able to take it apart and put it together again in the dark.

Rommy handed the line to him.

"Here's a little present for you. *Ay-ouch-nem!*"

Paul slipped the line over his shoulder with a mournful grimace and picked up the refrain.

"Ay-ouch-nem! Ay-ouch-nem!"

At eleven o'clock we reached the great lock which drops the west-bound boats from the canal to the level of Sweden's largest lake, Vaner. A small light burned dimly in the watchman's tower. Arvid hallooed loudly. Presently, a grey, tousled head appeared in the square of light.

"What do you want? Don't you know the lock closes at nine? You'll have to wait until morning."

We disliked the thought of spending an entire night motionless. Already we had lost so much time. There were still so many thousands of miles ahead. But now Ellen's voice came softly from the main cabin roof.

"Please, we're in such a hurry to get through."

This illogical argument evidently appealed to the watchman's romantic nature. For how often does a lonely man awaken to such a lovely voice calling to him from out of the night? We could actually hear the snap of the fellow's braces as he hurried into his trousers.

Under the dim light of the watch tower Rommy, Heino, Paul, and I manned the hand gears which closed and opened the locks. Two long, horizontal bars formed a cross like a turnstile. By pushing these around and around, horse-mill style, the mechanism of the gates was set in motion. Soon the *Erma* had passed through the eight chambers of the lock and reached the level of Lake Vaner.

Within a couple of hours we floated among the reflected stars on the mirror-like surface of the lake. The stillness of the night was broken only by an occasional "jug-a-rum" of a distant bull frog and the whir of invisible insects. The *Erma's* ghostly mainsail rose against the stars, beautiful but lifeless. We were becalmed.

After a few hours sleep, we awoke in a world of mist reddened by the rising sun. Heino had barely lit the primus and put on the coffee when a sudden wind ripped away the veil of lake fog. The breeze grew stronger. The *Erma* swung around, bow to the wind, and tugged at her anchor. Harry and Arvid, half-dressed, tumbled out of their cabins.

"Up with that anchor!" Harry yelled happily. "Here we go!"

Heino and I leaped to the bow to give Arvid a hand with the windlass. The wind was dead astern. Lembit and Paul slacked away the mainsail and in a few seconds we were fleeing westward with the last shadowy remnants of the fog. The shore was visible now and the trees seemed to sweep by with dizzying speed. Overhead the sky was alive with the soft blue and pink shafts of sunrise. The exhilarating burst of forward motion, after the long days of plodding along the canal, was too much for Lembit. He filled his lungs and burst into the first song that came into his head, one that dated back to the days of the Nazi occupation:

"Once in the shop windows were silk and lace,
Now you have to stare at Hitler's face.
Oh, my darling, if you only knew
How soon you'll like the cod bone stew."

The rest of us joined him in the swinging chorus.

The children came bouncing up from their cabins, and began jumping up and down on the deck, adding their piping voices to the general uproar.

The wind held steady from the east throughout the day and after fifteen hours of brisk sailing we reached the western shore. The town of Vanersborg lay directly ahead of us. With his binoculars, Arvid picked up the entrance to the Gota Canal. The wind was coming in strong gusts. Rain squalls blotted out the shore.

"We'll come about," Arvid ordered. "Lower the mainsail and go in with the jib."

At the wheel, Harry brought the bow into the wind. Caught for a moment in the crosswind, the *Erma* lurched with a sideward, rolling motion. There was a sudden, shrill scream from the fore cabin. I stuck my head down the companionway.

"What's wrong?" I called.

"It's Ulla," Nora said. "She's been burned. Tell Arvid to come quickly.

But Arvid was busy with the mainsail so I hopped down the few steps into the cabin. I found Ulla sobbing with pain. The *Erma's* sudden lurch had upset the coffee pot which had been boiling on the stove in the centre of the floor—the only available space in the crowded cabin. The boiling liquid had scalded Ulla's leg from the knee to the ankle.

Nora had already fished a tube of salve from the first-aid kit and began gently applying a thick layer to the angry, scorched skin. Ulla bravely stifled her tears and actually helped us wind a single layer of light gauze over the ointment. She was a mighty plucky three-year-old.

On deck, I found that we were close to the canal entrance. In a minute Arvid dropped the jib and tossed a line to the feet of a curious onlooker.

53

"Give us a pull, please," he called in Swedish.

The man picked up the line and with the aid of several friends hauled the *Erma* to the side of the embankment. Arvid turned to Rommy and Heino.

"All right, boys," he said, "you can play Volga boatmen again. There's still a few hours of daylight left." He turned to me. "What's the matter below?"

I told him what had happened and Arvid leaped for the companionway. As we wearily picked up the tow line to begin the last five-mile canal haul before the Gota River, Rommy mumbled gloomily: "What's going to happen when we get out on the ocean?"

Even Lembit had no answer for this one and we trudged along without a single *Ay-ouch-nem*. At Trollhattan, where the canal ends, *Erma* was dropped sixty feet by a series of locks to the Gota River. As she entered the second lock, which was more than forty feet deep, the top of her mast was several feet below us. From this bird's-eye view, she looked terribly small, like a toy boat afloat in a washtub.

Rommy stood with folded arms looking down on her from the summit of the lock.

"So we are going to cross the Atlantic in that?" he said softly. "Do you know what I think? I think we're crazy."

The night proved to be windy and starless but Harry and Arvid decided to risk a tricky sailing passage down the Gota River rather than lose more time by waiting until daylight. So for the last thirty-five miles, the *Erma* picked her way through the blackness of the river with reefed mainsail and jib.

In the grey light of early morning we sighted the white and red houses of Kungälv at the mouth of the Gota. Beyond that, we knew, lay the Skagerrak and the North Sea.

★ 6 ★

WHEN WE went shopping the next morning, we created something of a sensation. The clerk in the Kungälv grocery store stared at us wide-eyed as Ellen asked calmly for a thousand pounds of potatoes.

"One thousand pounds!" he echoed. *"Min Gud!"*

The eyes of every one of Kungälv's thirty-five hundred inhabitants seemed glued on us as we led the delivery boy and his pushcart through the streets to the *Erma.* We had deliberately chosen to anchor at a rotting, abandoned pier, some distance from the heart of the waterfront, but our attempt to avoid attention had failed dismally. The *Queen Mary* could hardly have created a greater furore. Ever since our arrival, the ancient dock had been thronged with friendly questioners.

"Where are you from?"

"Where are you going?"

"Are you Germans?"

"Are you Russians?"

Harry was getting worried.

"Another day of this," he moaned, "and all the Marine Police in Sweden will be down here asking questions. I don't like it."

But the two-day stop at Kungälv was a risk we had to take. According to our present plan, sponsored jointly by Harry and Arvid, this was to be our last port before a sea voyage of some six thousand miles which would take us around the northern tip of Scotland and then southward to the trade winds for the Atlantic crossing.

55

Before leaving Stockholm we had heard a rumour that the French Government had recently forced a large group of Lithuanian political refugees to return to their Russian-controlled country. So, at the last moment, Harry had changed his original plan to pass through the English Channel to the Bay of Biscay. We did not want to be picked up in French waters.

Now Kungälv was our last chance to provision the *Erma* for some fifty or sixty days at sea. Potatoes were cheap, so we bought plenty of them. They were the one thing we were to share in common. Three cartloads were dumped into the cockpit space near the after cabin.

The five bachelors did their own shopping. I managed to pick up four five-pound cans of venison, one can of pork, six small bags of oatmeal, eight pounds of sugar, five pounds of flour, seventeen two-pound packets of Swedish hard bread, one pint of concentrated lemon juice, small quantities of powdered milk, salt, coffee, and tea. After buying five bottles of denatured alcohol for the stove, I was flat broke.

Paul, Lembit, Rommy, and Heino had about the same stock of food. We stored it away very carefully under the bunks in individual piles.

The other cabins had somewhat more. Especially important were the canned fruits for the children and twelve carefully hoarded pint tins of condensed milk. This latter item was very scarce in Sweden, and Ellen had scoured all of Stockholm for those twelve cans. She and Nora planned to give each of the four children a small quantity each day, diluted with water.

This last-minute shopping in Kungälv practically exhausted our combined funds. Harry still had a small reserve to be used for the purchase of diesel oil. In our trip across Sweden we had been unable to buy a single gallon. It was even rarer than condensed milk.

Both Harry and Arvid seemed deeply concerned with the slim stock of food and began working out a system of strict rationing for both cabins. With two meals a day for adults, and three for the children, they decided there was just enough for fifty-five days. The ton of fresh water in the *Erma's* tanks was rationed at the rate of one quart per day for each person. The bachelors' cabin unanimously decided against rationing. As Heino philosophically put it:

"I don't believe I have enough to last for fifty days and I'd rather not know about it beforehand."

At dusk of our second day in Kungälv, Arvid returned from a shopping trip with Nora, and I saw at once that something had happened to shatter his usual calm. As soon as he came aboard, he summoned all hands for a hurried conference around the after cabin doghouse.

"A patrol boat of the Marine Police pulled into the harbour just a few minutes ago," he announced. "I understand that this is their first visit to Kungälv in more than two years. They very seldom come up the river from the coast unless there's a good reason."

He paused significantly and then added:

"They have already made inquiries about the *Erma*. My guess is that they'll be down here first thing in the morning—if not before."

He turned to Harry.

"Do you think we could clear to-night?"

Harry's answer was another question.

"What else can we do?"

And then for the first time in years I heard Harry let loose with an Estonian swear word.

"Do you think you can get the engine going with this filthy diesel oil?" he asked Paul.

57

"After all that work?" Paul groaned. "I can probably get her started, but she'll clog up again in no time. How far is it to the sea?"

"Ten miles," Harry answered. "On a dead night like this we'll need the engine every foot of the way."

Paul heaved himself off the doghouse roof and down the after cabin companionway. Lembit followed him. A few minutes later we heard the hiss of the blow-lamp and saw the livid blue of the reflected flame. Heino, Rommy, and I stood ready to cast off the lines from the dock.

Twenty minutes went by before Paul attempted to turn over the engine. For another ten minutes there was nothing but a series of sickening, hollow wheezes. At last, deafening in the still night, a single explosion roared and died away.

"We might as well be signalling with a cannon," observed Heino. "The whole town will be down to wave good-bye."

The semi-diesel exploded again and then settled down to an uncertain, quavering chug-chug. Lembit called softly from the companionway:

"Paul says that's the best he can do."

"All right," Harry answered. "Cast off the lines."

We slipped the mooring and leaped to the deck. The *Erma* moved with a halting, jolting motion out into the river. Harry switched on the running lights. Over the rooftops of Kungälv a red moon was beginning its climb from the horizon, but its light was still shadowy and uncertain.

We were in the northern branch of the Gota now and here the river flowed west to the sea through flat marshland. The navigable channel, at times, narrowed dangerously. The ailing engine barely gave us steerageway through swirling cross-currents. Kungälv was less than an hour astern when we heard the mournful wail of a locomotive whistle. In the helmsman's cockpit Arvid's flashlight blinked as he took a swift look at the chart.

"Drawbridge ahead," he called to Harry. "The damned thing is probably down for that train. Better cut the engine before we rip off the mast."

Suddenly, less than three hundred yards ahead, the low, iron framework of the bridge loomed against the sky.

"Reverse!" Harry ordered.

The gears of the engine grated wildly as Paul jerked back on the lever. The forward momentum of the *Erma* was checked slightly but not enough. To avoid shearing the mast, Arvid spun the wheel to starboard. Almost instantly there was a sickening thud and I felt myself hurled forward against the main cabin.

I thought at first that we had struck the bridge. But after getting to my feet, I found we were still at least fifty yards away. Harry and Arvid scrambled forward Hurrying after them, I discovered what had happened. We had rammed head-on into a long, low, wooden pier jutting far out into the river. With the light of the moon behind us, it had been invisible against the dark shore.

No one spoke for at least a minute. Over the bridge, the freight train, which had caused all our trouble, rumbled away into the night. Ellen and Nora came running from their cabins.

"What happened?" Nora asked. "The children were knocked out of their bunks. Every dish in the cabin is smashed."

"I hope that's all that was smashed," Arvid said, taking his flashlight and climbing over the bow to the pier. "I hate to look."

Remembering the crackling sound of breaking timbers, I fully expected to see the entire bow stove in. Instead, it was the pier which had given way. The only sign of damage to the *Erma's* blunt nose was an inch-deep dent in the solid oak bow stem.

Rommy clapped me cheerfully on the shoulder.

"She may be fat and slow," he said, "but she's a sturdy old party."

Harry and Arvid, however, took a gloomier view.

"A blow like that," Arvid said, "could loosen the caulking. It may fall out like rotten cheese."

The engine miraculously started with a single crank, and we backed away, and swung into mid-river. The surface of the water was calm, but the *Erma* now moved forward with a peculiar, slow, rolling motion. In the moonlight we could see that the river ahead was widening, and I realized that this motion was the rhythmic breathing of the sea. The world around us was flat and still. Now and then, frightened by the sound of our engine, a bird arose from the great, shadowy reed beds along the shore, and flew low over our heads.

Maia, Heino, and I sat on the fore cabin roof silently watching this silver world slip by the *Erma's* bow.

"Somehow," Maia said, "I thought the actual moment of our departure from land would be more dramatic than this. As it is, I can't even see the land. It's like saying good-bye to a ghost."

"It *is* a ghost," Heino said slowly, "a ghost we'll probably never see again. Our families, too, are ghosts, and our friends, and most of the things we have known all our lives."

There was a slight tremor in his voice and I realized for the first time that Heino, despite his usual bantering good humour, had a deeply emotional side.

"I don't believe it's that bad," I said. "We'll all return some day—after the Russians are driven back."

"After they're driven back," Heino echoed bitterly. "Who's going to drive them back? A million Estonians against a hundred and seventy million Russians. It seems a bit improbable."

At dawn we were running parallel with the chalky, grey coast of Sweden.

"Somehow," Heino observed over breakfast oatmeal, "this doesn't seem quite right to me. I thought the general idea was to get away from Sweden as quickly as possible, not to cruise up and down the coast."

"Actually," Paul said, "we're heading south-west. The wind is from the north-west and——"

He was cut short by Rommy's bellow from the bow. "Torpedo boat!"

We rushed on deck. Rommy was pointing toward the coast. Less than a mile away, a small, rakish vessel was bearing down on us at tremendous speed. The women and children, aroused by Rommy's cry, came tumbling from the cabins.

"Everyone below," Arvid ordered sharply. "And keep the children quiet. Very quiet."

As we ducked back into the after cabin, I saw that the torpedo boat carried the colours of the Swedish Navy. Paul closed the companionway doors.

"Why the devil," he asked, "should a man-of-war stop us? Do you suppose the Russians have taken over Sweden?"

We heard the idling engines of the torpedo boat, and then a voice shouting something in Swedish. Was this the end of our voyage? Had the Russians protested to the Swedish Foreign Office? It seemed very likely. Whatever it was, the conference took only a moment. The powerful engine of the man-of-war turned over faster. The *Erma* rolled in her wake. Then Arvid called:

"All right! You can all come up now!"

As we rushed on deck, he was squinting indifferently at the skies.

"What did they want?" Rommy asked.

"Nothing very much," Arvid answered. "It seems that the Swedish Navy is having gunnery practice this morning and we're cruising right in the heart of the target area. The firing begins in less than half an hour, so they advised us to head northward."

"Good Lord!" said Nora.

7

As THE *Erma* rolled and pitched in her curious fashion out of the Bay of Marstrand and into the Skagerrak, the sea was a bluish green. Aunt Juliana Altenbrun was a pale green. So was Heino. So was I. The three of us sat on the roof of the centre cabin, trying desperately to control that revolting feeling. Grandmother Paalberg stood by with a jug of hot tea, laced with canned lemon juice.

"After a while," she predicted firmly, "you will keep it down." Aunt Juliana was not so sure.

"Ten years ago," she said, "I went to sea with my husband for a four-day cruise. I was seasick for exactly four days. And that was on a seven-thousand-ton liner. I might just as well accustom myself, and everyone else, to the fact that I will be seasick all the time until we get to America. But I must be allowed to suffer quietly in the cabin instead of sitting out here, getting drenched."

"Nonsense," said Grandmother Paalberg indignantly. "You'll be all right in a day or two. A small boat is better than a big boat for seasickness. When we get out of this choppy water, the *Erma* will rise and fall steadily with the longer seas. There will be no more of this bobbing about. In that liner, you undoubtedly stayed in your cabin every foot of the way. No wonder you were seasick."

Heino abruptly left our little group and went to the side. The children, who had been playing with their dolls on the fore cabin roof, promptly dropped everything to cheer him on.

"Uncle Heino is sick again!" chanted Yuta.

"Uncle Heino is sick again!" echoed Ulla.

They did this every time. Even for Aunt Juliana. Heino glared wanly in their direction and returned to sip his tea and lemon juice.

Arvid came up from his cabin, carrying a coil of half-inch manilla line.

"Ulla and Yuta!" he bellowed. "Come here!"

The children trotted up immediately. For some mysterious reason, they always obeyed Arvid without question. Possibly it was because he never wheedled, never scolded, seldom treated them as children.

"Up to now," he said in his matter-of-fact voice, "you have been allowed to romp around the boat because there hasn't been too much danger. But now we are heading into the open sea and there is a little danger. You can't swim. We have no life-belts on board. Nothing but that big doughnut over there."

He pointed to the large, round life-belt fixed to the *Erma's* port rail. It was made of cork, covered with cracked, painted canvas. The children regarded it solemnly.

"But wouldn't that save them if they fell overboard, Father?" Aimi asked.

"If we could get to it fast enough, and toss it to the exact spot, and if they managed to come to the surface to catch it, then it *might* save them," Arvid explained patiently. "But, you understand, all of these things would be very difficult to do. If you happened to fall overboard on a rough day, or even a fairly calm day," he continued to the three-year-olds, "it would be many minutes before we could bring the boat about, to circle and come back to the spot where you fell in. And when there are even very small waves, it would be hard to see one of your little heads. Do you understand?"

64

Maia (standing), Nora, Aunt Juliana, Arvid and the children.

Aimi, Yuta, Ulla and Inga.

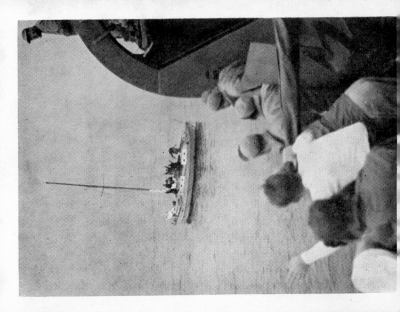

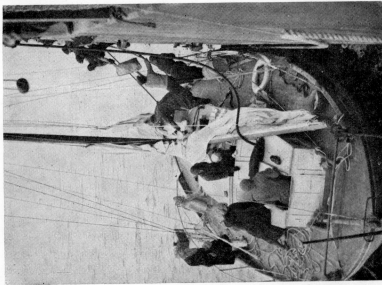

Receiving supplies 100 miles off shore from the *John P. Gray*. John McMahon, the ship's radarman, spotted the *Erma* in her distress.

"Why couldn't someone jump in and save them?" Aimi asked. "Uncle Rommy or Uncle Paul or Uncle Heino? Or you?"

"And perhaps lose his life, too? No, Aimi, when we are at sea we must learn to look out for ourselves, to work together, not to cause trouble. Each one of you is a member of the crew, the same as the grown-ups. Do you understand, Aimi? And you, Inga? And you, Ulla? And you, Yuta?"

The four nodded in turn. During the entire lecture, there had not been a single squirm or giggle.

"All right, then," Arvid said, "I'm going to make life lines for you two."

With his clasp knife, Arvid cut a length of rope about ten feet long, tied it around Yuta's middle, and then secured the other end to the mast. Ulla screamed delightedly:

"Like a puppy dog."

Within a few minutes Ulla and Yuta were tied to the mast and playing again with their dolls. The rope was long enough to allow them to jump on and off the roof and play in the narrow passage between the fore and main cabins.

"They won't drown," Heino observed, "but they may hang themselves."

The wind, which had been west-north-west all morning, was now slowly turning to west-south-west, and increasing in velocity. Harry, manning the wheel, kept glancing at the sky. It was still blue and cloudless, but the air seemed clearer, sharper. The sea, which had been choppy but comparatively calm, was suddenly alive with white-caps. Inga, standing on the main cabin roof, called, "There are rabbits in the water."

The crests of the short, choppy seas did look like rabbits. It was as though thousands of them had suddenly come to the surface and were racing toward us. The sea was already spraying over the port side. Aunt Juliana had had enough.

"I am much better," she said. "Anyway, I would rather be seasick than have this salt water ruin my only good dress."

Grandmother Paalberg snorted but she picked up the jug of tea and followed Aunt Juliana down the companionway.

With the wind from the west-south-west, Harry and Arvid were having considerable difficulty in holding the *Erma* to a westerly course. She was beginning to pound; the wind was steadily increasing in force. Rommy and Lembit came up from the after cabin where, as usual, they had been helping Paul work on the engine. Rommy's face, I noticed, was also on the green side, but he still attempted a swagger.

"What's the matter with you two?" he asked Heino and me. "You're not sick, are you?"

"Not at all," lied Heino. "We're just sitting here watching the rabbits play. It's fun."

*   *   *

By sunset the wind increased to gale force. Spindrift from the boiling crests of ten-foot seas drove in misty, red sheets across the *Erma's* decks. We were quartering the seas which bore down on the *Erma's* port bow with the hissing and roaring of an express train. Over most of them, the old lady rose with astonishing ease, but now and then a churning sea crashed solidly against her bow, flooding the decks with swirling, foaming water.

The sun was nearly below the horizon when Paul, sticking his head out of the after cabin hatchway, called to Harry:

"The bilge water is lapping at the engine! Coming up through the floorboards!"

Harry turned to Rommy.

"Did you pump her dry in that last watch?" he asked sharply.

Rommy was indignant.

"Of course. She sucked air after one hundred strokes."

Harry frowned.

"And that was less than an hour ago," he said to Arvid.

Ordinarily, it took two hundred strokes of the pump during each four-hour watch to keep the bilge fairly dry.

"We've been taking a lot of water over the side," Arvid said, "but, even so, it shouldn't fill that fast. We'd better reef the mainsail and take it a little easier."

Harry's orders came fast:

"Val! Rommy! Man the roller-reefing gear. Heino, take over at the pump!"

There was a curious urgency in Harry's usually calm voice which cut through our seasickness, and brought us to our feet. Rommy and I inched our way across the heaving deck, and wrapped our arms around the mast.

"What do we do now?" Rommy yelled.

I looked up at the towering spar, weaving crazily across the sky. The effect was not good. When the retching had subsided, I picked up the crank, and inserted it in the boom.

"The general idea," I tried to explain above the roar of the sea, "is for one of us to loosen the sail while the other cranks up the slack."

Rommy could pick the strangest times to be inquisitive.

67

"Why?" he wanted to know.

"To reduce the sail area, and consequently the strain on the vessel," I explained, quoting a book entitled *Sailing for Beginners*, which I had read before leaving Stockholm. "You loosen the halyard and let down the sail. I'll crank."

A second later, I was nearly smothered in canvas as the gale whipped the sail, tearing the halyard from Rommy's hands. As the canvas was raised from my head, I saw that both Arvid and Rommy were tugging at the halyard. Rommy was on the defensive.

"The wind is too strong for reefing," he insisted.

"Do you suppose we reef only in calm weather?" roared Arvid. "What a crew! It's a wonder we didn't lose the mainsail."

Taking the halyard in his left hand, he spun the roller crank expertly with his right, rapidly reducing the sail area to about one-half. The barren, sail-less end of the boom pointed up like a bony finger. With her speed cut, *Erma* seemed to take the pounding seas more easily in her stride.

All eyes turned now to Heino, who was still bobbing up and down at the pump. The bailing mechanism was an ancient device. It consisted very simply of a small copper can, attached to the end of a three-foot iron rod. Each upward stroke tripped the can at deck level, removing about a pint of water from the bilge.

The pump was set in the starboard deck, midway between the centre and after cabins. Since there was nothing to cling to but the pump handle itself, the operation, in stormy weather, was a hazardous procedure. When the *Erma* rolled violently to starboard, there was always the danger that the pump rod might snap, hurling the operator overboard and leaving the pumpless *Erma* to the mercy of the sea.

68

Heino's feet were spread as wide as possible, and he used his knees as shock absorbers against the rolling of the vessel.

"How many so far, Heino?" Arvid called.

"One hundred and fifty!" Heino panted. "And no air. All water!"

Now, as he bobbed up and down, we counted under our breaths. Two hundred. Two hundred and fifty. Three hundred! Harry and Arvid exchanged worried glances. The old lady was shipping water at three times her usual rate! At the three hundred and twenty-eighth stroke, Heino called:

"Hurrah! She's sucking air now."

With that he practically collapsed on the after cabin roof.

Nora's head emerged from the fore cabin companionway. The gale tore at her long, brown hair, streaming it pennant-wise nearly to the starboard rail. Against the wind, her voice sounded weak and far away:

"Arvid! The bread . . . it is soaking wet. . . . The flour bags. . . ."

The rest was lost in the roar of wind and water. Arvid scrambled hurriedly out of the cockpit, made his way catlike over the heaving deck, and disappeared down the companionway. A moment later we heard his strong voice call above the wind:

"Harry! Send down a flashlight. Quick! There's a leak in the port bow!"

Wordlessly, Harry handed me the *Erma's* only flashlight from the small compartment in the steering cockpit. The dark red light of sunset was leaving the sky and water now. Below, in the fore cabin, it was quite dark. In the white light of the hand torch, I saw Arvid quickly removing food packages and bags from the tapering forward sides of the cabin. From the bunks Nora and the three children watched him silently. Handing the flashlight to Nora, I helped Arvid stow the food bags in the port bunk.

"Is it bad?" I asked.

"Bad enough," Arvid answered shortly. "I'm afraid this heavy sea has pounded the caulking out of the old girl. The water is coming in in half a dozen spots below the waterline and along the keel. No wonder she's filling up."

He had a section of the floorboard loosened now, and we could hear the ominous gurgle of the sea as it flowed into the bilge.

"Tell Paul to bring his hammer, a screwdriver, some rags and caulking compound," Arvid ordered. "And ask Rommy or Lembit to stay at the pump."

As I ducked out of the companionway, he shouted after me:

"And tell Harry to change our course to north-east. We'll have to run before the wind because of the port bow. It may be a rotten plank."

But despite the caulking and our changed course, the bilge continued to fill rapidly.

"She's probably sprung all along the keel," said Harry wearily. "We'll have to put into Norway. We'll run parallel with the coast to-night and make a landfall in the morning."

I felt my heart go down to the bilge. So this was the end of our escape from the old world to the new. Norway instead of America!

"It seems a shame after all this," I said, "to end our voyage so soon."

"End it!" Arvid laughed. "Hell, we're not going to end it. We're just going to put in for repairs before we go on to New York."

8

LIKE A fat old party getting out of the bathtub, *Erma* grunted and groaned up the shipyard railway until her bottom was entirely clear of the water. As she sat there, with the sea dripping from her sides, we stared in speechless wonder at the old girl's bottom. It was in terrible shape. Ellen was the first to put her thoughts into words.

"Good Heavens, Harry!" she said. "No wonder she leaks. She's full of patches."

Harry smiled somewhat wanly. "It's not so bad," he said.

Arvid was more brazen.

"They look like perfectly good copper patches to me," he grinned. "What the devil did you expect to see? Hand-rubbed teak? After all, don't forget she's nearing seventy. You might expect a patch or two."

Heino and I circled the *Erma* slowly, counting the patches. There were seven beneath the waterline of the port bow, four on the starboard bow, and three aft. Heino whistled.

"Look," he said, "even some of the patches are worn out."

He touched the frayed edges of two on the port bow. Crusted with patina, they had come loose from the planking. Arvid picked up a hammer and struck a resounding blow on the *Erma's* side. There was a solid bong.

"See?" he cried happily. "She's sound. Good Swedish white oak. What's a patch or two between friends?"

Harry brightened, and ran his hand affectionately over her bottom.

"That's right, Arvid," he said. "This oak planking is an inch and a quarter thick. They don't build boats like this to-day."

Heino whispered to me:

"Personally, I think they're both crazy. Do you suppose they really believe we can cross the Atlantic in this, in this——"

At a loss for the proper word, he finished the sentence in a spluttering hiss.

The owner of the Kragerö shipyard at which we had put the *Erma* in dry dock, came up from the storehouse with a long sheet of copper, some oakum, and caulking tools.

"There you are," he said to Arvid in Norwegian, "if you need anything else just ask the watchman for it. You can work on her to-day and to-morrow, but she has to be off the railway by Monday morning. We have a lot of work ahead of us. Things sort of piled up, you know, during the German occupation."

It was now after ten o'clock on Saturday morning.

"We can make it all right," Arvid replied. "There's not too much to do. Just a few patches."

The Norwegian's leathery face split in a wide grin.

"Not room for too many more, is there?" he asked.

As soon as he had gone, Arvid and Harry assigned us to various jobs. Throughout the morning, we scraped blistered paint from the Erma's bottom, removed old caulking, hammered in new. Arvid, who had worked in shipyards before, expertly removed two ancient, worn patches from the port bow.

"This is where it really poured in the other night," he said.

Beneath the tin, the planking seemed somewhat

72

spongy. He poked the edges tentatively with a chisel. Heino and I, who had been watching over his shoulder, were startled to see a black ant emerge from between the planks. There was a second, a third, and then a regular parade.

Heino whistled shrilly between his teeth.

"Why, she's full of ants!" he cried.

Arvid, none too gently, stuck an elbow into Heino's ribs.

"Quiet!" he warned. "It's just as well if the women don't see this. No sense in worrying them over a few ants."

"But it means the wood's rotten, doesn't it?" Heino asked.

Arvid frowned.

"Not entirely rotten. A little spongy, that's all."

He tapped with his hammer around the outer edges of the old patch, searching for sound planks to hold the new copper. The fresh patch, I saw, was at least twice as large as the old one.

"Does that mean the rot is spreading?" I asked.

"Not at all," said Arvid blithely. "It simply means that I put on a bigger patch, with the nails in good, solid oak."

When he had finished, Arvid stepped back to admire his handiwork. There were now nine copper patches on the port bow alone.

"I suppose you'd call that good, solid oak," said Heino. "It looks to me as though she's put together with tin cans."

"Don't worry, my lad," said Arvid easily. "We'll be in America long before those patches fall off."

"I suppose," said Heino, "if the nails fall out, the ants will hold the patches on?"

Arvid laughed.

"Do you know," he said, "that's not as funny as you think. I once heard of an old Estonian fishing boat that sprang a leak during a bad storm. For some mysterious reason it suddenly stopped leaking and the crew made it to shore. Next day, when they examined the bilge, they discovered the leak had been stopped by a huge cluster of ants, clinging like marine glue to the planking."

Heino snorted violently.

"You wouldn't be trying to kid me, would you?" he asked.

Arvid was very solemn.

"Of course not, Heino. And do you know what? They say that Swedish ants are among the best leak pluggers in the world. Almost as good as Estonian ants."

By sunset, with seven men on the job, the work on the *Erma's* bottom was well under control. That evening, as we five bachelors of the after cabin sat down to our supper of pork soup, we felt pleasantly exhausted, and completely at peace with the world. As we sipped our coffee, the strains of dance music floated across the water. We noticed then that one of the piers, less than half a mile down the waterfront, was lighted with gay lanterns.

"What do you say we stroll over?" observed Paul. "I wouldn't mind a dance or two with one of these beautiful Norwegian blondes I've heard so much about."

"Nor would I," said Heino, getting to his feet. "Let's go."

"Wait a minute," said Rommy, "you're going to get into trouble. Suppose they ask us to produce papers?"

"At a Saturday night dance?" laughed Heino. "Not a chance."

74

Lembit and I voted with Heino and Paul, and a few minutes later all five of us were scaling the locked shipyard gates. By the time we found the road, the moon was high, and we had no difficulty in reaching the dance pavilion. Less than two minutes after our arrival, Heino and Paul were whirling with great abandon around the dance floor. Paul had his tall blonde. Heino had picked out a smart little blonde. As the rest of us stood watching from the sidelines, Rommy nudged me.

"Get ready for trouble," he warned. "Look over there."

I turned in the direction of his nod. A group of about twenty Norwegian youths were watching Heino and Paul intently.

"International complications," I said.

At the same moment Heino looked around, then said something to his girl. They stopped dancing and left the platform. Rommy smiled. "Heino's smart," he said. "Let's get out of here before something happens."

But it was too late. When the three-piece orchestra stopped, the Norwegians formed a circle around Paul.

"Who are you?" one of them demanded. "Where are you from?"

Paul got the general drift of the questioning.

"We are Estonians," he said with a broad smile. "Great pals of the Norwegians."

"Ha!" said one of the questioners. "Germans! Just as I thought. Let's get them back to the prison camp."

Lembit, Rommy, and I made our way through the circle.

"We are not Germans," I tried to explain. "We are from Estonia. We have escaped from the Germans— and the Russians."

"Ha!" said the ringleader of the Norwegians. "They

75

say they are Russians. Russian spies, probably."

I decided to try another tack.

"We are yachtsmen from Stockholm," I said. "We arrived to-day. Our boat is at the shipyard being repaired. We are cruising."

The youth, who spoke Swedish, translated for the others. There was a brief conference and then he turned back to me.

"If you are yachtsmen," he said in Swedish even worse than my own, "why do you wear such clothes?"

"We have been working on our boat," I explained. "Do you expect us to wear white flannel pants?"

There was another huddle and then the translator said:

"Perhaps you had better go back and work on your boat some more. There have been a lot of escaped German prisoners of war around here lately—and they're not very popular. Things happen to them!"

"All right," I said. "We'll go back and work on our boat."

The circle parted, and we trudged away from the pavilion. The group of twenty young Norwegians followed at a short distance. There were no words exchanged but we knew we were being escorted.

"What's the matter with them?" Paul demanded.

"They think we're Germans," I explained.

Paul was furious. He whirled around and began roaring in Estonian:

"We are not Germans! We are Estonians. We fought against the Germans the same as the Norwegians. I, myself, was a pilot in the Norwegian Army, volunteered in 1940."

"Take it easy," I said. "They can't understand a word."

76

Grumbling to himself, Paul gradually lapsed into silence. When at last we scrambled back over the shipyard fence, our escort vanished into the night. A few minutes later, as we stood there dejectedly admiring the moonlight on the calm sea, we heard a piping feminine voice call from somewhere out of the darkness:

"Good night, Paul! Good night!"

"It's the little blonde," Paul said happily.

"But where did she learn to speak Estonian?" I asked.

"I taught her," said Paul proudly.

The next morning we sanded the *Erma*, and applied a coat of red paint to her bottom. Above the waterline, we gave her a fresh coat of light grey paint. Sitting there in the bright sun, the old lady looked quite gay. Even her multitude of patches seemed to sparkle.

As we painted, the women washed clothing in tubs beneath the shipyard tap. After that, we warmed water on the stoves, and there was a much-needed bath for all hands.

Grandmother Paalberg remarked, "This may be our last bath before we reach America."

Early on Monday morning the shipyard owner told us that we could leave the *Erma* in dry dock until late afternoon. Since the paint was not quite dry, we took advantage of his offer, and set out on a shopping expedition in Kragerö. Our funds were extremely limited, but so were the shops. There was no milk to be had, no butter, no meat. From each of the storekeepers we received the same apology:

"You know how it is: those Germans!"

There was plenty of fish in the markets along the quay, but the price in Swedish kroner—the only kind of money the merchants would accept—was prohibitive. In a search for canned milk for the children, Nora and Ellen visited every grocery store in Kragerö.

"Canned milk!" the clerks exclaimed. "We haven't had canned milk since 1940."

Returning to the boat, we found Harry and Arvid talking with a tall, spare man in a black uniform.

"The police," Arvid explained shortly. "He wants to see all passports."

The official seemed puzzled by our red-backed Swedish alien passports. These were, of course, valid only in Sweden, and explicitly forbade the holder to leave the country without special permission. I saw him glance at this phrase and then at the one which read: "This passport is not valid for return to Sweden without proper authorization."

"You are cruising?" he asked politely after a moment.

"Yes," Arvid answered, "we are cruising."

"To where?"

Arvid gestured rather vaguely toward the west.

"To England, perhaps," he answered. "Or to Ireland."

The officer smiled slowly but understandingly.

"Anywhere, I suppose," he said, "but to Russia?"

"That's about it," Arvid grinned.

The Norwegian was really a nice chap.

"Well," he said, extending his hand, "your passports seem perfectly all right to me. Good luck and a good voyage. I know what it is to live in an occupied country."

When he had gone, Arvid turned to Paul, Heino, and me.

"Look alive, boys!" he smiled. "We have thirty-five gallons of pure diesel oil to pick up here. A very special concession from the shipyard boss."

Paul was overjoyed. This was milk for his baby.

"Thirty-five gallons!" he said. "Let's get going!"

By the time we had lugged the oil to the *Erma's* fuel tank from a huge barrel in the shipyard shed, it was nearly four o'clock. Then Harry and Arvid let the *Erma* slide back down the railway into the water.

"And now," said Harry, "get out your extra sugar, shirts, dresses, underclothing. Anything you can possibly spare. We have to pay the shipyard owner for the paint, oil, and use of his docking facilities. And don't be stingy! This diesel oil alone is worth a fortune."

The Kuun cabin led the way with two complete sets of children's clothing, two pairs of shoes, and a house dress. The main cabin donated three dresses, a man's shirt, and a kilo of sugar. From the after cabin, the five bachelors managed to part with a pair of shoes, a pair of trousers, two fairly new shirts, a kilo of sugar, and the bottom part of a pair of pyjamas. The latter item belonged to Heino.

"I'd give him the top, too," he explained to Harry, "but I haven't got it. Never wear one."

The Norwegian seemed overwhelmed at this flow of goods. It was really very little, but he realized it was the best we could do.

"Tack so mycket, tack so mycket!" he said, shaking hands all around.

It was five o'clock when Paul turned over the engine, and we began to move slowly out of Kragerö harbour.

"She runs like a charm," Paul shouted happily. "This is really good fuel."

As we passed the white lighthouse outside Kragerö, the wife of the supervisor, Joachim Andersen, stood outside her tiny house waving a huge Norwegian flag. On the way into Kragerö, we had stopped at the lighthouse to ask the way to the nearest shipyard. The

Andersens had been very kind, and had insisted on serving cakes and coffee to the *Erma's* crew.

As we waved good-bye, we saw a boy hop into a rowing boat, and head for the *Erma*. Paul shut off the engine and we waited until he drew alongside. It was the Andersen's son bringing us a farewell gift: a five-gallon can of diesel oil. Before we could say, *"Tack so mycket,"* he had shoved off, and was half-way back to the lighthouse. It was a moving gesture.

"They've been so nice to us," said Maia, "that I feel like crying."

"They're fine people, these Norwegians," said Heino.

Paul began to whistle one of the tunes we had heard at the dance hall on Saturday evening.

"Especially the blondes," he said.

* * *

As we beat our way against a strong north-westerly wind along the southern coast of Norway, Harry ordered a twenty-four-hour mine watch. The Andersens had told us that a number of Norwegian fishing boats had disappeared without a trace since the war's end.

"The British Air Force sowed hundreds of floating mines along our coast during the war," he said, "and it will be a long time before the waters are really safe. They are very difficult to see until a boat is practically on top of them."

So from dawn until darkness set in, one of us stood on the heaving fore deck of the *Erma* peering ahead for the shining black metal which might blow us to bits. It was Rommy who spotted one at dusk of our second night out of Kragerö.

"Mine off the port bow!" he shouted. "Less than ten feet away!"

Arvid instantly brought the helm over hard. The mine slid past our side so close that any of us might have leaned over and touched it. If our course had not been changed at that very instant, we would certainly have crashed into it head-on. Rommy was the hero of the hour.

"I thought at first," he said, "that it was a dolphin—until I saw the little knobs on top. They're very hard to spot, particularly in the twilight."

He turned to Harry as though something had suddenly occurred to him.

"What do we do after dark?" he asked. "We will be blind in the dark."

Harry shrugged.

"There's nothing we can do," he said. "We'll just have to take our chances."

After that, none of us slept too soundly off the Norwegian coast.

That night at sunset, as we rolled over the choppy North Sea, we passed very close to a fast, trim destroyer, flying the Polish flag. It was undoubtedly one of those Polish men-of-war which had fought so bravely with the British Navy, and was now returning to her homeland. The sailors, leaning over her low rails, waved to us. We could hear the far-away sound of singing voices.

"Happy because they're going home," said Paul. "The poor devils. If they only knew how the Soviets have already taken over their country, they would turn around and go back to England."

"Give them time to find out what it's like—this life under the Russians," said Heino, "and they'll turn around fast enough."

"By then," said Lembit, "it will be too late. The Russians will have their destroyer, and the sailors will be on their way to Siberia."

9

I AWOKE at three in the morning to find Paul shaking me by the shoulder. The engine had stopped and I could feel the *Erma* rolling heavily as though in the trough of the sea.

"Arvid wants us on deck," Paul said. "We're running into a gale."

Someone had switched on the five-watt extension lamp over the motor. In its feeble glow, I saw Rommy climbing into his leather trousers and high army boots.

"Anything wrong?" I asked.

"Just that we're shipping tons of water over the starboard side," Paul answered.

It was then I noticed that my blanket was as thoroughly soaked as if it had been dipped into the sea. Looking up, I saw that the water was running in rivulets through the chinks in the cabin sides.

"The gale is hitting us from the north-west," explained Paul, "and Harry is stubbornly keeping her headed straight for the west. Wait until you get on deck. It's like riding a submarine."

As Rommy and I lurched through the companionway the unexpected force of the wind very nearly sent both of us sprawling. It was our first experience with the tremendous strength of a gale on the open sea. For a moment we both clung to the main traveller, bending our heads to the wind, fighting to catch our breath.

The beam of a flashlight shot suddenly from the steering cockpit, swept the after deck and settled on our cowering figures.

"Rommy! Val!" Arvid's voice roared at us from the cockpit.

"Hello!" I gasped.

"What the hell are you doing back there? We need you up here!"

Clinging to the edge of the after cabin roof as well as to each other, we managed to reach the cockpit. Harry, ankle-deep in water, was at the helm. Under the light of Arvid's torch, Paul and Lembit were unrolling a bolt of heavy canvas which had been brought with us for sail repair.

As my eyes grew accustomed to the curious half-light of the false dawn at sea, I saw that the *Erma* was rolling with what seemed to be terrifying speed through towering, white-capped seas. We were quartering the wind and, from time to time, as a giant sea crashed against the starboard bow, the entire deck was flooded with a swirling mass of water.

Overhead the gale shrieked and moaned. As I looked up, the mast itself seemed to bend under the terrible pressure of the wind-taut sails.

"Has something gone wrong with the sails?" I shouted in Harry's ear. "Will we be able to stay afloat?"

"Stay afloat?" Harry laughed. "Well, I should hope so. We're making excellent time with this wind. Better than five knots. If we can keep it up, we'll be across the North Sea in two days."

"Come on!" called Arvid. "Give us a hand with this canvas."

I looked up at the mainsail. To my surprise, it was still intact.

"What we're going to try to do," explained Arvid, "is to fasten the canvas to the lifeline. You see, the reason we're shipping so much water is because the

Erma's freeboard is too low amidships for this kind of sailing."

He pointed to the steel cable mounted on stanchions which ran for about twenty feet on both sides of the *Erma's* deck. It was three feet high in the centre, tapering gradually to about ten inches at either end.

"If we can secure the canvas to the rails," he continued, "it should stop some of the seas from coming aboard."

"If we had spring-hooks," said Paul, "it would be simple. As it is, we'll have to sew short pieces of line along the edges and secure them to the rail."

Opening his tool kit, Paul produced a packet of large sail-maker's needles, a leather sewing palm and several spools of heavy thread. His long, dexterous fingers made a quick job of fastening an eighteen-inch piece of quarter-inch rope to the edge of the canvas.

"There," he said triumphantly, "one of those every twenty-four inches should hold her to the rail in any wind."

Crouching in the shelter of the main cabin, Lembit, Rommy, and I tried to imitate Paul's handiwork. It was not as easy as he made it look. In that howling gale, with the *Erma* pitching crazily from side to side, threading the needle was in itself a major operation. The process of shoving the needle through both the rope and the heavy canvas called for tough fingers and a martyr's soul. By the time we had finished, the canvas was liberally spattered with blood from our pricked fingertips, and we had exhausted our repertoire of profanity.

To decrease its resistance to the wind and make it easier to handle, the canvas was once more rolled up, and then hoisted to the outside of the railing by Arvid and Paul. As they unrolled it, foot by foot, Rommy, Lembit, and I fastened the ropes to the posts and cable of the handrail. Time after time the sea broke with full force against us, tearing the canvas from our hands, and sending one or the other of us toppling back into the cockpit.

At last, the job was done. No longer did the seas sweep unhindered over the deck. The canvas barrier successfully shouldered them back into the ocean. Some water still came in along the bottom and over the top but, compared to the previous deluge, it was a mere trickle.

"Now," said Arvid, "let's see what we can do about the cockpit. That coaming is far too low."

Two ten-inch planks which we had picked up at a lumber-yard in Smedslatten were swiftly sawn into halves, and then fastened to the sides of the cockpit between the main and after cabins. In that way, the height of the coaming was raised about twenty inches and gave excellent protection against the sea and the wind.

The sun was now high above the horizon and shone dazzlingly through scattered wind clouds, on the pale-green, mountainous seas. With the mainsail reefed to a quarter of its normal size, Harry sailed the *Erma* as close to the wind as he dared. From time to time, a sea, larger than the others, slammed over the bow with a thunderous crash.

Shortly before noon, while the gale was still at its zenith, I was astounded to see Grandmother Paalberg and Aunt Juliana emerge from the main cabin. They were bundled in heavy coats with woollen scarves wrapped around their heads, and stood for a time peering over the cabin roof at the heaving sea.

"How are you feeling, Aunt Juliana?" I asked.

"She's feeling fine," answered Grandmother P. "Aren't you, Juliana?"

"Strangely enough," said Aunt Juliana, "I am. And I don't know why. I've been thrown out of my bed, soaked to the skin, and yet I haven't had a single arthritic pain all morning."

"And she hasn't been sick since last night," added Grandmother P. "Just finished two bowls of vegetable soup."

"You must be right about the sea air being good for arthritis," Aunt Juliana said to Arvid. "Really, I haven't felt so well in years. Do you suppose it could be the effect of the salt water?"

Arvid looked quickly at the compass.

"Undoubtedly," he said. "Yes. I'm sure that must be it. You've heard of salt water baths? It seems there are certain properties in salt water that are very beneficial to sufferers from rheumatism and arthritis. I remember meeting an old Norwegian sea captain, master of a freighter on the South American run, who told me that the only time he was free from his rheumatism was when he put to sea. The moment he set foot on land he could barely walk."

"Remarkable!" said Aunt Juliana happily. "Simply remarkable!"

When the two ladies had returned below, I said to Arvid, "Do you know, it really is remarkable. We had to carry her on board, and now look at her, getting around like an old sea dog."

Arvid, with an eye on the mainsail leech, eased the helm a trifle.

"Damnedest thing I ever heard of," he agreed.

*   *   *

On the third day when we came on deck the gale

86

had blown itself out. We were cutting merrily through a calm sea, pointing toward a sunlit shoreline not very far away.

"Scotland," said Harry. "Here we are—Fraserburgh." He indicated on his chart the harbour that was opening out before us.

The women and children swarmed from the cabins to take advantage of the sun, their arms filled with water-soaked clothing and blankets. Ignoring Harry's protests, they proceeded to hang their wet clothes from every available stay and shroud.

"A fine thing to do," Harry observed sourly. "We look like a floating gypsy camp or a laundry boat."

"Would you rather be proud or have our clothing ruined by mildew?" snorted Grandmother Paalberg.

"And whose fault is it?" demanded Ellen. "If you had sailed with the wind instead of against it. . . ."

Against this unanswerable feminine logic, Harry gave in.

"At least," he smiled, "you might hang those from the back stay instead of the jib."

He pointed to a fairly roomy pair of lady's underdrawers flapping defiantly from the jib stay.

"Aunt Juliana's drawers," said Grandmother Paalberg firmly, "will stay where they are. They are nothing to be ashamed of."

With our laundry flying proudly, we chugged through the harbour waters to the customs and immigration dock. As we made the *Erma* fast, I could see that Harry and Arvid were a little on the nervous side. I knew that they were wondering what our reception might be. After all, Great Britain and the U.S.S.R. were allies.

The immigration officer, a stocky, broad-shouldered

man with a sunburned face and a heavy moustache, squinted at our passports, then at us, and then back again to the passports.

"You are Swedes?" he asked.

Arvid, who had had previous experience with the Scottish accent, acted as spokesman.

"No," he answered, "we are Estonians."

"But these are Swedish passports."

"Swedish alien passports," Arvid said. "We have left our homes in Estonia. We are political refugees who have decided we do not wish to live under the Soviet government."

To our amazement, the official calmly accepted Arvid's brief explanation.

"You wish to remain here in Scotland?" he asked.

"No," Arvid answered, "we plan to go on to the United States. Some of us have relatives there."

"To the United States!" He jerked his head toward the *Erma*. "You're not going to cross the Atlantic in that—that skiff? With these women and children? Why, man, that's lunacy!"

Arvid grinned.

"It probably is," he agreed, "but it's the only thing we can do."

"I suppose it's your own business," said the Scot, beginning to stamp the passports, "but I don't know why you don't stay here and become citizens of the United Kingdom. What does the United States have that we haven't?"

"Plenty of distance," Arvid said.

The Scot tugged at his moustache.

"Distance?"

"From the Soviets."

The immigration man smiled.

"You really have the wind up, haven't you? I can't

believe it's as bad as all that." He returned the last of the passports.

"Now, if you're going to stay for a few days there's the matter of the harbour fee. Customs will take care of that. Johnny!"

At his call, a young, smooth-shaven man came into the office from an adjoining room.

"Pilgrims on their way to the United States," explained the immigration man. "They're waiting for you to relieve them of the harbour fee."

The fee, based on net tonnage, was quickly computed. It came to two pounds sterling. Only Harry's reddening ear tips, as he fished for his wallet, indicated the severity of the blow.

"So you're really going to the States," said the customs official as he changed Harry's five-pound note. "South through the Channel, I suppose?"

"No," answered Harry, "we plan to head north through the Pentland Firth and then south."

"But why? It's much shorter going through the Channel."

"It may sound strange to you," Harry said slowly, "but we would like to stay as far away as possible from the French ports."

The customs man was mystified. Here, in this free, friendly country, it was difficult to understand our fears of the far-reaching Soviet tentacles.

"You see," I tried to explain, "there is an agreement between the French government and the U.S.S.R. which permits the Soviet to repatriate all Baltic citizens who have fled to France. Before we left Sweden, we had letters from friends in Marseilles. They told us the French police are helping Soviet agents round up these political refugees for return to Russia."

89

The older Scot interrupted:

"Do you mean they're sent back against their will?"

"That's right," I answered. "And they'll be murdered or shipped off to labour camps in Siberia."

His eyebrows went up incredulously. I had to admit that here in Scotland this sort of talk did sound incredible.

"Anyway," I finished somewhat lamely, "we want to avoid the possibility of being forced to land in a French port."

The younger man pointed to a map on the wall.

"In that case," he said, "why don't you go on through the Caledonian Canal? It's a bit north of here, leads through the Highland lakes to the Irish Sea. That's much shorter than sailing clear around Scotland."

"I thought the Caledonian had been closed to shipping years ago," Harry said.

"Not at all. Of course it's too small for modern, larger vessels but there's considerable small boat traffic. Beautiful scenery. Sixty miles of it. It'll be a bit rough sailing through the west coast currents but, after that, you'll have a regular pleasure cruise south to the Trades."

"It's an excellent idea," said Harry, catching the customs man's enthusiasm.

For a moment, I thought he was going to add: "Well worth two pounds sterling." But even Harry's enthusiasm had its limits.

* * *

The next afternoon, as Paul, Lembit, and I strolled back to the *Erma* from a sight-seeing trip to the town, Paul's eye caught a weather-beaten sign hanging over the door of a waterfront pub:

THE BALACLAVA

"Curious name for a Scottish pub," he observed.

"Probably has something to do with the Crimean War," said Lembit.

Paul suggested practical research so we went in for a glass of dark stout and several platters of fish and chips. It was a good thing we did, for apart from the fact that the stout was excellent, it was in the Balaclava that we met Bill.

We had been at our table for only a few minutes when Bill came over and introduced himself. All we ever understood was "Bill." His last name was one of those unpronounceable things—for a Balt—beginning with "Mc" or "Mac." He was about thirty, dressed in a Royal Navy uniform, and his ruddy, weathered face seemed to radiate good health.

"You're from the Swedish sloop, aren't you?" he asked. "Saw you pull in yesterday. Well, greetings from His Majesty's Navy! A wonderful country, Sweden. Cheers!"

We drank to Sweden and then I explained that we were Estonians. That made no difference to Bill. One foreign country, obviously, was the same as another. Bill ordered another round and we drank to Estonia.

After the third stout, I noticed a curious thing. Despite the fact that Paul's English was limited to a vocabulary of perhaps five words, he and Bill were carrying on a lengthy and spirited conversation.

The key to this strange dialogue seemed to be an occasional international word such as *America*, *England*, *Russia*, *motor*, or *diesel*. Having blurted out one of these key words, Paul or Bill would then let loose with a triumphant torrent of Estonian or English while the other sat by grinning happily. The conversation seemed to be helped along considerably by fearful grimacing, gesticulating, and back slapping.

At one point, as Paul was giving a masterful imitation of the effect of poor oil on *Erma's* diesel, Bill grabbed him suddenly by the shoulder.

"Come along," he ordered. "We'll get some medicine for that damned engine."

They left the Balaclava arm-in-arm, returning about half an hour later with two five-gallon cans.

"Look," said Paul, removing the cap of one of the tins, "one hundred per cent pure diesel oil!"

He poured a little out in the palm of his hand and lifted it to his nose. For a moment, I thought he was going to drink it.

"Ah-h-h," he breathed in ecstasy. "Wait until the old girl gets this in her stomach!"

"Where the devil did you find it?" asked Lembit.

Paul and Bill winked coyly at each other.

"There's plenty more to be had," Paul said evasively. "But first, let's get this in the tanks."

The children were delighted with Bill. He tossed them high in the air, gave them bags of sweets, and quickly mastered the Estonian equivalent for "nice kid."

"*Ilus laps!*" he shouted. "*Ilus laps!*"

During the afternoon, Paul and Bill made at least half a dozen trips to their mysterious source of supply. Each time they returned loaded down with more diesel oil and such sundry items as sea soap, manilla rope, clay water bottles, and the works of Sir Arthur Conan Doyle.

That night, at Bill's invitation, Paul, Lembit, Heino, Rommy, and I slept aboard a British destroyer which was destined for the scrap heap. After three weeks of sleeping in our cramped bunks, the destroyer's hammocks seemed luxurious.

The next morning, as we made our way back to the *Erma*, we passed two captured German submarines. On the dock near one of them stood two, strangely familiar, five-gallon oil cans.

"So that's it!" Lembit said to Paul.

Paul evidently did not hear him. He was too busy talking with Bill.

10

AFTER YEARS of furtive existence under the guardianship of the Gestapo and the M.V.D., and our cramped life in Sweden within the shadow of the Soviet, we found the free air of Scotland a trifle too rich for comfortable breathing. Like people who had been shut up for too long in a darkened cellar we were, at first, dazzled and frightened by the brightness of a free country.

Our first scare came one night as we lay in the Moray Firth at the entrance to the Caledonian Canal, feasting on crabs which the resourceful Paul had caught in a home-made trap. At ten o'clock, Harry switched on the radio for the Scottish Regional news. The very first item caught our attention:

"Sixteen Estonians, men, women, and children, who plan to cross the Atlantic to America in a 37-foot sloop, have arrived in Fraserburgh after a passage across the North Sea from Sweden. They are now entering the Caledonian Canal and will cross Scotland within the next few days. The tiny craft is under the command of Captain Harry Paalberg and. . . ."

After listening in amazement to the first few sentences, Harry instinctively silenced the radio.

"That's a hell of a thing to do," he said angrily. "*Broadcasting* our plans!"

"But what harm can it do?" asked Ellen.

"Do you think the Russians are going to sit back and let us get away so easily?" said Harry darkly. "They will protest to the British Foreign Office and, since England and Russia are allies, we will be sent back to Estonia."

"I don't believe it," said Maia. "You've lived too long under the Germans and the Russians, Harry. The British don't do things like that. This is a democratic country—not a dictatorship."

"But they *could* do it," Arvid said. "After all, they could hardly ignore an official protest."

Rommy was even more ominous.

"Or Russian agents might stop us without British consent," he contributed cheerfully.

"That's silly," said Lembit.

"Is it?" Rommy asked. "Moscow has officially declared Harry's father an enemy of the people. The M.V.D. has had a warrant for my arrest for years and for Paul's, too. In fact, all of us, since we refuse to return to the Soviet, are *wanted* by the Soviet. Look at what happened to those Lithuanians in France. Why are we any different?"

As we sat there in the darkness of the Scottish night, almost anything seemed possible, and I began to realize that it takes a long, long time to shake off the fear instilled by a police state.

Early the next morning, however, as we entered the first of the hand-geared locks at Inverness, we were overwhelmed not by Russian agents but by the generosity of the local Scots. As the *Erma* floated in the lock chamber, we were amazed to see a throng of at least a hundred people gather on the banks above.

Despite rationing and food shortages, it seemed as though each of them had a gift for us. We were deluged with carrots, cabbages, beets, lettuce, loaves of bread, scones, sweets, tiny packets of sugar. Some actually lowered bottles of fresh milk to us with pieces of twine. One man tossed down a woollen blanket.

"For the children!" he shouted. "To keep 'em warm! God bless 'em!"

The radio broadcast also brought to Inverness a squadron of newspapermen and photographers from Glasgow and Edinburgh. There was even a correspondent from the London *Times*. Harry watched them sourly as they clambered on to the *Erma's* deck.

"Tell them," he said, drawing me aside, "that we don't want our pictures taken."

"But we can't do that," I said. "We might hurt their feelings."

It was the representative of the London *Times* who finally penetrated Harry's reserve.

"You don't seriously believe our government would allow you to be sent packing without your consent?" he asked.

The reporter had spoken with just the right air of righteous indignation so that you could almost hear the British lion roaring at the temerity of the Russian bear. Within the next five minutes, the *Times* man had persuaded Harry to pose with Ellen and Yuta on the main cabin roof—complete with smile.

"*Pravda*, please copy," grinned Rommy.

*　　　*　　　*

Our passage through Loch Ness, which lies so tranquilly between high, rugged cliffs and undulating, pine-covered mountains, was like a ride through fairyland. Soothed by the pure diesel oil that we had obtained in Fraserburgh, the diesel purred contentedly through the long, sunlit, summer afternoon. We sat on the deck or on the cabin floors, sleepily watching the enamelled reflections of the steep shores in the silver and black waters of the lake, half

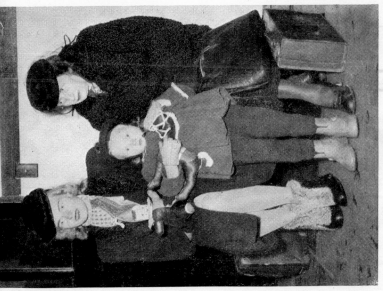

Top: The *Erma*, drying her sails. *(Photo: Elizabeth N. Laurent)*
Bottom: Ellen, Yuta and Grandma P., at Norfolk. *(Photo: Jim Taylor)*

(Photo: Jim Taylor)

The *Erma* at the end of her voyage.

listening to the tales which Arvid and Maia were spinning for the children.

It was nearly midnight when we reached the far end of the loch and began to grope in the blackness for the entrance to the canal. Heino, kneeling in the bow with a boathook out-thrust to warn of shallow water, called suddenly, "Listen! Do you hear that? The sound of bells!"

Somewhere, far in the distance, growing louder and louder, a bell was tolling. Lighting his flashlight, Harry studied the chart we had bought at Fraserburgh.

"That must be the Benedictine abbey. It's at a place called Fort Augustus, not far from the canal entrance. We'll steer towards the bells."

With the engine in low gear, we moved very slowly for perhaps five minutes in the direction of the bells.

"Bottom," Heino shouted abruptly. Paul, who had been standing with his head and shoulders out of the after cabin companionway, instantly threw the engine into reverse. But it was too late. There was a soft thump as the *Erma* stuck her nose into the bottom.

Luckily, as we had been moving very slowly and the bottom was muddy, we suffered no damage. After fifteen minutes of grunting over the boathook, aided by the groaning of the temperamental engine, we managed to float clear. By this time, the sound of the bells had died away.

"We'll drop anchor and wait until morning," Harry decided. "We might do more damage to the *Erma* here than we would on the open sea."

* * *

Early the next morning, as we were washing the breakfast dishes over the side, we were somewhat startled to see two monks, in a small skiff, rowing towards us from the shore. The man at the oars had his robe tucked high above his knees, and rowed with the long, smooth sweep of the expert.

"Good morning!" he called as he brought the skiff skilfully alongside. "Is this the *Erma*?"

Harry acknowledged that it was.

"Well, then, welcome to the Abbey of St. Benedictus! We heard your engine during the night and thought you might be in trouble."

Rommy and Paul helped tie the skiff to the side, and the two monks easily clambered aboard. They were both under thirty, stalwart six-footers with lean, suntanned faces, and broad shoulders which seemed emphasized by the cord drawn tightly around the waist of their robes.

"Mama!" cried Inga from the forward companionway, "there are two men here dressed like ladies." It was fortunate that she spoke in her native Estonian.

When everyone had been introduced, Grandmother Paalberg poured some coffee for our visitors.

"We had hoped," one of them said, "that you might find time to visit the abbey this morning. As you know, there are five locks in the canal here, and there are several boats already ahead of you."

From somewhere under the voluminous robe, he produced a packet of cigarettes, passed them round, and then lit one for himself.

"Naturally," he continued, "we are anxious for news of the Church under the Soviet. We have heard many rumours, of course, but we seldom get a chance to talk with someone who has actually lived in a Soviet-occupied country."

"Is it true that there is freedom of worship in the Soviet?" asked the other monk. "We have heard that the Soviet constitution actually recognizes the existence of the Church."

It was Maia who answered. In hesitant but understandable college English, she briefly sketched the clever campaign of the Soviet against the churches in Estonia. She told how, in the first Russian occupation, two clergymen and twenty-seven members of parish councils of the Estonian Lutheran Church had been murdered. In the second occupation, only seventy-seven out of two hundred and fifty clergymen remained in the country. The others had fled abroad. She told of the Red Army "destruction battalions" which had razed eleven churches in a single week.

"The ironic part of the Soviet war against the Church," she explained, "is that officially the authorities pretend to recognize freedom of worship. But the Church, in fact, is being taxed out of existence. Church properties have been nationalized. The clergy are forced to pay exorbitant rents, fantastic rates—ten times the average—for such public utilities as gas and electricity. So gradually the Church is being starved to death."

But sitting there in the brightness of the morning, looking out over the clear, still waters of Loch Ness, it seemed almost impossible to believe that for thousands of our countrymen these horrors were still real.

"I'VE NEVER seen so much life on the water," Aunt Juliana said. And right she was. Small auks shuttled here and there like wound-up toys, gulls and terns soared about us, and seals dived and reappeared in competition with the auks. Large greyish gannets with black wing tips darted down to the water with such a splash that columns of spray rose as though bombs were exploding, and storm swallows fluttered low over the water, their long legs treading the surface.

All of us were watching the antics of the birds, sorry to say goodbye to the fairy-tale Highland scenery. After a three-day passage we were now in the Firth of Lorne and the *Erma* shivered, shook, and bounced in the unruly tidal stream.

"Aren't these rather dangerous waters?" Aunt Juliana asked Harry, looking around us with anxious eyes.

"Slightly," he answered. "These straits of the Inner Hebrides are exposed to the whole might of the Atlantic tides. Twice a day the water surges back and forth, making eddies and counter currents. Less than forty miles ahead is Corryvreckan, one of the largest whirlpools in the world."

"Do we have to go through it?" Aunt Juliana asked, worried.

"No, we'll pass to the east and sail south-west into the Sound of Jura."

Throughout the afternoon we sailed at a fair speed, aided by light, quartering breezes. The wind died down about sunset, and at ten o'clock a fog came up.

By midnight it was so thick that we could not see anything. Traffic was quite light, but still we heard occasional fog horns sounding around us.

Because of battery failure we were unable to switch on our running lights or sound the horn. After a while, Arvid and Harry agreed that it was too risky to advance, so Arvid and Heino went forward and dropped the anchor. We were lying in the lee of Seil, but could not see it in the darkness and fog.

The stream flowed quietly beneath us now. It was low tide. Despite the late hour several of us were still on deck, inwardly excited by the impressions of the last few hours. This strange primitive world of rocky shores and islands seemed barren of any life but that of the sea and air. The waters had been in turn savagely violent and deceptively placid, wrapped in a misty twilight during the day and since dark smothered with a foggy blanket so thick that we could barely see each other's shadowy forms.

*　　*　　*

When Arvid and Lembit came on deck at four in the morning, the first dim glow of dawn was seeping through the thinning grey of the fog. But still it was thick and dark enough to bar any attempt to get under way. Arvid went back to his cabin leaving instructions to call him if the wind should rise or the fog clear. Some twenty minutes later, Lembit opened the fore cabin slide and called, "The fog is lifting."

Arvid, who always seemed to sleep with one ear open, instantly left his bunk. Light gusts of wind blew, and the fog banks were thinning in the slowly growing dawn. As Lembit cranked the windlass and Arvid pulled on the main halyard, patches of sea opened around the *Erma's* bow, and by the time her jib had filled there was clear water ahead, shining in the half-darkness. The breeze was light, vacillating from the south-east. There were heavy banks of fog to leeward and astern, but the *Erma* made headway, however slowly, and the dawn grew lighter in the typical snail-like pace of the northern latitudes. Soon, the wind began to freshen and to steady. It blew now directly from the south. Arvid called to Lembit: "Close-haul the sheets!"

Lembit, an eager and talented disciple in sailing, promptly started to re-trim, and first eased off the jib sheet, in order to prevent the mainsail from becoming backwinded. After hauling in the main, Lembit pulled on the jib sheet, but then he failed to recognize the correct trim.

"Draw it in a bit more," Arvid said.

As he spoke, the air flow from the jib hit the luff of the mainsail and set it slatting again. Lembit instantly understood.

"I get it," he called. "The idea is to ease it back until the flapping stops. Right?"

Arvid nodded, and the *Erma* edged forward close-hauled on her port tack, following the now clearly discernible contours of the Isle of Seil to the left. The wavelets could not have caused her occasional jerks.

"The flood tide is running in," Arvid explained. "It will be slow sailing soon."

The sunrise was not very bright since the air was still misty, although the fog had risen higher, forming low stratus clouds. Harry appeared from below, carrying the shore chart. He laid it on the cabin top and set his binoculars on it.

"The barometer is falling," he remarked casually, then settled down to study the chart.

We were nearing a small promontory, the western corner of the irregular, lozenge-shaped island of Seil. Around the corner, to the south of the promontory, the chart showed the shoreline bending back to the south-east for a stretch, then to the east, then almost due south. Opposite that south-easterly stretch, only a quarter of a mile from the tip of the promontory, a smaller island hugged Seil, separated from it by a narrow channel, nowhere wider than half a mile.

"That's the island of Easdale," Harry said, tapping the chart with his index finger. "We have to sail through this little sound."

Arvid looked up at the fluttering pennant.

"I'm afraid it will be a difficult bit of sailing," he said. "Hope it won't be necessary to tack. It's no fun with counter-running tides."

Arvid's fears, however, were quickly realized. It was all right at first as the shore bent westward to the tip of the promontory. That allowed us to slack off, and sail with the wind abeam. But as soon as we came out from the shelter of the headland, the wind, funnelling through the channel, rose in strength and swung to the south-east. The small island lay there high-banked and quite near. The entrance of the passage seemed extremely narrow.

"How about sailing around the island instead?" Arvid suggested.

Harry thought it unnecessary. So we continued west-south-west, on a close reach, the wind coming in a trifle forward of our beam until we approached Easdale's north-eastern corner. Then Arvid swung *Erma* into the wind. Soon the jib filled on the opposite tack, the boom went over, and down *Erma* bore toward Seil, close-hauled to bring her as far into the channel as possible. The eddying tide ran against her, and the fresh south-easterly breeze was so far ahead that the luff of the mainsail shivered constantly. Occasionally she shuddered all over, startled at the slightest bump.

"The leeward drift must be tremendous," Arvid said to Harry.

"It is," Harry agreed, "but we're still making headway. It will be fifteen minutes before we come about again, and the tide is running out fast. It should be entirely out in an hour and a half. But to be on the safe side we had better have the engine ready."

He yanked open the after cabin's slide and called: "Paul! Light the blowlamp and stand by to start the engine!"

Even the children, sensing that something was up, were now on deck. We entered the channel less than two hundred yards away from the landward curving coast of Seil, our lee shore. We were getting ready to come about, and Lembit had already stationed himself at the lee jib sheet when something unforeseen happened. Like a racehorse lashed by the whip, the *Erma* suddenly went through a series of jerks and shudders, then leaped forward with a terrific burst of speed. The children screamed delightedly.

"What the hell's happened?" Lembit demanded.

Even Arvid, at the wheel, seemed puzzled. Harry turned from the railing and grinned:

"It's a counter-current along the shore, created by the rush of the main stream. It often happens in narrow straits. A lucky break for us. Now we can come about without too much trouble."

And it was high time. The steep, dark shore appeared threateningly close. Opposite there was a break in the shore, exposing horizontal layers of black slate which looked like an abandoned quarry. Arvid whirled the wheel and the *Erma* slowly turned into the wind.

Although our progress was slow, the shore of Easdale loomed ahead all too quickly. Harry, on the starboard side, scanned it closely. It was only a little lower than Seil. We could spot several buildings, but it seemed bare and empty of human life. The only inhabitants were birds; gulls, terns, and stormy petrels, as well as giant gannets that sent up tower-high pinnacles of spray as they dived for fish. Suddenly Harry called out, "Get ready to come about."

"What's up?" Arvid yelled, startled because the shore was still about three hundred yards away.

"Reefs!" Harry shouted.

As Arvid quickly put down the helm, Grandma P. appeared in the companionway and stood watching the operation with a critical eye. As the bow slowly moved into the wind and the jib sheet failed to catch it, Grandma P., apparently unable to contain herself any longer, suddenly yelled:

"She's in irons and making sternway! Put the helm down!"

The *Erma*, indeed, was beginning to be swept slowly back with the tide. She was always a trifle awkward at going about with head seas or currents. Arvid, with a wide grin, put down the helm and ordered Lembit to sheet the jib to port in order to bring her back on the old tack. After what seemed an interminable time the *Erma's* bow swung to starboard.

"Sheet the jib to starboard! Fast!" yelled Arvid.

But Harry was already there, pulling the line taut and cleating it down. While he was doing it, Grandma P. called excitedly: "Wear her! Bring her about completely so we can go on the new tack!"

Arvid, with another quick grin, worked the wheel. As Harry shoved the boom across, and the mainsail and the loosened jib filled, the *Erma* was less than fifty yards from the foaming shoals.

Harry decided not to take any further chances, and ordered Paul to begin heating the engine. We would be safe for a while because on our starboard tack we had nothing to fear as there was a favourable counter-current along Seil and no shoals. But it was prudent to be ready for an emergency. We changed to the port tack and started a new zig toward Easdale. When we approached the shoaling waters of the island again, the flood tide was so slow that Arvid decided not to start the engine, but to try to come about instead of wearing. The manœuvre succeeded. The *Erma* turned steadily through the wind without getting stuck, the jib and main boom went over, and off she sailed on her starboard tack.

We were now coming out of the channel. The wind changed to the south again, and we could steer east-south-east on a long onshore tack into a deep bay off Seil. Tacking through that swirling passage without using the engine had been a fine piece of seamanship. Even Grandma P. smiled approvingly.

The wind was contrary and fickle. All day it kept heading us, following our every move and forever blowing straight into our eyes. In the afternoon, as we tacked down in the Sound of Jura with the mountainous island to starboard, the wind kept stiffening, and soon we had to start the engine to offset the impact of the swirling flood tide. The skies had cleared and the foam and spray crested dazzlingly white from the pale green tops of the twisted seas. It swept continuously over the bow, wetting the foot of the jib.

Then evening came. The majestic, green shores of Jura and of its southern neighbour, Islay, cast their vast shadows over the sound so that we sailed enveloped in twilight, while the peaks of the islands still burned in the setting sun. Soon the wind reached gale strength, and we lowered the mainsail.

Despite the use of both engine and jib, our progress was slow. The *Erma* shook and pitched badly, and every once in a while the propeller shot clear of the water and threshed wildly in the air. The will-o'-the-wisp lights of Ireland beckoned as Harry forced her over the hacking sea. At about midnight he resignedly brought her about and we raced downwind toward the shelter of sandy Kintyre Mull. There was nothing else to do—the old girl just didn't like this sort of weather. In the feeble light of a nearby airfield we felt our way into a little cove on the western shore of the peninsula. At once, the hoarse roar of the breakers quietened. We luffed, shut off the engine, lowered the soaked jib and dropped anchor. The wind still shrieked in the rigging, but we had a curious feeling of security despite the pitching of our craft.

At first, it was a snug, sweet feeling, but we soon grew tired of the cold wet discomfort of our sardine-box existence. It was four days before we could haul up the anchor, crawl stiffly out and make for the green and amber hills of Ireland.

12

FOR MORE than two weeks we were delayed in the Irish Sea by recurring south-westerlies which made us seek shelter. During one four-day period we were forced to stay in Strangford Lough, where the citizens of Portaferry and Strangford very kindly presented us with a quantity of food, particularly Irish potatoes. Then in the afternoon of 23 September, after tacking laboriously southward against contrary winds, we sought shelter near the harbour of Dun Laoghaire to the south of Dublin. From our anchorage we could see the lights of the Irish coast winking softly in the blackness, obscured at times by a thin veil of mist which drifted shorewards from the sea.

At midnight, as Heino came up to relieve my watch, a full, shapeless moon rose slowly in the east, lighting the dense clouds with a peculiarly ominous yellow glow. Then suddenly in the western skies, somewhere between the coast and the reflected lights of Dublin, two gigantic rainbows arched across the night.

"Rainbows in the moonlight!" Heino said softly. "No wonder the Irish are superstitious."

Neither of us had ever seen such a thing before. We stood watching silently until the brilliant colours faded into the blackness.

"The radio forecasts a gale for to-night," Heino said uneasily. "I wonder if there's any connection between the storm and these rainbows?"

"I don't know," I answered, "but you had better not doze off. Harry told me to call him the instant the wind picked up."

"No danger of that," Heino laughed. "The night's too spooky."

As I opened the companionway slide and ducked below, I noticed that the breeze from the south-west was dying away, and that suddenly the air seemed colder. I pulled the blanket over my head to shut out the gentle snoring of the others, and instantly fell asleep.

Two hours later, I awakened to find myself sprawling, half in and half out of my bunk. The *Erma* was pitching violently. The cabin seemed filled with a constant, thunderous roar. Once, as a boy, I had been trapped inside a rain barrel while playmates pounded with clubs on the outside. It was like that now.

Pulling myself back into the bunk, I braced one arm against the engine box, and listened. The snoring had stopped, so the others, too, must be awake. Overhead, I heard the clump of heavy shoes. Since Heino was wearing rubber-soled sneakers, I knew that either Harry or Arvid had gone up from below.

A moment later, the companionway slide was pushed back, and Harry shouted:

"Paul! Start the engine! Quickly! Everyone else on deck!"

A blast of cold wind and spray roared through the open companionway. Paul, springing out of his bunk, hastily tore the plywood cover from the motor, and deposited it on my head. Switching on the bulb over the engine, he began to fill the blowlamp pan with petrol.

"Shut that slide!" he yelled as the rest of us tumbled out of the cabin, "or I'll never get this damned thing lighted."

Outside, the peaceful waters of a few hours before had been transformed into the wildest seascape imaginable. The gale, coming straight from the shore, whipped the shallow water into a tempest of boiling, whirling foam, and sent it hurtling seaward like a blizzard driving across a great plain. Further out, near the anchorage of the *Erma*, the wind lifted the sea into short, twisted waves, and flung the spindrift like icy particles across the deck. Above, the moon shone clear and cold in a cloudless, starless sky.

On the open deck, the force of the wind was so great, the sting of the flying spray so painful, that it was impossible to face to windward for more than a few seconds at a time. In the bow, I saw the figures of Arvid and Heino bending over the windlass. The clank of the anchor chain sounded dull and far away.

I realized then that we were dragging anchor, and were being blown helplessly toward the harbour wall to the south. The massive corner tower rose threateningly in the moonlight less than a hundred yards from our stern. It seemed inevitable that we should be pounded to bits against its concrete bast.

Arvid's voice came from the bow:

"The anchor's all out, Harry, but she's still drifting!"

Foot by foot, dragging thirty fathoms of anchor chain and her two-hundred-pound anchor, the *Erma* edged towards the breakwater.

"Lembit! Rommy! Give me a hand with the mainsail!" Harry's voice, I noticed, was surprisingly calm. As the men tugged at the halyard, the sail slatted wildly in the wind, crackling like a battery of anti-aircraft guns. Halfway up the mast, with a shrill whizzing sound, the canvas parted from the slides like tissue paper.

In the next moment, there was a yellowish burst of

flame from the after cabin companionway. I hurried aft to find Paul smothering the engine with blankets which, fortunately, had been well dampened by the spray.

"Tried to pump the damned blowlamp too soon and set fire to the whole works," he gasped.

The oil around the base of the semi-diesel was burning fiercely, lapping over the floor boards with every lurch of the boat. A fire extinguisher was among the many extras the *Erma* lacked. I grabbed a blanket and helped Paul beat out the fire.

"Now, shut the slide," Paul ordered, "and I'll have another go at it."

As I closed the companionway, I saw that the breakwater was less than fifty yards astern. Paul saw it, too. With steady fingers, he refilled the heating pan with petrol, pumped up the pressure, lighted the petrol, and opened the valve. The finger of flame darted from the lamp and hissed from yellow to bright blue. Paul showed me how to play the blowlamp over the iron of the cylinder head.

"It's too early to crank," he said, "but I'm going under and crank her anyway. Maybe the fire heated her up a little."

He wriggled under the cockpit, and began cranking the heavy flywheel. Nothing happened. There was only a sickening, sluggish gurgle. For at least five minutes, Paul spun the wheel steadily. In the light of the blowlamp, I could see the sweat pouring from his grimy face and neck.

"You hold the lamp," I shouted, "and I'll crank."

"No time to change," he panted.

Suddenly, there was a heartening sputter. Another and another, and the engine started with a full-throated roar. Completely exhausted, Paul let his head droop forward on his arm. The spinning flywheel sent a spray of oily bilge over his face and hair.

"Throw her into gear!" he yelled, as he began wriggling from the cockpit. "And open her up!"

I pulled the gear lever back and advanced the throttle. The *Erma* seemed to shudder as she faced the storm. Paul drew back the companionway slide, and we saw that we were less than twenty feet from the breakwater tower. Even then, with the engine going at full speed, it was all the *Erma* could do to inch her way back against the tremendous force of the gale. The short, choppy waves beat a thunderous barrage against her hull, and I found myself wondering about the safety of those ants in the port bow.

As we gained steerageway, Harry brought the helm over so that, on the backward drift, we would clear the south end of the harbour wall. With this manœuvre successfully completed, we had about two miles of comparatively clear water between us and the rocky shoals which rimmed the bay.

The gale reached its peak about four in the morning. At that time, despite the labouring efforts of the engine, the *Erma* was forced to retreat, dragging her anchor and its thirty fathoms of chain. Behind us, silver in the fading moonlight, lay the encircling shoals from which there was no escape.

"Our only chance," said Harry, "is that the gale will blow itself out."

At dawn, it was impossible to stand on the deck or to make our way from one cabin to another. The force of the spray was like that of a hundred powerful fire-hoses sweeping the *Erma's* decks. For more than two hours we were unable to man the pump. In the cabins, the bilge water had risen at least eight inches above the floorboards. Everything was afloat. But not one of the children had awakened. And then, at last, as the sun came up over the horizon, the roar of the wind began to lessen; the curtain of spray, which had obscured the Irish shore throughout the night, thinned and dropped away.

A few hours later, as we cleared the bilge, and made coffee on our stove, the Dublin radio told us that the gale had reached Force Eleven on the Beaufort scale. Approaching hurricane intensity, it had sent two freighters and a large yacht aground on the Irish coast, and forced the *Queen Elizabeth* to return to port.

After breakfast we entered the harbour, dropped anchor, and took inventory of the damage to our stores. It was considerable. Most of the flour, sugar and bread had been ruined by salt water. Two five-gallon cans of paraffin for the stoves had opened and emptied into the bilges and in the storage space behind the after cabin, the potatoes were liberally coated with a greasy mixture of oil and sea water.

Finally, when the boat was in order, and our things had once more been put to dry in the rigging, Harry summoned everyone to his cabin for a council of war. It was not a happy session.

"First," he said, "we must find out exactly how much money we have left."

One by one, we reported on the state of our finances. The five bachelors in the after cabin had a total of eight shillings. Aunt Juliana miraculously produced two pounds which she had been hoarding for an emergency. Harry's wallet contained two pounds, ten shillings. That was it.

"I think," Harry said slowly, "that we had better plan to spend the winter here in Ireland. We'll get jobs, save our money, and then continue the voyage in the spring."

113

Everyone was silent. For some inexplicable reason, the children began to cry.

"It's not just the scantiness of our supplies," Harry continued. "It's the fact that the weather is turning against us. We left Sweden six weeks behind schedule, lost time in Norway, and now we seem to be stranded here in the Irish Sea. Every day lost lessens our chances for a successful Trade Wind passage."

"But if we stay here," Nora wanted to know, "where would we live?"

"Here on the *Erma*," Harry answered.

"But the children would freeze to death!" wailed Ellen. "There's no heat. Why, even to-day, they're cold and chilly. And Yuta's nose is running."

"It might be warmer at the pier," said Harry. "Perhaps we could even install stoves."

We five bachelors regarded each other sourly, and I knew we were all thinking about the prospect of sleeping through six winter months in those miniature bunks.

"Harry is right, of course," Arvid said. "Even with the best of luck, we'll undoubtedly run into contrary winds off the American coast. Without sufficient supplies, we may starve."

Grandmother Paalberg, who had been sewing the torn, red mainsail, looked up from her work.

"I wonder what the relations are between the Irish government and the Soviet?" she asked quietly. "Do you think we will be allowed to stay on here? To find work?"

"We'll have to apply for temporary visas, of course," Harry answered. "I hardly believe the Irish will refuse."

"Aren't you afraid," said Maia, "that after all this publicity, the Soviet may take some drastic action?

114

You know, we're not exactly the best sort of advertising for the U.S.S.R."

"Personally," Rommy said with a frown, "I'd rather put a little more distance between the *Erma* and the Kremlin."

"And who wouldn't?" said Harry impatiently. "All I'm trying to point out is that we are short of supplies, short of money, and short of time. Therefore the sensible thing to do is to stay on here, and cross to America in the spring."

At that moment, Lembit, who had been working at the pump, stuck his head down the companionway.

"As closely as I can figure it, Harry," he reported, "she seems to be leaking at the rate of about three gallons an hour."

"Another patch has probably worked loose," said Arvid glumly. "We had getter go over the side this afternoon and have a look."

Altogether it was not a happy session. It looked as if our voyage was over, at least until spring.

13

THE NEXT morning the world was quite suddenly transformed into a much brighter and more cheerful place. The weather, an anti-cyclone high which moved into Ireland on the heels of the gale, may have had something to do with it, but chiefly it was the appearance of Paddy Shortall. At the oars of a light rowing boat Paddy came skimming over the calm waters of the harbour just as the church bells of Dun Laoghaire began calling the worshippers to Sunday morning devotions. The slight, ruddy-faced man brought his boat to a stop a few yards from the *Erma's* side, and politely removed an ancient, peaked cap.

"Good morning," he said with a gallant, old-fashioned bow to the ladies, "I am Paddy Shortall, the boatman, at your service. If there are any errands you'd be wanting done ashore, I'll be glad to oblige."

Not knowing exactly how to cope with such impressive formality, Harry, too, removed his cap and bowed. The rest of us followed his lead. Paddy's face wrinkled in a smile, and I noticed that his blue eyes were as clear and gay as a child's. Reaching under the folds of a long, knee-length ulster, he produced two folded newspapers.

"I thought you might be wanting to see these. The Dublin papers of last evening."

Harry, undecided as to whether he should take the papers without paying for them, hesitated.

"I'm afraid," he said apologetically, "that we can't afford to pay for the services of a boatman. You see——"

Paddy, apparently, was somewhat hard of hearing. He tossed the newspapers to Harry and, a moment later, followed them aboard. There was a series of introductions, a round of general hand-shaking, a bow for each of the ladies, and a quick pat on the head for every child.

"A regular floating kindergarten, that's what it is," chuckled Paddy. "Or are you running a sort of a floating orphan asylum?"

Briefly, Arvid explained the purpose of our voyage. Paddy, head cocked sharply to one side, listened with narrowing eyes. His reaction was immediate and explosively vehement.

"Them damn Russians!" he stormed, clenching his fist and raising it above his head. "So that's what they're up to! Persecuting their subjects! I knew you couldn't trust them. Said so right along!"

When his indignation had burned away, that peculiarly charming pixie-like smile again lighted his face.

"It is insane, of course," he said, "to think of crossing the Atlantic in a boat like this with women and children aboard, but it's a magnificent venture, and I must admire you for it."

Heino, who, like most of us, was unable to understand much of what Paddy was saying, grinned broadly, and again shook the Irishman's hand vigorously.

"I see you don't like the Russians, either," he said in fluent Estonian.

Paddy looked puzzled.

"Damn Russians!" said Heino, proud of his rapidly expanding English vocabulary.

"That's right," agreed Paddy. "Those damn Russians are no good."

They shook hands again, and beamed at each other. Paddy turned to Arvid.

"There must be something we can do for you here," he said simply. "Are you sure there's nothing you need in the way of supplies? Milk for the children? Potatoes? Bread?"

"Well, you see," Arvid began, "we——"

"No," Harry broke in quickly, "there's nothing we need."

There was a deep, stubborn pride in Harry. And Paddy sensed it at once.

"At least," he said lightly, "you will see something of Dun Laoghaire? It's an old town, one of the most beautiful in all Ireland."

He pointed toward the shore.

"You might be tying up over there at the southern pier, alongside that small steamer. Then every one of you can go ashore for a sight-seeing trip."

"But we have no visas," Harry protested weakly.

"Visas! And why should you need visas to step ashore for a few hours?"

Paddy spoke in such a grand manner, that argument was difficult.

"You are fleeing from oppression, aren't you?" he asked. "Then what should be more natural than that you should find haven in an Irish town?"

I knew that Harry, who was having difficulty following Paddy's broad brogue, was now completely mystified.

"Why shouldn't we go ashore, Harry?" cried Ellen. "For heaven's sake, don't be so stubborn!"

"And so proud," said his mother softly. "You must think of the children, Harry."

Harry, red to the ear tips, as usual, gave in to the women. As Paul went below to warm up his engine, Paddy rowed back across the bay to explain our mooring to the captain of the steamer. When he had gone,

118

Heino and Rommy began questioning Arvid. "Who is he?" Rommy asked. "The mayor of the town?"

Arvid explained that Paddy was simply a boatman who made his living by supplying the wants of ships anchored in the harbour.

"Is that all?" Rommy was disappointed. "The way he acted, I thought he was some kind of official."

"I thought he was one of the authorities, too," said Heino.

"In Ireland," Arvid said, "every man is an authority."

* * *

The following morning we had barely finished breakfast when Paddy appeared, ready to lead us on an expedition through the shops of Dun Laoghaire.

"It will be better," he said, "if we split into two groups; the women and children in one, the men in the other."

This struck us as rather odd, but we readily agreed. Before separating, our fund of four pounds, eighteen shillings was divided between Harry and Ellen. The women, it was decided, would shop exclusively for canned milk, oatmeal, and dried fish. The men would purchase the bulkier articles such as potatoes.

About a hundred yards from the waterfront we entered a broad, fashionable avenue, lined with well-tended trees. As the women and children "oh'd" and "ah'd" at the magnificent palms, the first they had ever seen, Paddy proudly explained the history of the Victorian statues which seemed to lurk at the base of every tree. Further along, we turned into a more commercial thoroughfare where trams rumbled impressively past well-stocked shops.

"And now," said Paddy, lifting his hat to the ladies, "if you'll just turn here to the left, you'll find a fine selection of shops with very reasonable prices."

The primary reason for Paddy's insistence on the segregation of males from females became apparent before we had taken another ten steps. Throwing back his shoulders, he executed a smart right face, and led the way into a spacious pub. Even at that comparatively early hour of the day it was well filled with local seamen. They greeted Paddy enthusiastically, and regarded the rest of us curiously.

"Friends of mine," Paddy announced grandly as he waved us toward the long marble bar. "Fleeing from the Russian oppressor, they are! Eight glasses of the best Irish Republican Guinness, if you please."

The next half-hour was a hectic one. Like all seamen who had sailed to foreign ports, the patrons of the pub had a smattering of many languages—Swedish, German, French, Italian, Spanish, Norwegian. There was even one red-faced fellow who knew the Russian words for "more beer" and "illegitimate offspring."

In rapid order, we toasted the Irish Republic, the Estonian Republic, the Irish nation at large, the Estonian nation at large, the United States as an Irish-Estonian institution, Lord Kitchener, and George Bernard Shaw. After all our fellow tars had stood treat, Paddy slapped on his cap and said, "Let's be getting on with the shopping business."

As we walked along the street toward the shops, I suddenly realized that Heino was no longer with us.

"Have you seen him?" I asked Harry.

"No," he answered, "I haven't noticed him for the last ten minutes. He's probably still in the pub."

Hurrying back, I stuck my head through the

doorway. There was an instant barrage of hearty greetings but no sign of Heino.

"Maybe he went back to the boat," Harry said as I rejoined the others. "That Guinness is powerful stuff."

With Paddy in the lead we rolled along the sunlit street until we came to a large grocery store.

"Best grocery in all Ireland," said Paddy, waving us in, "and the proprietor is a friend of mine."

The grocer, a huge, bald-headed man, shook hands with Paddy and then with each of us.

Harry made our slender resources go as far as he could, and the friendly grocer slipped in an extra bag or two of sweets for the children. We each shouldered a package and followed Paddy towards the water front.

As we turned a corner I nearly dropped my bag for coming towards us, dwarfed by two giant policemen, was Heino! Seeing him, between the neatly uniformed officer and a plainclothesman, I realized for the first time what an odd-appearing lot we of the *Erma* really were.

It was at least a month since Heino had last shaved, and he had acquired a fairly luxuriant golden growth of beard. Since his hair had been allowed to go un-clipped for much longer than that, his general appearance was somewhat startling. In addition to this excess of hair, he wore one of those old-fashioned cloche mantles which drooped cape-like from his shoulders to his knees. The mantle, which Heino had picked up in a Stockholm second-hand clothing shop, originally had been black, but was now, after considerable exposure to salt water, a curious whitish green. On top of his bumper crop of curls, he wore a small, battered cap, at least two sizes too small.

Immediately Paddy put down his crate and rushed to the rescue.

"What are you doing with my friend?" he shouted to the policemen.

"Do you know this man?" one of the officers asked in surprise.

"Know him?" roared Paddy. "Of course I know him. And he's innocent of whatever it is."

"Take it easy, Paddy, take it easy," the policeman grinned. "We're not charging him with anything. Just taking him along for questioning. Can't make head or tail of what he says. What is he, anyway?"

"An Estonian," said Paddy. "Fleeing from the persecution of the Russians to a free land. And a fine, free land this is when a man can't stroll down the street in the broad daylight without being molested by the secret police!"

"We only wanted to have a look at his passport and papers," protested the other officer mildly. "If the boy's off a ship here, he should have a visa to come ashore."

"A visa! Papers!" Paddy's voice rose several notches and he began to talk so furiously that it was impossible for anyone but a fellow Irishman to follow him. Now and then, I caught such words as "tolerance," "freedom," "freedom of worship," "liberty," "Russian slaver," "Cossacks."

The harangue ended suddenly when one of the officers reached over and patted Paddy on the shoulder.

"As long as you say he's all right," he said soothingly, "it's all right with us."

With that the two patrolmen lifted their hands and strolled off.

"What happened?" we asked. "Why did you leave us in the pub?"

"Well," Heino explained as we walked along, "it was like this. After the third beer, for some reason or

122

other, I suddenly began to wonder if there was a Y.M.C.A. in town. You know I've always been a very active Y member back home, and I thought it would be nice to drop in at the branch here and say hallo.

"After walking along for a while without seeing a sign, I decided to look in the telephone book, so I walked into a place that I thought was a restaurant, and asked if I could see the telephone book, but nobody could understand me and the harder I tried to explain, the bigger the crowd grew. Then a plain-clothesman came, together with the policeman in uniform."

"And no wonder," laughed Arvid. "In that cape you look like a bomb-throwing revolutionary—to say nothing of the beard."

Heino's eyes, which were about all you could see of his face, looked hurt. He was very fond of that cape.

Dinner that night, with Paddy as guest of honour, was a merry affair. The barometer was still rising. A steady, moderate wind from the north-west rocked the *Erma* gently at her anchorage. And when Harry finally announced we would sail southward the next morning our happiness was really complete.

"To America!" toasted Paddy, raising his beer bottle. "And a safe voyage!"

"To Paddy," said Arvid quietly, "to Paddy of the good heart."

Paddy, for the first time since we had met him, seemed at a loss for words. Heino's beard arose from the other side of the table.

"Damn Russians," he said solemnly, clinking his bottle against Paddy's.

"Damn Russians!" agreed Paddy.

★ 14 ★

FOUR DAYS out of Ireland we met the eternal warmth and languor of the South. For hours on end the *Erma's* massive bow made a series of gleaming, pewter ripples which seemed to travel, completely unbroken, for miles on either side. Except for the peculiar, heaving motion of the low ground swell, our wake was the only disturbance on the shining surface of the sea.

There was something almost hypnotic about this peaceful, slowly swinging seascape. Here in the pond-like quiet, the sea was a foggy mirror, reflecting our thoughts, our dreams. To each of us, it seemed to con-jure up a different image. To Heino, it brought back the great rye fields of northern Estonia, rolling under the warm sun at blossom-time. To Nora, it was the lawns and terraces, the gardens and fields of Narva; to me, the shady, peaceful lawns of the University of Tartu seen in the early morning.

When, on the morning of October 7, for the first time since leaving Ireland, we saw the smoke of steamers rising on the horizon, we were almost startled at their intrusion on our endless expanse of shim-mering waves.

"Four of them," Arvid said, studying the plumes through his binoculars. "We must be in the Azores shipping lanes."

As they came closer, one of the vessels left the convoy and headed straight for us. She came on swiftly.

"An American army transport," Arvid told us. "She's loaded to the rails with soldiers."

Soon, even with the naked eye, we could make out

124

her grey guns and the khaki-clad men swarming about the decks. As she swung about in a great circle, the sun struck the Stars and Stripes fluttering over the stern. For several of us this was our first glimpse of the American flag.

About a hundred yards off the port beam, a strong, megaphoned voice shouted, "Are you all right?"

Arvid cupped his hands and answered, "We are all right!"

As the great vessel crossed our wake and ploughed again toward the western horizon, we could read the name across her stern, *Isaac Sharpness*.

"Goodbye, Isaac!" Nora called. "We'll see you in America!"

It was on the morning after we had met the Americans that most of us really began to appreciate the odds of the gamble on which we were staking our lives. Up to this time we had regarded death by shipwreck or drowning as an even chance, but it had not occurred to us that our adventure might end in death by thirst or starvation.

On this day we were astonished to find that our supplies were alarmingly low. Except for a few butt-end crusts, our bread had vanished. The oatmeal was so affected by moisture that it had acquired a rank smell and was practically inedible. The only food we had in quantity was the potatoes given us three weeks earlier by the kindly people of Ireland. Then it had seemed to us that with the gifts of our Irish friends we would have plenty of supplies to last until we reached Madeira, where we would restock for the long stretch across the Atlantic. But we had not counted on these extra days. Most terrifying of all, however, was the scarcity of water. We had never wasted it and had not used water from the tank since we reached Scotland;

we had depended on our small cask and demijohns which we could fill ourselves without the aid—and the expense—of a tank ship. The tank was a large one and there should have been plenty of water in it to last until we reached Madeira, so we hoarded the little money we had left and took what seemed to us a very small risk. Now the casks and demijohns were empty and the tank measured less than four days' supply.

It was a worried little group that gathered around the main cabin roof to watch Harry shoot the sun and make his daily calculation of our position.

"Three days ago," Aunt Juliana said plaintively, "Harry told us we would land in Madeira on the morning of the eighth."

"So?" Grandma P. uttered the monosyllable with a frigidity that might have silenced anyone else. Criticism of Harry was something she reserved almost exclusively for herself.

"Well," Aunt Juliana continued blindly, "here it is the eighth and we haven't even sighted land."

"Naturally," Grandma P. snapped. "We have been slowed down by contrary winds and calms."

"But suppose Harry has made a mistake in his calculations?" Aunt Juliana persisted. "Madeira is such a little pin point. It would be quite easy to miss it, I should think."

"Don't be ridiculous," interrupted Grandma P. "Harry couldn't make a mistake like that."

"But the sextant is such an old one. They say the mirrors are worn and need resilvering."

Harry, by this time, had returned the sextant tenderly to its battered case and was busy computing our position. We watched him silently. Finally, he made a small pencil dot on his large map. Ellen, who

126

had been watching over his shoulder, gasped in dismay.

"But we're still a long way from Madeira!" she said.

"Not too far," Harry replied cheerfully. "About a hundred miles, that's all. We'll be there to-morrow afternoon."

The next morning everyone looked until his eyes smarted. At one o'clock, nothing—at one thirty, nothing. Aunt Juliana said, "I do not feel well."

Some minutes later there was a false alarm from Maia.

"There, there," she pointed to the south, but Harry, after a careful look, dismissed her discovery as just a bunch of clouds on the horizon.

Finally, at three ten Arvid leaped from the forward cabin and called out loudly and clearly, "Land, land . . . ahead . . . there! I just saw it through the toilet's bullseye."

There it was: two conical hazy blue heights which at first sight looked like clouds. Harry took their bearings and said, "This is the smaller island. The main one is not yet in sight." But to us this was not important; we were no longer lost in the endless sea.

Two hours later Harry sighted the blue, cloud-piercing peaks of Madeira, the main island of the archipelago. They rose slowly over the rim of the horizon as we approached, and, by sunset, those with the sharpest vision, Grandma P., Harry, and Arvid, said they could distinguish the mountainsides below the great cumulus turban. As the peaks rose higher out of the sea, so did our opinion of Harry and Arvid as navigators. Even Aunt Juliana would have sworn by that battered sextant now.

After our anxiety had vanished, instead of gloomily turning over in our minds the chances of survival, we feasted our eyes on the blessed land. Silently, we watched the sulphur-coloured peaks glow vividly with the colours of sunset and then die to ashen grey as the far-away lightning criss-crossed the mushrooming layers of clouds above the island.

Our sleep that night was peaceful and deep, almost as it once had been, far away and long ago, in a peaceful Estonia. The next morning everyone was up far earlier than usual to watch the sunrise lighting the cloud banks around the craggy back of the still distant island. The whole sweep of the moisture-drenched western horizon was splashed with varying shades of blue, azure, indigo, and cobalt, and the island itself was veiled in a blue haze.

A light westerly breeze came with the sunrise and grew stronger with the morning. Aided by the engine, the *Erma* gained speed, and the small, shouldering waves, rippling in the brilliant sunlight, lapped musically against her bow. The smaller island we had spotted yesterday appeared to be a barren, deserted cliff with a sad, wrinkled profile.

"That's Porto Santo," Harry told us. "They say Columbus lived here in his youth, and that along these shores he found trunks and twigs of unknown trees. It was these trees that first made him believe there was land beyond the western ocean."

We looked at the rugged island with new interest. It was exciting to think that Columbus once had stood on these very shores, that it was here his dream of the westward passage had been born.

"So we're already on the threshold of the New World!" Maia exclaimed with a tremor of excitement.

"Some threshold," Rommy muttered sardonically. "All we have to do now is cross the Atlantic."

"How long do you think it will take us to reach America?" Ellen wanted to know.

"About four to five weeks," Harry answered. "If we don't run into contrary winds, we should be able to make it in about that time."

"How many sea miles have we covered up to now?" Rommy asked.

"The mileage itself doesn't mean too much. The canal passages, our stay in Norway and the storms in the Irish Sea have made it seem pretty long, but actually, we've covered only about twenty-six hundred miles."

"And there's how much to go?" Rommy persisted.

"Let's see," Harry calculated airily. "First we'll sail some six or seven hundred miles to the southwest to catch the Trade winds, then we head due west for about three thousand miles to the American coast. After that we'll sail north for New York about a thousand miles. That makes a total of about forty-seven hundred sea miles."

"In other words, it has taken us two months to cover twenty-six hundred miles, and you say we'll cover about five thousand miles in five weeks!" Rommy was obviously sceptical.

The 6,000-foot volcanic mass of Madeira approached with painful slowness, but by ten o'clock we were able to pick out the lines of its mountainous ridges. By noon, we could tell that the tiny, pink and white spots were buildings. Meanwhile, we went through all the excitement accompanying a landfall. Everyone talked louder and faster than usual; the children ran shouting about the deck; and the hair-do's of the women became almost magically glossy and well groomed. Nora, Ellen, and Maia appeared in gay dresses that we hadn't seen since the last sunny days in the Caledonian Canal. Grandma P. and Aunt Juliana blossomed forth in bright red and blue bandannas.

In the afternoon, the children were taken below and carefully dressed in their Estonian national costumes. All four were soon mincing proudly around the deck in their pleated woollen skirts and white blouses with intricate flower patterns of embroidery. Even we men began to preen ourselves. One by one, we knelt beside the after cabin, steadied a pocket mirror on the roof, and soaked our week-old beards with sea water and soap. It was like shaving with glue—and twice as painful. The irrepressible Rommy approached me brandishing a pair of clippers which Arvid had brought along to trim his daughter's hair.

"If you'll cut my hair, I'll cut yours," he offered.

"No, thanks," I declined. "The shave was enough for me. I'm still bleeding."

"Then, how about cutting mine?" he persisted.

"I've never done it," I hedged, "but maybe I could trim your neck, if that's all you want."

"No, I want a regular hair-cut, a short one about an inch high on top and clipped around the sides."

"Like von Stroheim?" I suggested, hoping to scare him out of it.

"That's the idea," Rommy said enthusiastically. "Let's go."

Rommy was a most persuasive fellow. Soon, I found myself kneeling behind him, ploughing virgin white stripes above his tanned neck and across his black hair. The barbering quickly attracted the children. All four shouted with glee every time I tossed a clipperful of hair into the sea. Presently even the adults were watching from the sidelines, offering advice and unflattering comments.

"He looks too much like a Soviet deserter," Maia criticized at one stage. "It's too square in the back. Run the clippers up a little higher."

What with the advice, the criticism, the rolling of the *Erma*, and the fact that I had never before cut so much as a single hair, the situation soon got out of control. In attempting to make a smooth transition from the back of Rommy's well-shaped cranium to the crown, I found myself gradually fighting a losing battle. There was still some hair in front, but the rear was quite barren. Rommy, sensing my panic, thoughtfully stroked his dome.

"I told you I wasn't good at this," I tried to apologize. "Better let Heino try it. He's clever with his hands."

With a stoical grunt, Rommy let Heino take over.

"Make an Indian out of him," Ellen advised. "It's all you can do now. A warlock and clip off the rest."

"Don't bother fussing around," said the patient calmly. "Just clip it all off."

Within a matter of minutes, the last hair on Rommy's head had swirled away with the wind. As he arose to his feet even the children were silent and somewhat frightened. Above his tanned, weather-beaten face his white scalp seemed to glow with a sickly phosphorescence. For days, every time I saw him without his beret I felt a pang of conscience.

*   *   *

The closer we came, the mightier and more impressive the island looked. At times the cliffs of the shore seemed to rise almost perpendicularly into the clouds. They were bare, rocky, partially covered with a pine scrub growth. Further inland we could see canyon-like gorges between steep valleys with hazy cloud flocks drifting through ravines; and winding up the hillsides at different levels were several villages.

At four o'clock, when there was no longer any hope of reaching the island's southern coast before nightfall, Harry decided we would sail throughout the night, despite the wind, and cover the remaining fifty miles to Funchal before daybreak. The gnawing in our stomachs, the desire for a good, cool drink of fresh water, was the main reason for this decision.

At seven o'clock the next morning, after we arrived and dropped anchor in the harbour of Funchal, the sun came out with dazzling brightness and incredible warmth. It lacquered the chalk-white and ochre stucco buildings with a glaring lustre, and gleamed on banana groves and sugar-cane fields on the lower level of the mountains. To the east, where the harbour opened, a medieval, fort-like dock jutted out into the sea. In the harbour that it protected, three medium-sized steamers and a dozen motor-boats and small yachts rode at anchor.

15

As WE stood drinking in the satisfying land smells, a drab, black motor-boat knifed its way swiftly toward us. We could read the name, *Argus*, painted on the bow. It manœuvred expertly alongside, and a squat, heavy-browed man, gloomily dressed in black, and a slighter, blond young man in somewhat gayer clothing, leaped aboard. For at least a full minute, the heavier one stood without speaking, scrutinizing us closely. I was suddenly, and painfully, reminded of the time I had been questioned by an N.K.V.D. man in Tallin.

The silent scrutiny seemed to have the same effect on the children, who immediately began to hide their faces in the folds of their mothers' dresses. At last, the younger official spoke.

"We're from the immigration police. We saw you coming while you were still out at sea."

He gestured toward a very youthful man who was still in the boat.

"And that's the port doctor. He's going to examine you."

As he spoke, the doctor rose to his feet, grasped the *Erma's* railing, and regarded us solemnly through his thick-lensed glasses. Suddenly he nodded to the officers, resumed his seat, and began lighting a cigarette. Whether we were overwhelmingly healthy, or ready for the undertaker, the inspection was obviously over. It was the briefest group medical examination I had ever seen.

The English of the younger, blond immigration

officer was excellent. He said, "Your passports, please. And the ship's papers."

Arvid and Harry collected the various documents, and handed them over. The two officials went over them carefully. The difference between Harry's black-covered Estonian passport and the red Swedish alien passports caught their attention at once.

"What's this?" the younger one asked suspiciously.

"An Estonian passport," answered Harry. "The others had their passports taken away from them by the Russians, but at that time I was in hiding, and managed to save mine."

The two officers exchanged confused glances.

"What is all this?" demanded the blond. "Russians . . . hiding . . . and Estonia. What is Estonia?"

"The Republic of Estonia is a country east of Sweden," Harry tried to explain, "on the opposite side of the Baltic."

"So you are not a Swede!" The official's voice was accusing.

"No, I'm an Estonian."

The immigration man waved his arm somewhat wildly towards the rest of us.

"And these people? Are they Swedes?"

"No, they're Estonians, too."

The officer's voice rose sharply.

"But they have Swedish passports. How do you account for that?"

"They are not Swedish passports," Harry explained. "They are Swedish alien passports. You see, we are all Estonians who lived temporarily in Sweden as war refugees."

Harry's calmness seemed to infuriate both men. After several minutes of study, the young Portuguese asked coldly, "What kind of government do they have in Estonia?"

"It was a republic," Harry answered slowly, and I noticed that his ear lobes were getting red. "A democratic republic. Temporarily, it is occupied by the Russians."

"So!" The Portuguese fairly hissed the sibilant. "By the Russians! So Estonia is a communistic country!"

"Not at all. It is occupied by the Communists, but the people are not Communists."

The official was impatient of such reasoning.

"People and rulers, what is the difference? A country must be either one thing or another. Why didn't you like the Russians?"

"Would you like anyone who walked into your country, arrested your family, and destroyed your home?" Harry asked. "But, as a matter of fact, when most of us left Estonia the country was occupied by another conqueror—the Germans."

Harry, as usual, was being painfully truthful. I noticed Arvid wince. The face of the squat Portuguese was absolutely expressionless, but the blond one flushed.

"So you escaped from the Germans," he said slowly. "I see." But it was quite clear that he did not.

The situation was getting more muddled every moment. The more we tried to explain, the more complicated everything seemed. After thinking all these things over, the blond officer said accusingly, "You seem to be stateless persons with no proper passports or visas. I'm taking the passports with me. You will get them back when you leave. Meanwhile, no one will be allowed ashore."

"In that event," Harry snapped, "your government

will be obliged to pay for our winter expenses here. It is absolutely necessary for us to go ashore to buy supplies and diesel oil if we are to continue our journey."

"And our children need fresh milk and exercise," Ellen called. "They should be taken ashore."

"We shall see," the officer said. "I'll have to consult my superiors."

The two climbed into their boat and roared shoreward.

Early the next morning we were awakened by a foghorn "Hallo!" A broad-shouldered young man with a battered straw hat pulled at a rakish angle over one eye leaned on his oars a few yards from the *Erma's* side.

"This is the harbour boatman," he announced with quiet pride. "Anything you wish from shore, I will get it for you."

After the reception the day before, his friendly smile was like a springtime sun. Arvid at once invited him to tie up and come aboard. When this was done, he flashed his white-toothed smile and began to chatter away.

"You're going to America, yes? A most wonderful country. Very okay. I have been there many times—twice—as a seaman on Portuguese boats. I learn English-American there. See? Like a regular son-of-a-gun, eh?"

He pushed back his hat and laughed uproariously, revealing more sound, white teeth than I had ever seen outside a horse's mouth.

Harry told him that we did expect to do some shopping. We were down to our last few dollars, but he planned to cable his father in New York for enough money to re-provision us and buy more diesel oil. First, however, we wanted to know the prices of various staples.

"Sure," the boatman grinned, "I understand. To-day I will get a price list of everything from the stores."

"Do you know how much diesel fuel is a gallon?" Arvid asked.

The Portuguese looked astonished.

"Diesel oil! No such thing here. The war make it very scare." He gestured expansively, "Not on the whole island will you find it," he gestured. "But there is plenty of petrol. You can use petrol, yes?"

Harry seemed stunned.

"There must be some diesel oil somewhere on the island. We'll have to go ashore to find it."

But the boatman was still muttering, "No oil, no oil," as he rowed away.

Within a matter of minutes after he had gone, a bevy of small rowing boats clustered around the *Erma*. They were manned by noisy, desperate-looking characters attired in colourful rags. As they came alongside, they loudly chanted something which sounded to us like *"Chincho fo chincho! Chincho fo chincho!"*

Then they rested on their oars and we saw that the boats were filled with a weird assortment of goods: fruits, wine, wicker furniture, souvenir post cards, assorted handicraft, anything and everything.

"Change for change! That's what they're yelling," cried Rommy triumphantly. "They want to trade stuff with us. Look at that fruit! Let's go, boys!"

He dived into the bachelor's cabin, and reappeared almost instantly clutching an old pair of army boots. One of the *chincho-fo-chincho* men, a huge, black-mustachioed fellow immediately held up a battered, wicker arm-chair. Rommy vigorously indicated his lack of interest, but the Portuguese hoisted the clumsy piece on to the *Erma's* rail, and reached for the boots.

With a sudden push, Rommy returned the chair to the boat, nearly knocking the tradesman off his feet. This seemed to irritate the merchant beyond endurance. Thrusting forth his long neck and formidable chin, he began upbraiding Rommy in such rapid Portuguese that his moustaches flapped furiously like the wings of a crow flying against the wind. Finally, completely out of breath, he subsided for a moment, and then clutched the *Erma's* railing.

The brawny Rommy, however, was ready for him. Rolling up his sweater sleeves, he began to flex his arm muscles until they swelled terrifyingly. The Portuguese abruptly changed his mind, and removed his hand from the rail. The victory became a rout when Rommy, with an irritated gesture, swept off his beret, baring his freshly-clipped scalp. The peddler grabbed his oars, and frantically rowed away, his eyes glued to Rommy's head in horror-stricken fascination.

Then after a brief session of bartering, Rommy exchanged the boots for a huge basket of glittering red apples. The fruit was no sooner over the side than Aimi, Inga, Ulla, and Yuta were munching away furiously.

Now we were all hurrying below, rummaging through our belongings for odds and ends to trade with the *chincho-fo-chincho* men. The men found shirts and shoes, razor blades, underwear, neckties. Heino, Harry and I each decided to part with one of our two suits of clothes. Nora sacrificed a pair of high-heeled dancing slippers.

For some reason, the slippers with their rhinestone buckles seemed to have a fatal attraction for one grey-bearded gaffer. Pushing the other boatmen aside, he offered Nora two fair-sized baskets of apples and bananas. But obviously, Nora was a horsetrader from away back. She shook her head from side to side so violently that her blonde hair escaped her bandanna and streamed in the wind.

But the old owl was a worthy opponent. With a gesture to show his overwhelming generosity, he offered her a basket of pears. When Nora refused and indicated that she wanted still a fourth basket, the man flew into his native language to deliver either a long prayer or a curse.

Ignoring him, Nora dangled the shoes before one of the younger traders, turning on her radiant, half-Nordic, half-Slavic charm. The Portuguese, hynotized either by the shoes or Nora's smiling eyes, pointed to four large baskets of assorted fruits. But before the deal could be concluded, the bearded gentleman thrust the boy aside and signalled his agreement to Nora's demands.

16

FOR THREE days we sat around hopefully awaiting word from the immigration officials which would allow us to go ashore. In desperation, Harry finally composed a strong letter to the Chief of Police and sent it ashore by the boatman, "Yank."

On the fourth morning, a tall quiet Dane came out in Yank's boat, and introduced himself as Andreasson, the Scandinavian Consul in Madeira.

"I'm trying to straighten things out," he told Harry, "but it may take a little more time. In the meanwhile, is there anything I can do for you? I have the authorities' permission to take the children ashore for a little outing."

Harry composed a cable to his father and gave it to the consul, while Aimi, Inga, Ulla, and Yuta were hurriedly scrubbed from head to toe and attired in their Estonian national holiday costumes. Then the four youngsters, squealing with delight, took off with their new "Uncle Consul."

They were back late in the afternoon with enthusiastic tales of how "Uncle Consul" had driven them in a two-horse carriage through a veritable fairyland of palm trees, fine houses, sweet shops, and ice-cream parlours. Judging by the children's description, Madeira was one large ice-cream cone, dotted with palm trees. Heino and Rommy were frankly envious. So, to be perfectly frank, were the rest of us. As Lembit put it bitterly, "These Portuguese seem to have an age limit for Communists."

That night, so strong was our yearning to go ashore

that Paul put on his swimming trunks and, fortified with a few swigs of Madeira Malvasia, swam to the nearest embankment, holding his dungarees above his head. He was back within half an hour to report a policeman patrolling the docks.

On the morning of the eighth day, October 18, just as our stomachs were beginning to heave like accordions from the lopsided diet of fruit and wine, the *Argus* swept alongside.

"Captain Paalberg, Captain Kuun, and Mr. Veedam will be permitted ashore," announced the blond Portuguese.

"Mr. Veedam!" chorused Rommy, Heino, and Paul.

"Yes, the newspaper correspondent," answered the immigration man. "Which one is he?"

As I stepped forward, he said, "You wrote to the chief of police saying you were a representative of some British newspapers?"

Four days before, I had written a brief note, claiming that I was to write an account of the voyage for a Scottish newspaper, and asking if I might be allowed a brief glimpse of Madeira. I had nearly forgotten about it, however, and was now as astounded by my good fortune as any of the others. Without looking at my cabin mates, I hopped in beside Arvid and Harry.

"The power of the press!" Heino yelled derisively as we took off.

As soon as we docked, Harry and Arvid, escorted by the squat, swarthy officer, set off for the Danish Consulate, where two hundred dollars from Captain Paalberg was awaiting them. Breathing deeply of the sweet shore smells, I followed our blond friend down a palm-lined boulevard to the Madeira police headquarters. The chief, a young man of less than thirty, sat behind a desk beneath an enormous portrait of Salazar, the strong man of Portugal.

"So, you are a newspaper correspondent?" he inquired in excellent English.

"Yes," I answered, and then tried to explain how I had been asked to mail a story now and then about our trip.

The more I tried to explain, the more confused my English became. Finally, with a few dying-fish gestures, I lapsed into silence.

"Your newspaper accounts must be extremely interesting," he said after a considerable pause. "Tell me, what language do you write them in?"

"English," I stammered.

"That, in itself," he remarked drily, "should make your articles practically phenomenal."

Then he extended a well-manicured hand, and the interview was at an end. As we walked back to the water front, the immigration officer gave me a quick, amused glance.

"You're really rather lucky," he said.

"How's that?" I asked.

"He might have arrested you as an impostor. You want to be more careful when you're dealing with a chief of police."

I began explaining that it was easier for me to write in English than to speak it, but the official presently silenced me by absent-mindedly beginning to whistle some abominable Portuguese ditty.

It was hours before Arvid and Harry returned to the dock. Finally, they appeared, looking dusty, tired, and rather grim. Their dark-complexioned guide looked even grimmer, and I noticed, with considerable pleasure, that he was perspiring with a will.

"We've been from one end of the city to the other,"

Arvid said despondently, "and we can't find a drop of diesel oil. I'm afraid Yank was telling the truth."

Harry seemed equally glum.

"What about supplies?" I asked.

"We managed to get a fair amount," he answered briefly. "Yank will bring the stuff out in the morning."

We rode in silence out to the *Erma*. As soon as they stepped aboard both Harry and Arvid went directly to the helm cockpit and unscrewed the cap of the fuel tank. The measuring stick showed less than two inches of oil.

That night, after the children had been put to bed, Harry asked us all to come up on deck for a conference.

"To be perfectly frank," he began, "neither Arvid nor I want to make the decision as to whether we should continue our voyage——"

"Not continue?" cried Rommy. "Why not? What else can we do?"

"Well," Harry answered, "we spend the winter here in Madeira or go back to Scotland or Ireland. Now, suppose I tell you just how matters stand, and then we can put it to a vote."

There was a murmur of assent.

"When we started on the trip," Harry began, "neither Arvid nor I calculated on so many delays. By this time, we really thought we would be half-way across the Atlantic. But here it is nearly the end of October, and we're still in Madeira with about five thousand miles to go."

It was almost dusk now and from the shore came the voice of a lone singer. It was one of the ancient Portuguese folk songs with a haunting, melancholy strain. Harry waited absent-mindedly until the singer's voice had drifted from a high to a lower note, and then he continued:

"As far as food is concerned, we'll have to live mainly on potatoes and rice. They're cheap here, and we were able to buy fairly large quantities of both. For the first few weeks, of course, we'll have bread, butter, ham, and a little pork. But after that, it will be potatoes and rice, mixed with olive oil."

Rommy, the heaviest eater of us all, interrupted:

"We can stand it. After all, it won't be for too long."

"That's just the trouble," said Harry soberly. "There's no way of telling exactly how long we may be at sea. At this time of the year, the Atlantic is a tricky place. When we get into the Gulf Stream, off the American coast, it will certainly be well past the middle of November. By then we may run into gales. And gales in the North Atlantic, with winter coming on, are not too pleasant."

"Do you think the *Erma* can weather them?" Paul asked.

"I don't know," Harry answered bluntly. "It's a gamble."

"And the water supply?" Lembit asked.

"With rationing," Harry said, "we should have enough—if the trip doesn't take too long. Everything, of course, depends on the time element."

The voice of the far-off Portuguese singing seemed more doleful than ever. Whether it was because of the song or Harry's frank words, we were beginning to feel decidedly gloomy. It was Grandma P.'s caustic comment that finally perked us up.

"Personally, I can't see any problem at all," she said bitingly. "Here we are practically at the half-way mark —on the threshold of America as you said the other day—and suddenly we begin this talk of turning back."

"But we planned on filling the tank with diesel oil," said Harry quietly. "If we had diesel fuel, we could

144

count on the engine taking us through calms and contrary winds."

"Oh, bother the diesel oil," snapped his mother. "Did your grandfather have engines when he sailed his barquentines to South America and half-way around the world? Not a bit of it! He sailed every foot of the way—contrary winds or fair! And we should be able to do the same!"

"And if we returned to Scotland," roared Rommy, "how do we know we won't be sent back to Sweden, and then to Estonia, and finally to Siberia? The Lord knows I hate the ocean, but I'd rather be eaten by an octopus than by Father Stalin!"

There was a vigorous chorus of approval. Harry turned to Aunt Juliana who had been sitting quietly with eyes half closed, listening more, I suspected, to the singer than to the argument.

"What about you, Aunt Juliana?" Harry asked. "Are you ready to risk your life?"

"My life?" asked Aunt Juliana absently. "Oh, yes. Of course. You see I've been prepared to die ever since I first set foot in this horrible boat, so it wouldn't be too much of a shock for me. Anyway," she added after a moment, "it would be a deal pleasanter to die than to go back, wouldn't it?"

*　　　*　　　*

We were up at sunrise the next morning to ready the *Erma* for our departure. Breakfast was barely finished when Yank arrived with the provisions Harry had ordered the day before. As the Portuguese lifted them over the side, Arvid ticked off the articles on the list: eight sacks of potatoes, four sacks of rice, twenty-five kilos of sugar, sixteen small tins of Argentine butter, four quarts of olive oil, eight cans of condensed milk, an eight-pound ham, a ten-pound slab of pork, less than a dozen assorted cans of luncheon meat and sardines. There was also a box of white bread and a blackish variety of hard-tack.

"Doesn't look like too much for sixteen people, does it?" Heino asked wryly as we stored the stuff below.

"We won't put on weight, that's certain," Rommy predicted. "But I'm surprised Harry didn't buy any onions. They must be quite cheap here in Madeira, and they're full of vitamins."

"Onions!" echoed Lembit. "That's one thing we can do without. It's bad enough to have four of us stuffed into that cubbyhole, but to have you gnawing at onions every hour of the day and night! God forbid!"

"Nevertheless," Rommy said firmly, "I'm going to ask Harry to get me some onions when he goes ashore. They prevent scurvy."

"You're thinking of lemons," scoffed Paul.

"Anyway, what are you going to do for money?" Heino asked. "Onions may be cheap, but no one's giving them away, you know."

For answer, Rommy reached in his pocket and pulled out three crumpled Portuguese *escudo* notes.

"Yank has been teaching me a game called poker dice," he explained. "He won most of my underwear, and a sweater, but I got these."

But now he regarded them dubiously.

"To tell the truth," he added, "I don't know whether they'd be worth a bushel of onions—or a hundred."

As Harry and Yank pushed off for shore to make the last of our purchases—two fifty-pound sacks of flour—Rommy pressed the money into Harry's hand.

"Here's my contribution to the ship's stores," he

said. "I want you to spend it on onions—large, juicy, Madeira onions."

Harry shuddered slightly, but agreed to make the purchase despite the vehement protests of Lembit. The rowing boat was about half-way to shore when the harbour tank-ship pulled alongside to replenish *Erma's* water supply. Arvid and Lembit took the big hose from a tall, skinny, hawk-nosed man, and carried it below to the water-tank openings in the main cabin. After that, the small cask and the three clay demijohns lashed to the deck rail were filled.

"That makes at least a ton and a fifth of fresh water," Arvid estimated. "It should be enough—with rationing."

After the tank-ship headed toward its anchorage, the *Argus* came roaring from the shore. As it circled us slowly, the blond immigration officer suddenly heaved a packet on to our deck, and then, clasping both hands over his head in boxer-fashion, bade us both hail and farewell.

"Probably a going-away present," said Nora cheerfully. "Now, wasn't that nice of them?"

Lembit untied the parcel and held up the farewell gift—our passports.

At eighty-thirty, Harry and Yank returned with the flour, and four lumpy sacks. Holding one hand ostentatiously to his nose, Lembit helped hoist them aboard. Rommy instantly ripped open one of the bags, and held aloft a great, crimson-skinned onion, somewhat smaller than a grapefruit but certainly larger than an orange.

"Beauties!" he declaimed. "Ravishing beauties!"

A few minutes later, after we had all shaken hands with Yank, Lembit and Paul loosed the bow and stern lines from the mooring buoys, and the *Erma* floated free of her Madeira anchorage. At a signal from Arvid, at the helm, Harry hoisted the mainsail. Slowly, with a tiny breeze half filling the canvas, we nosed toward the southern pier of the harbour. Yank chased us for a while, alternately rowing madly and waving farewell. As we neared the end of the pier, Aimi spotted a tall figure, running along the dock, waving with one hand and shielding his eyes from the glaring sun with the other.

"It's Uncle Consul!" she screamed. "Goodbye, Uncle Consul, goodbye!"

Like high-pitched sirens, all four children screamed their farewells and thanks to the good-hearted Dane. Soon we were moving into the open sea, through an armada of *chincho-fo-chincho* men. They were obviously awaiting the arrival of the British cargo-ship, which was approaching the harbour, still protected by her grey war-camouflage and heavily armed. Heino pointed to a grey-bearded boatman, nearly hidden behind piles of wine bottles and heaps of sundry goods.

"Look at that rascal!" he said. "He's wearing my best blue shirt!"

"And the one behind him, the fruit pedlar, has on my trousers," moaned Lembit. "The good ones I was going to wear on the day we landed in America."

As we sailed through their midst, the boatmen greeted us enthusiastically, rising to their feet, and flourishing their straw hats in elaborate bows.

"They're a gallant lot of thieves," grinned Paul. "But God help the British. They don't know what they're walking into."

The morning was dry and sunny. The canopy of clouds, drifting high across the mountain tops, seemed small and fluffy. As we drew almost abreast the freighter at the mouth of the harbour even the slight breeze died away. Soon, it seemed as though the ocean swell was carrying us back to shore. Finally, after a motionless half-hour, Harry reluctantly signalled Paul to start the engine.

Twenty minutes later the familiar chug-chug sounded from the after cabin, and the *Erma* nosed forward into the gently heaving sea. At our three-knot speed, the massive house-studded island seemed to be following us out to sea.

"We'll be able to make out the mountains until sunset," Grandma P. predicted, "but by morning everything will be well out of sight. So take a good look at your last land for four or five thousand miles."

Most of us unconsciously took a deep breath. Five thousand miles! Wasn't the diameter of the entire earth only some eight thousand? Suddenly the voyage which lay ahead seemed to assume almost astronomical proportions, and America became a far-away planet in outer space.

149

17

IN THE late afternoon of our third day out of Madeira, a steady north-north-east wind set in, and soon the *Erma's* wake shimmered wide and foaming in the sunset. All about us the sea was lumpy and fringed with whitecaps. Heino was having a turn at the wheel.

"Could this be the Trades?" he asked Harry. "The wind seems steady and in the right direction."

"I hardly think so," Harry answered doubtfully. "Probably just another north-easterly. We can't expect the Trades much before the twenty-fifth latitude."

"Where are we now?" Ellen asked.

"Just passed the twenty-ninth. Didn't you see it?"

"What?" Both Ellen and Maia looked quickly around.

"A white post with a green sign," Harry teased. "They have them at every latitude line, don't they, Arvid?"

"I thought it was the other way around," Arvid answered, "a green post with a white sign."

"Just the same," put in Grandma P., "I wouldn't be too cocky. Your father always said there are two things no man can predict, the start of the Trades and the heart of a woman. We may be in the Trades, no matter what your signposts say."

As the hours passed, it began to look as though Grandma P. was right. The north-easterly blew on and on at the same steady strength, and even the seas seemed to stabilize themselves to a regulation height. At last Harry himself was almost convinced that we had actually reached the Trades.

"At least," he said cautiously, "we have all the symptoms."

"That's good enough for me, doctor," Paul announced. "If no one objects, we'll celebrate with my last bottle of Malvasia."

No one objected, and a few minutes later the beginning of the Trades was clearly marked by an empty bottle.

*   *   *

For several days, as we sailed south-west for the twentieth latitude, we had the wind directly astern. To take full advantage of it, Arvid and Harry shifted the jib from the forestay and set it in a goose-wing position across the port deck. A two-by-four, fastened to the railing, acted as a jury boom. The mainsail was then slackened so that the boom pointed almost at right angles to starboard, the starboard runner having been eased out of the way. The boom, held clear of the waves by the topping lift, was connected to the forward end of the handrail by a preventer rope in order to avoid gybing. This increased our speed to about four knots, but Arvid was still not satisfied. On the morning of our seventh day out of Madeira, I watched him as he checked the tautness of the back stay, and then walked to the cockpit to study the spray wetting the foot of the mainsail.

"Something wrong?" I asked.

Arvid lighted a brown Madeira cigarette, cupping the match in the shelter of his palm.

"Looks lop-sided, doesn't it?" he asked, jerking his cigarette towards the wide mainsail on one side and the narrow jib on the other. "Like a bird flapping along with a crippled wing."

He turned to Harry, who was at the helm.

151

"This fore-and-aft rigging isn't suited at all to the Trades. Square sails would be the ticket for this running before the wind. Faster—and no danger of gybing."

"Or a set of light sails," Harry added. "We ought to have a good spinnaker in place of the jib."

Arvid puffed silently at his cigarette, watching the canvas bulge as we rode a crest, and then sag when we slid down into the trough. Suddenly, he sent his cigarette arching into the wind, and whirled on Harry.

"I've got it!" he cried. "Why not use *both* our mainsails? We could spread the red one to port in place of the jib, enlarge the sail area, and balance the rig. What do you say to that?"

For Arvid, who rarely raised his quiet tenor above a conversational pitch, this enthusiastic outburst was practically unparalleled. Harry, however, merely squinted a little more into the sun, and ran his tongue thoughtfully over his front teeth.

"Seems like a good idea," he admitted finally, "but it may be rather complicated. In the first place, we'd need a stouter jury boom."

"What's the matter with using that six-foot timber?" Arvid said. He pointed to a stout, oak beam which we had brought with us from Sweden. "We could lash that to the two-by-four and make a much stronger jury boom."

Harry, holding the wheel lightly, considered the idea, keeping his eyes straight ahead as though we were passing through mined waters.

"It's certainly worth a try," Arvid argued. "The red sail should increase our speed by at least a knot or more."

"All right," Harry agreed at last, "let's give it a try."

To clear the deck for the work ahead, the women

152

and children were ordered below, but most of them continued to peep excitedly over the companionways. First, the goose-winged jib was taken down, and returned to the forestay. The twelve-foot two-by-four and the six-foot oaken timber were then firmly lashed together. After that the double, reinforced section was fastened to the foot of the mast. The single end, extending over the railing, was partially supported by short timbers to relieve pressure on the rail.

"Okay!" called Arvid. "There's our new jury boom. Now for the red mainsail!"

Lembit carried the red sail from the after cockpit to the mast. Arvid tied a line to its clew, and Lembit, stretching out full length on the boom, connected the clew end of the sail to the end of the two-by-four. Turning the wheel over to Rommy, Harry clambered forward, and tossed Lembit a long piece of half-inch manilla.

"Fasten that to the end of the boom," he ordered. "We'll run it down to the gunwale to reduce the pull of the sail. There's going to be a terrific strain on that two-by-four!"

"Watch her now!" Arvid warned Rommy. "She'll handle awkwardly."

Moving swiftly and expertly, Arvid and Harry took the jib from the forestay and unfastened the halyard and sheet. Harry secured the halyard-block to the top of the red sail, and Arvid simultaneously connected the jib sheet to the tack end.

As Harry lifted the canvas with smooth, powerful pulls on the halyard, Arvid close-hauled the sheet. Within seconds, the great, red sail, clapping loudly, filled and stretched taut in the wind. The *Erma*, now fitted with two balanced wings instead of one and a half, responded with a surging leap. From the companionways, the women and children sent up an ear-splitting cheer.

With her new rigging, the *Erma* put on an intoxicating burst of speed. Spray flew high over her bow in a silvery, transparent *V*. The rush of the green and white waters along her sides was like that of swift-flowing rivers. In her widened wake the white foam bubbled and hissed.

"What would you say our speed is now?" Heino asked with a glance over the side, "About seven knots?"

"At least!" Lembit agreed enthusiastically. "We seem to be going twice as fast."

Arvid crumpled an empty cigarette packet and tossed it over the side. He watched it recede in our wake, counting slowly to himself.

"Not quite that much. I'd put it at about six knots. What would you say, Harry?"

"Just about," Harry agreed. "It's a nice pickup though."

The increase in sail area, however, created new problems for the helmsman. Each silver, gurgling crest that swept the *Erma* forward, tried to force her to yaw violently. Deep in the troughs of the waves, which now were consistently running at least ten feet high, the great spread of canvas tended to flap. But Arvid and Harry, with a skilful touch on the helm, brought her around so that every wave and trough bore us south-westward. The rest of us never tired of the magnificent sight.

But ten hours later, as the sea was reddening in the sunset, we caught Harry and Arvid anxiously eyeing the jury boom. To our dismay we saw that the two-by-four to which the sail's clew was fastened was bending dangerously upward with each bellying of the sail.

"It'll hold," Lembit said encouragingly. "It's good, strong timber."

But at nine o'clock, as the ocean glittered under a rising full moon, the *Erma's* new rigging met with complete disaster. With a sickening, splintering sound, the long timber cracked in two. As Arvid heroically struggled to keep the unbalanced *Erma* from falling into the wind, Harry sprang forward and quickly doused the slatting sail.

That night, under the glorious full moon, the *Erma* ploughed forward with the jib back in its old, goose-wing position, tied to the stump of the broken timber. It was a saddening change of pace. With the cracking two-by-four our dream of a twenty-day Trade Wind passage vanished completely. And once again America seemed as far away as the brassy moon.

"But it may be all for the best," Nora said, patting the roof of the main cabin. "After all, the old lady's getting on and the fast life might have been too much for her."

* * *

During those first days of the Trades, particularly on days when the wind quartered our course, and the seas were relatively calm, Heino, Lembit, Paul, Rommy, and I tried our hands at the helm. Of the five of us, Lembit had the surest, most natural touch. He sat there calmly, grasping the wheel lightly, and was seldom tricked into the exaggerated corrective motions which plagued the rest of us.

Rommy, on the other hand, was an indifferent pupil. During his trick at the helm, if the wind was moderate, he liked to study his English grammar.

"Why should I waste time staring at the empty sea?" he demanded after Harry protested. "When we get to

155

America, I want to be able to get a job—and how can I get a job if I don't speak English? No sense wasting valuable time."

After a while, Rommy developed a special technique for steering with his feet. One afternoon, Arvid came up from below to find him sitting atop the after cabin with his legs dangling into the helm cockpit, and his toes gripping the spokes of the steering wheel. Now and then, he glanced up from his studies to meet the compass card directions.

"What the devil are you doing?" roared Arvid. "A fine sailor you are!"

"What's the matter?" asked Rommy calmly. "I'm on course to a hair, and this is a very comfortable way to steer. The trouble with you, Arvid, is that you're steeped in tradition. Just because no one has ever steered with his toes before, you think it's all wrong."

As Arvid continued to stare at him, Rommy slowly abandoned his comfortable perch, and assumed a more conventional position at the helm.

"Anyway," he grumbled, "I have no ambition whatever to become a sailor. In fact, if we ever do get to America, I'll never step inside a boat again as long as I live."

18

THERE WAS a peculiar, trancelike charm about those Trade Wind days. As the *Erma* rolled on through the immense, sun-filled expanse, we could literally feel our hearts lighten, and the blackness that all of us had known for so many evil years, lift from our spirits.

Yet these days were eventful, too, for one morning as I was lying on the after-cabin roof, soaking in the warmth of the late October sunlight, half listening to the children as they carefully repeated English words and phrases that Maia was teaching them, I became aware of a curious, long-drawn, puffing sound, something like that of a steam locomotive labouring up a steep grade. Lembit, who had been sitting with Arvid in the helm cockpit, sprang to his feet.

"What was that?"

Arvid also had stood up and was looking to starboard. I looked too, half expecting to see a steamer on the horizon, but there was nothing. The great, majestic rollers of the Trades swept by, blue and white in the morning sun.

Then, much closer, the mysterious rumbling sound was repeated. Aimi, standing on the fore-cabin roof, spotted the cause.

"Look!" she cried in a frightened voice, pointing to the starboard. "It's a monster."

Less than fifty yards astern a whale was ploughing the waves with his bulldozer-like, broad forepart and closing in on us in a parallel course about fifty yards off our starboard.

"A sperm whale," Arvid exclaimed.

"What was that noise he made?" Aimi asked fearfully. "Was it his usual voice?"

"No, whales haven't any voice," Arvid answered. "That, probably, was the sound of his spouting, letting out his breath."

The big, shining hulk now reached us, then slowed down and swam a parallel course to starboard. By this time almost everyone was on deck, looking with awe and curiosity at our first whale. He overreached the *Erma's* length, although he could not have been much more than fifty feet. But more than his length, the bulk and massiveness of his body, especially his head, impressed us as it heaved half out of the water in surging waves.

"It's an old bull," Arvid told us. "Only the old bulls swim alone. Some younger competitor has taken over his harem and driven him away."

The whale suddenly changed his course and swam directly toward us. As he came closer and closer to the starboard bow our excited talk died down. The mountain of flesh seemed about to ram us. But just before a collision became unavoidable, he swerved and slowly swam across our bow to the port side and continued forward. Everyone breathed easier.

Soon afterwards a fantastic thing happened. The whale accelerated his speed, then, when he was less than a hundred yards ahead of us, bent and unbent with a terrific splash and, as if catapulted by a tremendous spring, left the water and leaped high up in the air, almost in an upright position, until he seemed to be higher than the *Erma's* mast. His heavy, backward-tapering body shone as though lacquered in blacks and browns. Then it arched over his truncated, oversize head and dived into the mushrooming spray of water. Spray flew over the deck, and after some moments, when the surge of his fall hit us, the boat rocked so hard that Inga fell and started to cry. When we were able to look around once more, we spotted the whale as he was diving again a little farther ahead. His wide, two-fluked tail waved us farewell and then he was gone. For about half an hour we scanned the waters around us, but there was not a sign of him.

*　　　*　　　*

In the dry air and hot sun of the Trade Winds, we cooled the deck of the *Erma* each morning and afternoon with buckets of sea water. The children loved this. As the man with the bucket sloshed the water over the decks, the bare-footed small fry ran up and down screaming at the tops of their lungs.

But one Sunday morning, the children had jammed themselves into the after cabin to watch Lembit make pancakes; so when Paul took the bucket and went forward to slosh the decks, the only other person in sight was the helmsman, Arvid.

With the goose-winged jib and mainsail, we were running free before the wind at about five knots. The froth of the ten-foot waves gurgled at the stern and ran hissing along the *Erma's* sides. Going to the starboard bow where he was hidden from Arvid's view by the mainsail, Paul tossed the bucket over the side and began to haul it in with the rope that was attached to the handle. The pail was out of the water when the rope broke. As he saw the bucket, our only good one, slowly sinking into the sea, Paul dived over the side. When he came to the surface, he was already ten yards astern of the *Erma*. He called out, not very loudly and almost jokingly to Arvid, but the wind and the sea drowned his voice.

At that moment, Ellen happened to come up from

the mid-cabin. As she walked aft, she saw Paul's arms flashing in the sun. By that time he was at least fifty yards away.

"Arvid! Harry!" Ellen screamed. "Someone's overboard!" Arvid leaped from his seat in the cockpit and looked astern.

"The damn fool!" he roared, and then louder, "Man overboard!"

At his shout everybody came tumbling up from below. As though they had rehearsed it a hundred times, Harry leaped into the cockpit and took over the helm while Arvid ran to the stern and began to haul in the billowing mainsail.

"Rommy, Val," Harry ordered, "keep your eyes on Paul. Don't lose sight of him for a moment." He put the helm up, but instead of coming about, the *Erma* continued to plough forward before the wind.

"Heino, Lembit, get the jib back on the forestay."

Paul's blond head was getting smaller by the minute. He was now at least five hundred yards astern, and completely hidden for long intervals when both he and the *Erma* were in the troughs.

Aunt Juliana began to weep, and the children too were crying. "Uncle Paul is gone, Uncle Paul has drowned."

Forward, Heino and Lembit unfastened the jib from the jury boom. As they attempted to attach its spring hooks to the forestay, the wind whipped the canvas from their hands. Arvid, darting forward from the stern, ran into Aimi, nearly knocking her over the side.

"Get below," he ordered, picking her up. "Quickly, every one of you women and children."

Working swiftly and expertly, Arvid had the jib back on the forestay in a matter of seconds.

"Up with it now!" he ordered.

Heino hauled on the halyard. The canvas filled with a crackling sound. Instantly, Harry spun the wheel, and the *Erma* began to turn into the wind. Dashing to the stern, Arvid tugged at the boom, bringing it amid ships and then over. As the *Erma* came about in a sweeping circle, both Rommy and I lost sight of Paul. At one moment, he was there, and then we could see nothing but the great rollers.

"He's gone!" I shouted.

"He can't be," Lembit answered. "Paul's a strong swimmer. He could stay afloat for hours."

Then Rommy picked up Paul's bobbing head again, at least three-quarters of a mile away. We were on a tack which would bring us to a point well beyond him. On the next tack, the *Erma* would sail down wind directly towards Paul. It was a ticklish bit of navigation, and I could see the strain on Harry's face as he made the calculations.

Slowly we beat back against the wind, plunging almost directly into the seas. Now and then, the froth of the combers broke over the forward deck, sending up clouds of spray which momentarily blotted Paul from our view.

Once more, Harry put the helm over. The *Erma's* bow moved into the wind, the sails flapped for a moment, and then as the boom swung over, she plunged forward on the new tack, running swiftly before the wind. From the fore-cabin roof Rommy and I signalled to Harry with our arms. If we missed Paul this time it would mean another half-hour of manoeuvring.

"Rommy," Harry called, "toss him the life-belt when we draw abreast. Lembit, throw him a line."

Rommy tore the ancient, doughnut-shaped life-belt

from the rail. As we bore down on Paul, he gave it a mighty heave over the bow. It landed inches from Paul's head, and my first thought was that Rommy had scored a direct hit. Harry skilfully brought the bow around into the wind, sheltering Paul in the lee. Ignoring the life-belt, Paul grasped Lembit's line. In a matter of seconds we hauled him over the side.

"What the hell's the matter with you?" Harry demanded. "Are you crazy?"

Despite his wide grin, Paul was very short of breath. Staying afloat that long while clothed had been no easy job.

"The bucket!" he panted. "I lost the damned bucket."

Harry's eyes flashed. This was one of the few times I had seen him angry.

"With the goose-winged jib, and in a sea like this," he exploded, "you go over the side for a lousy bucket! You should have your head examined!"

Paul grinned sheepishly.

"But it was our only bucket."

Harry turned away in disgust.

"Let's get the jib back," Arvid said impatiently. "If someone else doesn't decide to jump overboard, we may still cover a few miles to-day."

But Rommy, who had retrieved the life-belt, also had a bone to pick with our rescued shipmate.

"Why didn't you grab the life-belt?" he asked in a hurt tone. "I tossed it right on your nose."

Paul looked at the cracked canvas.

"To tell the truth," he said, "I didn't think the damned thing would float."

By this time, the women and children had come up from the cabins. Nora and Ellen threw their arms

162

around Paul. Grandmother Paalberg brought him a hot cup of tea. From the helm cockpit, Arvid watched all this commotion out of the corner of his eye.

"That's the women for you," he mumbled to me in disgust. "A man acts like a bloody fool, and what do they do? They make a hero of him!"

* * *

Bright, refreshing Trade days were followed by soft-breezed, romantic Trade nights in which the all-embracing darkness seemed to reduce even the rumble of the seas to a mere murmur. Orion's bow and belt glimmered ahead of us, and Sirius burned in a great flame above the horizon. Behind and beside us the Big and Little Dippers spread wide over the firmament. Now we could follow the movements of four planets every night. Ruby-red Mars and paler Saturn travelled side by side across the skies as if they were the two tail lights of an unseen car. Toward morning the white pair, Jupiter and Venus, appeared in the east and rolled along until they vanished in the glory of the sunrise. Sometimes the big full moon overtook them and covered the skies and the sea with a dreamy silver film.

These were nights to sit or lie on deck, dream and remember, talk of things past and friends lost. And to sing. Scarcely a night passed without our sitting on deck late, enjoying the velvety air, talking and singing. On special occasions we did not turn in until the small hours of the morning.

One of these special occasions was Harry's birthday. The sun had set in scarlet and gold and its afterglow drenched the skies. We began to sing about our old north country. Lembit led the men in a nineteenth-century song picturing a quiet evening in the Estonian woods.

> *Dusk settles on the water*
> *And gleams in golden flakes,*
> *A shepherd's fire is shining*
> *On the other side of the lake.*

Although I have a mediocre voice, I sometimes joined in the general harmonizing. Rommy wasn't much better but he occasionally surprised us with his thundering chest tones. Heino and Lembit, both fair tenors, alternated in the second voice, and Paul and Arvid sang the melody. Often, as now, Ellen and Nora joined us. The children were in their bunks. Harry, who never sang, had turned in to get some sleep because he took the watch at midnight.

After a while the songs got livelier. Heino started his "Bedbug Ballad," a charming, melancholy Russian melody that preserved the character of a love song to the very end.

> *My thoughs are always set on you through*
> *   every day and night.*
> *My sleep and dreams are full of you, you*
> *   hold me good and tight . . .*

etc. until, unexpectedly:

> *I wish for once I'd catch sight of you,*
> *But more than merely seeing,*
> *I hope I'll catch and make way with you,*
> *You bedbug, you loathsome being.*

When we sang our favourite bear-hunting song, Rommy's voice reached full gale force and seemed to

164

rip the mainsail. With the singing of the last verse a silence fell upon us. Heino peeked uneasily into the compass and fumbled with the wheel.

"What's the matter? Why don't you go on?" demanded Rommy.

"Well," Arvid said, "first let Heino put her back on the course. I think she got wrenched off during the last refrain."

Lembit coughed respectfully.

"How about reefing the sail, Rommy? That was quite a blow."

But Ellen didn't like our poking fun at Rommy and proposed that we stop. It was late and probably we had wakened the children. We were coming back out at midnight anyway.

*　　*　　*

A few minutes before twelve o'clock we were on deck again, joined by Aimi, who had managed to get permission to come to the birthday party. Actually, we were a little early for our opening ditty, when, suddenly—the boom gybed.

Rommy had just taken over the helm from Heino (according to Heino), or was just about to take it over (according to Rommy) so the question of "guilt" remained unsettled. Anyway, the boom slatted badly, the sails slatted, and the *Erma* was off her course. Even with an expert like Arvid lending a hand, it took a quarter of an hour to put everything back in order.

Then we proceeded according to plan. The main hatch was opened a trifle and we serenaded down it, "Don't sleep so many hours. Don't sleep your life away." Harry appeared, not looking sleepy at all. He had a mug of Malvasia in his hand. Ellen followed with a tray of sardine sandwiches, and Maia was with her.

After accepting our congratulations Harry went below again and returned with three small bottles. Paul recognized them in a flash.

"Beer!" he exclaimed.

Lembit was a bit sceptical; he grabbed one of the bottles and held it against the moonlight.

"Is this the real stuff?"

Harry smiled modestly. "It should be. I bought these bottles in Stockholm before we left and kept them in the bilge all the time. Maybe they are spoiled, though, for bilge water isn't much of a cooler."

"A little sour," Paul discovered, "but only a little. It's good lager beer."

The foam of the swell glistened in the moonlight and the boat rocked forward in soft, regular leaps. Occasionally the sail flapped or the boom creaked before the warm breeze. It was a charming night.

"This reminds me of the moonlit summer evenings when we were in Narva," Nora said. "We used to sit on a bench in our garden under an old birch tree."

"Aimi, do you remember those days?" Ellen asked.

"Of course I do," Aimi said. "It's only a year and a half since the Russians burned Narva—and our house. I remember even the first Russian time," she added proudly, "and that was four or five years ago."

"I didn't know you had a place in Narva. Why in the world did you live up there on the Russian border?" I asked Arvid.

"I like gardening," he answered, "and this was an attractive cottage in a little wood, pine and spruce mostly. Whenever I got time off from my ship I rushed to Narva and took out the spade and rake, but mostly it was Nora who kept the place going. The last time I came home I was just in time to snatch the family from the advancing Red Army. The artillery fire was

166

actually over-topping us, and when we looked back, flames were blazing over our grove. It must have been our cottage."

"Yes, half of Narva burned down in that one night." Nora sighed. "Best not to think of it."

19

BY THE first day of November the period of strong and even Trades and changelessly comfortable weather was past. As if wishing to compensate for our scant water rations, the skies started to send squalls upon us. But they did not compensate; they were too short and almost always too violent for water gathering. All we could have caught in a canvas would have been salt-water spray that flew high over the cabins.

The squalls formed once or twice almost every day —or night. Suddenly, a small patch of dark clouds would appear on one side of us or the other, behind or in front of us, and pour rain either in hazy vaporous columns or straight dark streaks, blackening the narrow section of the sea underneath while the sur-rounding expanse sparkled in bright sunshine. Some-times a couple of these little storms blew up on either side of the *Erma,* but as often they broke directly over her, giving her a really good push.

Usually they were even too short to permit us a bath. Once I tried to shampoo my hair but was left with it full of soap, the rain having stopped abruptly even before the cloud had passed. Rommy, looking at my soapy head, grinned and suggested that he shave it while it was lathered.

The winds were not so strong and steady now, occa-sionally they died to short calms, or again squalls turned them all around the compass. We sailed now directly west between the twentieth and twenty-first latitudes, slightly aided by the vast northern equatorial current at a rate of five or ten miles a day. Soon we reached the immense currentless part of the southern North Atlantic, usually called the Sargasso Sea. Here we met the first trails of Gulf weed on 3 November, just after passing the thirty-ninth longitude. Little Yuta's fancy was kindled at the sight of these yellow-brown floating ropes swimming by.

"Are those big snakes?" she asked. "Where do they come from?"

Harry had a hard time convincing her that they were just small sea plants stuck together, formed into rows by waves and growing, multiplying and dying in the sea.

The heat was becoming more intense. The women wore sun suits, the men and children shorts or swimming trunks. Heino and I cut off the legs of our old working pants, and used the remainder as shorts. We covered our heads, the men with old caps and berets, the women and children with bandannas.

Our meals were getting skimpier and skimpier. There was no bacon or ham left, the fruit was gone long ago, almost gone too were butter and the last bag of powered milk. Breakfast consisted of rice porridge with a spoonful of sugar; dinner, mostly of thin soup, potatoes, hash, and tea. For the first time during the trip thirst began to bother us, and our daily water ration of one quart seemed small.

With the routine becoming more monotonous every day our little community began to show signs of tension. Nothing serious happened, but minor differences of opinion were more irritating now than they had been. In short, we got on each other's nerves. Rommy and Paul intensified their half-joking, half-serious nagging about food which had started in the Irish Sea. As a result, Rommy had separated his supplies in Madeira. Rommy's original diet consisted mostly of flour cooked with olive oil plus bread and onions. Soon Paul developed an aversion for the smell of onions, probably because he had eaten too many of them himself, and, as they shared the same bunk, he often accused Rommy of trying to kill him with his breath. One morning Paul made a definite proposal.

"I'll give you three cans of meat and three cans of peas if you'll cut down your onion eating to one a day and throw away two-thirds of them. It's a big sacrifice on my part but I don't mind."

Rommy cut a big round off a coconut-sized onion, set it deliberately on a half-musty piece of hard bread and looked at it appraisingly. Finally, lifting the delicate treat to his mouth, he took a bite. Then, as if remembering Paul's proposition, he said, "I don't want your meat and peas. I prefer onions."

Paul was struck dumb. He recovered, however, and shouted angrily, "Come on, Rommy. I meant it seriously. Cut out your joking and take the bargain."

But all in vain; Rommy, calm and aloof, stuck to his odoriferous menu. Thus this particular tension continued until Rommy ran out of onions a couple of weeks later.

Of course, onions were not the only source of conflict. Ellen and Nora also became involved in a typical Sargasso Sea feud. Their argument started over the children. One still forenoon Ulla wished to play with Karunass, Yuta's teddy bear, but Yuta, unexpectedly, refused to lend it. Ulla, a determined child, resorted to direct action. She stuck out her hand, first missed, then succeeded in capturing the teddy bear. Yuta countered with a push. In the heat of the struggle they fell and instantly sent up a piercing, two-voiced wail.

The mothers, who reached the scene in no time,

disentangled their little darlings from the life lines, caressed and comforted them.

"Don't cry, Yuta," Ellen said, "Don't pay any attention to Ulla. She's a rough girl."

"It's all right now, Ulla," Nora retorted. "Don't pay any attention to Yuta. She is sometimes very naughty." Then to Ellen: "And Ulla is not a rough girl, mark that."

"And Yuta isn't naughty," Ellen countered. "Ulla often *is* rough, and, what's more, you know it."

The clash of mothers continued for some heated minutes, then ended abruptly when both took their little girls to their cabin. Under normal conditions that would have been the end of the matter, but conditions were not normal. Scarcely half an hour later when the mothers met again they somehow became involved in a discussion of educational methods, something about "pampering and spoiling children," on the one hand and "handling inborn bad temper in children" on the other. Before anyone could tell what it was all about, the criticism veered to their respective husbands. It started when Ellen brought up the question of command on the boat.

"After all," she said casually, "that's the domain of the captain, not the mate."

"What do you mean?" Nora demanded. "Isn't Arvid co-captain of the boat?"

Ellen shrugged and said very casually, "I think that's just in name. Who ever heard of a boat with two captains?"

That did it. Both women left abruptly and did not meet again that day. The next morning a rope was drawn from the mast to the port railing. This was the demarcation line; ahead of it—before the mast—was the playground of Nora's children, aft of it, along the main cabin, was Yuta's playground. The starboard side was not halved, but it was strictly understood that the demarcation line would continue to the railing. No social intercourse between the young of the fore and middle cabins!

During the first day the line was observed but then, curiously, the new order began to slacken. Ulla and Yuta forgot that they were supposed to be feuding, they talked to one another, crossed the line, fraternized openly until, a couple of days later, the rope was quietly taken down. The same day Ellen stepped down the forehatch and with a natural smile said, "Look, Nora, I remade this old beige dress. What do you think of taking out the shoulder pads?"

Usually these trying moods never outlasted the sun. At every twilight we gladly forgot the hot, calm, squally days and greeted the nights that poured balm on our harassed spirits.

* * *

The Trade Winds continued to weaken throughout November. They became fickle and fidgety, changing direction often, occasionally blowing up wild squalls but more frequently dying to calms. We had experienced short spells of calm and light breezes earlier in the month, but nothing like the dead calm which struck us on 16 November. The day before had been the hottest one yet, although the fresh breeze, deflected by the sails, had provided a cooling draught, but almost instantly after the sunset—following the usual short period of heavier swells that occurred at every sunset and sunrise—the wind and the seas had died down and the *Erma* just managed to keep steerageway.

This was the first night that it was definitely too hot to sleep below in the draughtless cabins. Arvid and

Heino were on duty and I sat with them in the cockpit. The *Erma's* deck had become so crowded with sleepers that there was no space left for us. Some time after midnight I went down, but in spite of sleeping naked it was a sweaty business; very little draught came down the open companionway. The three-quarter moon danced softly up and down above the opening and to my sleep-dazed eyes it looked like the flame of a blast furnace sending its reddish glow into the narrow cabin.

The next morning at sunrise there was a slight breeze, but when the crimson sun burst over the horizon and exploded into a fiery glow, the wind collapsed entirely and we lost steerageway. The sails slatted and the boom rattled with every slow roll. Then the *Erma* started to turn around lazily, making a full turn in about half an hour. There was no use holding the wheel so we lowered the sails.

This was an important day; we expected to pass the sixtieth longitude, which meant setting back our watches for another two hours as we had done at longitude thirty. Now our watches would be running on Eastern Standard Time, the time of the eastern seaboard of the United States. In a way this was like arriving in America. Heino, Paul and Lembit switched back their time pieces in the morning without waiting for the agreed hour of four o'clock in the afternoon. And when Heino relieved me at the beginning of the forenoon watch, he lifted his left arm to my eyes and pointed at his wrist watch.

"Six o'clock, New York time."

Lembit, bent over the railing, turned his head and declaimed loudly, with mock dramatics, "Soon the sun will set on the high towers of the Waldorf-Astoria." He had just finished his rice porridge and was holding the empty plate in the water to let passing waves rub against it. This, we had discovered, was the least strenuous method of washing dishes on shipboard. "It must be a regular palace," he continued, "all gleaming with gold and mirrors and full of rich visitors."

"The Americans really are drowning in money, aren't they?" Paul asked.

"Well, I don't know," Harry answered cautiously. "Some people in America have plenty of money and others haven't."

"Harry, empty this pot, please," Ellen said, appearing in the companionway and handing a white enamelled vessel to the captain. Harry took the one-eared object, poured its contents quickly overboard, then rinsed it and gave it back. In the beginning this morning routine had embarrassed him, but by now neither he nor anybody else noticed it.

"When I was a little boy," Heino said, "I knew an old carpenter who had bought himself an apartment house in Tallin with the money he had saved in the United States. He used to tell about the fast tempo on construction jobs and how carpenters who couldn't lay floors quickly enough were fired. He, himself, had been fired twice for this reason."

"Still, he made money enough to go back and buy an apartment house," Arvid pointed out.

"I guess we'll be all right too because Estonians are supposed to be so thrifty," Ellen said. She had come up to the port deck and lay sunning herself in her bathing suit, looking like a Wagnerian mermaid with the light on her yellow hair.

"When I visited New York," Arvid said, "I met at the Estonian Society some people who were *more* than thrifty. I remember two young carpenters who worked together on the same job and lived in the same flat, a

174

cold-water flat in an old, run-down East-Side building that cost them five dollars a month. They both earned forty to fifty dollars a week, but they rarely spent more than five dollars each. They bought cabbage and potatoes or sauerkraut, added bits of porks and made a soup that lasted five or six days. To keep their shares of meat separate they tied their pork in small canvas bags before they put it in the soup. They never went to the cinema or paid for any kind of entertainment. On Sundays, if they had no extra work, they walked around New York together. They didn't waste a single penny."

"I wouldn't want to lead such a life. It sounds awful," Ellen said.

"Not for them. There are many immigrants who live like that."

"What became of those two carpenters?" Heino asked.

"One of them, after saving ten thousand dollars, went back home and bought a large farm somewhere in South Estonia. The other stayed in New York, started to work on his own and is now a big contractor himself. I've heard he's worth millions, but that may be exaggerated."

20

AFTER the *Erma* had floated around for most of the afternoon, Paul, with the help of his brother, made a desperate attempt to start the engine. He filled an empty alcohol bottle with the dirty Swedish fuel that still lapped in our port tank, let it settle for a while, then poured it into the engine, little by little, while Lembit cranked the flywheel in the bilge. For the first fifteen minutes nothing happened, then the motor started to cough and sneeze and finally it actually ran. But only for a couple of minutes; after that it stopped and nothing could induce it to start again.

From the overhauling of the engine the afterdecks were filthy, covered with smudges and soot. So were Paul and Lembit. They threw pail after pail over the decks, but the soot stuck to the boards.

"We need some sea soap," Paul complained. There was a little of it left in the big wooden box that Bill had presented to us in Fraserburgh, but we were saving it now for washing the children.

"You know what?" Lembit proposed. "Nora had a bag of washing soda and quite a lot of it is left. I'll go and ask for some." He returned with the bag and then the clean-up started. Dressed in their swimming trunks, the brothers vigorously scrubbed the decks; Paul wielded the long-handled ship's broom, Lembit spread the soda over the boards and flushed them with water. Soon the deck was gleaming. And then, what with the water sloshing around, the sun scorching overhead and the boys being grimy and sweaty, it was only natural that they should decide to do an equally good job on themselves.

Lembit thought the soda might take off their skins, but Paul said, "Nonsense," and threw himself down on the deck, showing that he was eager to undergo the treatment. Lembit grabbed the soda bag and soon the deep tan on Paul's back disappeared under a white foam. As Rommy, handling the pail, provided a steady flow of water, Lembit wielded the broom over his brother's back which emerged gleaming like a seal's. Paul's grunting satisfaction encouraged the others. Rommy and Lembit could hardly wait for their turn.

"More water—give it a good rub," Rommy shouted. But just watching the heavy broom scraping over their flesh made me shudder. I had no courage to face the long broom and Rommy's heavy muscles.

For our children and women this was a highly emotional experience. The women, especially Maia, seemed awe-struck by the primitive ruggedness of our young Vikings. The children shouted, screamed and danced about, occasionally jumping over the bodies of the human seals.

After Rommy had taken his turn in the human laundry he tied the customary swimming line around his waist. As he stepped over the railing he suddenly stopped and turned towards Harry, who was sitting on the main cabin reading.

"Harry, don't you think we might go in without the line? It's dead calm and the boat is at a standstill."

"Yes," Harry answered, "you won't need the line today."

Four splashes quickly followed. When the boys pulled themselves aboard after a short swim, Paul, who was a fairly good diver, described what he had seen under water.

177

"The *Erma's* bottom is covered with seaweed and barnacles and they glitter in the sunny water. I saw two fish swimming away from them, two nice fish, like herrings, about a foot long."

"Bonitos, probably," said Harry.

"Why don't you try to catch some," Nora suggested. "The potatoes are almost gone. They won't last much longer than a week." She was in the after cockpit peeling a scant handful for dinner.

"That's true," Arvid added. "The sugar is running out, too, as well as the hard bread. After that's gone our menu will be skimpy with only rice and a few Stockholm tins."

"Look! Here are plenty of fish," Heino called from the starboard bow. "I see three or four swimming under the bottom. One is right alongside the boat."

Paul and Lembit rushed forward, their angler's instinct aroused. Heino went below to fetch hooks and lines. There were four hooks left; two had been lost in the fishing attempts before Madeira, lackadaisical and unproductive attempts that had not been spurred by hunger. Two were simple hooks, an inch and a half and an inch respectively. The remaining two were one-and-a-half-inch lures, shining fish-shaped trolls with tufts of red woollen yarn attached to them.

Heino set the hooks and sinkers on the lines and spread them from the stern. Paul and Lembit walked back and forth along the side of the boat, trailing the trolls. Occasionally the fish showed in abundance, and there were tense moments when they seemed to be biting the bread crumbs on the hooks or swallowing the lures, but never a fish was landed.

About half an hour after sunset an erratic breeze from the east began to ruffle the surface. The sails were set and the *Erma* caught the moving air currents.

The new wind was cooler than yesterday's and most of us went to sleep below. The anglers decided to set their lines for the night. They tied them all into four long lines and streamed them from the traveller; then they crawled into their bunks.

A little after midnight Heino woke, left the cabin and discovered that the hooks were gone: torn clean off the lines by the swiftly passing waters. This, of course, meant the end of our angling.

In the morning I awoke to the sound of clanking metal. It came from outside and was loud enough to vibrate the *Erma*'s shell. I jumped from my bunk over the sleeping Heino and looked out of the companionway.

The first thing I saw was Rommy's crew-cut head reaching over the house roof from beside the wheel. Then Ellen's honey-blonde head emerged from the main companionway with the morning sun glinting on it. As the clinking sound was repeated, Nora, Aimi and Inga popped up too. From the leeside of the peak came the sound of clanging metal. There, beside the windlass, the brothers were squatting. Lembit held a sheet of iron on one fluke of our heavy anchor; Paul worked on it with a cold chisel and hammer. He hammered slowly, methodically, with all his might, and the piercing sound of hammered metal seemed to spread over the whole Atlantic.

"For mercy's sake, what's going on?" Ellen asked. "You woke up Yuta."

Lembit's apology came glibly.

"A thousand regrets, madam. We thought the children would be up by this time. However, this harpoon will be used to catch fish for all of us."

Work on the harpoon lasted for about two hours. After cutting it out from the sheet, Paul filed the prongs sharp, then lashed the fork to the end of the boat-hook with a nail and a thick layer of cord. When it was finished he grabbed the harpoon and started to walk with it along the deck.

There were many fish about this morning, flying fish that had appeared again after a mysterious week-long absence. Their leaping and soaring was pleasant to watch, but nobody could spear them.

"I wonder why all the bonitos have disappeared," Arvid said, puzzled. Paul walked back and forth along the railing for more than half an hour, but then, seeing no chance of using his weapon, he went below.

At about ten o'clock, Harry called from the starboard bow, "Paul, come here if you want to see the world's most beautiful fish."

Paul and his harpoon were there in no time, and others came too. All we could see was a darting gold-silvery line of motion under the surface of the water. It glimmered for a moment, then disappeared.

"Here it comes again," Lembit shouted from the port side, "and it's moving like greased lightning."

The fish was rather large; its yellow, sparkling, long dorsal fin swished along the surface like a streak of liquid gold, and all we could make out was the outline of a slender long body coloured like the rainbow and sprayed with silver.

"It's a dolphin, a real dolphin," Harry shouted.

"But the dolphins we've seen were entirely different," Ellen said.

"Oh, those were porpoises. This is a real fish—a dorado."

The dolphin now scurried back to starboard. It kept moving up and down, back and forth, with the speed of a motor-boat. Sometimes it looked all blue under its long golden crest, the next moment it was a shimmering yellow with tens of additional shades from green to purple; then again it looked like an ordinary fish, greyish above and silvery beneath.

"It likes our company," Aimi shouted.

"But not enough to come close and stay still for a second," Paul grumbled. It seemed a hopeless business to try to spear this fast fish.

I went below. A little after eleven o'clock a sudden outburst of screams and the wild crying of the children brought me up again. Yuta and Ulla who had fled to the port side, as far away as their life lines allowed, were bawling with all their might. Aimi and Inga were disappearing into the companionway of the fore cabin as Harry and Grandma P. stuck frightened faces from the main cabin. No one was at the wheel because Lembit, who had been steering, had joined Paul and Heino in jumping, lunging and running after the big fish aboard. There was a spot of blood on the mainsail and more spots on the deck. While the frantically leaping fish attempted to flop overboard, Heino rushed down to the after cabin to the accompaniment of desperate cries from Paul.

"The hammer! Get the hammer! Quick!"

Heino reappeared with the hammer just in time, as the fish was beating and wriggling itself free from Paul's hold. A few hammer blows ended its struggles. During these last convulsions of death we witnessed what some of us had heard about, the change of colour of the fish's body. It was slender, between two and two and a half feet long, with a dark yellow dorsal fin and a deeply forked tail, but its head was rather heavy, broad and blunt nosed, with a small mouth that gave it a slight resemblance to a boxer dog. Its back under the fin was an intense ultramarine, and its sides and belly

181

yellow, ranging from lime green and lemon yellow to a burnished gold. Small round eyelet-like marks speckled it. These marks, as well as its entire body, were flickering as if afire. Weaker and weaker grew the golden tones, darker and darker the blue of its back, until, soon after its death, all that was left was a dull blue-grey on its back and a muddy leaden colour underneath. It was a fascinating transformation, but rather sad too.

Paul's magnificent catch took care of two days' meat supply. Harry, conservative as always, estimated that the fish weighed thirteen to fourteen pounds. We ate it for dinner and salted the remainder. Its flesh was white and very delicate; it tasted something like perch, but better. This was our last fish. On the few mild days that we experienced during the remainder of the voyage, Paul hopefully patrolled the deck with his harpoon, but he had no luck. When the sea was rough they probably stayed in deep water for we never saw them.

The next day, a little before noon, Grandma P. spotted a whale astern. It swam there for a while, suddenly disappeared, and about forty-five minutes later was discovered again to our port, only about two hundred yards away. It followed us for a few minutes, then it dived.

Shortly after noon Nora called out, "Look, there are two whales swimming with us." True enough, there they were, to the port side again, the one nearer to us less than a hundred yards away, and the other behind it at a distance of less than two hundred. They seemed to be what Arvid called "blue whales." Compared with our sperm whale they were lower or flatter of body, and their upper jaws were not so bulky but elongated and narrow—snoutlike. They were quite long, longer than the old sperm. Harry estimated the nearer one at sixty or seventy feet.

This time the whales were in no hurry to disappear. We had our dinner at about three o'clock and ate the last pieces of yesterday's dolphin while the whales still swam beside us, at exactly the same distance and in the same position. Ulla and Yuta wanted to feed them and cast small pieces of fish overboard, but apparently, the whales did not care for fish.

At the beginning of the first dog watch the enormous creatures were still there. By this time we all had started to regard them with something like affection. They accompanied us faithfully until almost sunset, then they were gone. They had an uncanny ability to come and go when we were not watching. Only once we saw them diving, but we never spied them coming up.

During the night we could see no signs of the whales although we scanned the moonlit waters. During the next forenoon they failed to reappear, but about twelve-thirty Aimi and Inga exclaimed joyfully, "Here they are again. Both of them."

Yes, there they were. But their positions were different; instead of accompanying us both on the same side as they had yesterday, they swam with us one on either side. They were considerably nearer, too, about fifty yards away. It was touching to see these huge beasts following us so affectionately. At least, they looked affectionate. Despite their great size, they seemed so friendly that we felt we might swim to them, climb on their backs, scratch their snouts and pat their heads. The children kept watching the whales and talking about them long after the grown-ups ceased to pay them any further attention.

"Oh, they've left us again," Aimi exclaimed plain

183

tively later in the afternoon. But scarcely five minutes later, when the men around the after cabin were busy with their soup and the girls had settled down for a quiet session with their dolls, a deep soughing sound made us look to starboard. One of our friends had appeared barely ten feet away, water parting on his neck and a column of water and spray spouting forward. A chorus of surprised outcries sounded from the mast. Inga and Aimi emerged from the shower, their bathing suits wet. Inga exclaimed, "The whale sprinkled me all over." Aimi, who had been reading *Snow White and the Seven Dwarfs,* shook the water from her book.

With all this excitement we had forgotten the other whale. When we remembered to look, he was there, surfaced, swimming abreast of the *Erma* again about fifty yards away. Our starboard whale, the naughty one, had discreetly withdrawn from our immediate vicinity. We followed them with our eyes, looking for an additional spout, but the most we could see when the deep soughing indicated their breathing, was just a little higher swirl of water above their submerged snouts.

The children christened the naughty one "Grumpy" and the other "Sneezy."

"The quiet one is a girl and the noisy one a boy," Arvid said. "Grumpy acts like a schoolboy, splashing water on us." This was a new angle on Grumpy and Sneezy and it fascinated the children.

About an hour later, without warning, the whales sank under the calm water and did not show again. Aimi and Inga, as well as the rest of us, kept looking for them, but this time they did not reappear.

21

It was a fine morning like those we met when we first hit the Trades; a moderate north-easterly was blowing, the sea purring contentedly. If our half-empty stomachs had not given us a feeling of vague restlessness that prevented us from enjoying it fully, we would have thought it as fine weather as we had experienced. But Aunt Juliana had a faintly achy feeling that meant a change was coming; she could feel it now since she was free of the arthritis that had ached continually. Nora joined us on deck after finishing her laundry. She was still amazed at Juliana's cure.

"It's a miracle!" she exclaimed.

"It *is* a miracle," Juliana agreed, laying her hand on the pocket-sized Bible in her lap.

It was the result of the warm sun, Rommy argued. The sun, according to him, was good for everything. But, Aunt Juliana pointed out, she had been well rid of her arthritis before we reached the Trades, in fact, even before we arrived at Madeira.

"You are a real mystery woman," Grandma P. said half jokingly. "Not only because of your arthritis but also because of your seasickness. In the old days you pretty nearly died every time you had to go to sea."

Harry, at the helm, had been listening to the conversation with one ear while he kept looking over his shoulder into the binnacle. Now he, too, ventured a theory.

"You know, Juliana, your healing may have come from the strong emotional strain, the unusual and sudden change of living conditions and your fright. All these things together must have shocked your system and licked both your arthritis and your seasickness."

"Maybe so," Juliana nodded earnestly. "But whatever it was, He did it." She ran her fingers over her Bible. "I know that without putting my faith in Him I couldn't have pulled through. I thought, 'If He wants to help me, He will, so I won't despair.'" Juliana's face lighted up. "I still can't help worrying a little about our trip, but I'm not really frightened any more. Whatever changes of weather we get, He'll send them and we won't have any say about it."

After a pause Harry said, "As a matter of fact we're due for a change. We're more than a month out of Madeira and should be leaving the Trades soon. Just a little more than a thousand miles and we'll be in New York." Harry made a thousand miles sound like nothing. He perked us up.

"Actually," he continued, "we are only three hundred miles from the nearest coast of America."

"Only three hundred miles!" Ellen exclaimed.

"Yes, the nearest American islands, the Bahamas, are only three hundred miles from our present position. The nearest point on the mainland is Miami, Florida, about five hundred and fifty miles. And, as I said, it's a thousand miles to New York. If we're lucky, we'll do it in ten days."

"If we're lucky," he repeated.

Ellen arose.

"I'll begin to put our things together."

Though we laughed at her haste, we suddenly felt that our goal was very near, and a current of excitement ran through all of us.

* * *

The change came. On the late afternoon of the same

day, 22 November, the wind started to veer. For more than two days it kept turning clockwise, making a full circle and keeping us busy with the sails and sheets. In the late afternoon a fierce squall suddenly leaped on us from west-south-west and in a few minutes the ocean was in an uproar, angrily biting the *Erma's* stubby bow. She held stubbornly to the north-west, plunging through the waves, spume, and spindrift, wetting everyone on deck. Then a breaker, rather small but sharp and fast as a cannonball, hit her port bow. There was a deafening crash, water and foam spurted over the port side and when it had passed we saw that the foremost part of the gunwale planking was gone, beaten out clean, without our seeing how it happened, without even seeing the plank in the sea. Arvid looked at the damage calmly and said, "It makes for a nice scupper." Nevertheless, the course was immediately changed to north.

The squall ended as suddenly as it began, but the wind still kept turning and about midnight had another tantrum. In a matter of minutes it shifted to north-west, blew up a new squall with a heavy downpour, then another and a third, forcing us to turn south.

A sudden calm followed, and as we were beaten mercilessly by heavy seas, and the sails had not been lowered, she was shaken thoroughly to her last wooden peg. Harry had called all hands when the last squall struck, and we struggled with the sails, first changing the tack, then reefing the main. After it blew over, all of us, wet and bedraggled, left the deck at once, so the sails remained up. Perhaps there was a little breeze at the time, but the last breath of wind died away, and the old *Erma* got a mean chopping in the heavy sea; I could feel it even in my sea-conditioned sleep.

After an hour or two, Arvid awoke, jumped out and lowered the sails.

"Damned land rats," he muttered. "Do they want her mast shaken off?" In the darkness he spotted the watchman, who happened to be Rommy, and demanded, "Who ordered the sails to stay on?"

"Nobody. Nobody ordered them down, either."

Arvid muttered a half-dozen salty words.

"She'll leak like a sieve again. This kind of shaking is just the thing to loosen up the caulking."

The change of weather did not make us forget that we were nearing our destination. On the contrary, it steadily reminded us of it. At four o'clock when another short squall ended in a new calm, Lembit, who had rushed out to lend a hand, came down stark naked, dripping wet and shivering. As he massaged himself to get warm he asked Heino, "Have you thought about our landing in the States? Do we really have to dock under the Swedish flag?"

The topic was not entirely new; once or twice it had been touched upon but not seriously because our landing had seemed very far away. Now suddenly it was real. Heino sat up on the edge of the bunk. It was evident that he was serious.

"I have nothing against the Swedish flag, but landing under it is a different matter. It makes no sense. If we do, we'll be traitors to our country. Why, it will looks as though we have no flag of our own any more, or that we have no right to use it."

"Or maybe that we haven't the courage to use it," added Paul. "What will the Americans think of us if we hesitate to use our own flag?" He called over to me, "They still recognize the Baltic republics, don't they?"

I shrugged. I wasn't sure. At least there had been no official declaration to the contrary as far as I knew.

"We are not landing under the Swedish flag and that's that," Paul declared.

It sounded very final. Lembit, however, touched a new angle of the subject.

"What about our captains? What do they think of it?"

Paul was surprised.

"What about them? Why should they think otherwise?"

"Well, for one thing, the *Erma* is a member of a Swedish yacht club and her papers say so. In other words she's a Swedish boat."

Paul dismissed this view instantly.

"Don't be fussy. The *Erma* is just a small yacht and can choose whatever flag she wants."

"It'll be better though to have a talk with Harry to-morrow," warned Lembit.

By the next morning the seas had calmed down considerably, and the sun was almost as hot as it had been before the change came, but the wind was from north-north-west. As it was only a moderate breeze, we made nice headway directly west sailing by the wind.

Before noon Heino, Lembit, and Paul went to Harry, who was having his trick at the wheel. Heino did the talking. Harry listened quietly, with an expressionless face. When Heino had finished, he looked at the sea, frowning as if trying to find the right words.

"The idea of flying the Estonian flag is a good one, but there are certain objections to it." The men's faces grew tense and Lembit asked, "What objections?"

"Well, according to international sea law there are strict regulations about the use of flags."

"But they can't be applied to such a small boat," Paul interrupted. "The *Erma* is no cargo ship, in fact, she's not a ship at all."

"There are rules for yachts, too."

"But don't you think our case is different? Everybody will understand our situation and think it only natural for us to hoist our own flag."

"That's what I hope, too, but I'm not sure," Harry answered. "It all depends on how we are received by the Americans. There is no sure way of telling. We just have to guess and hope for the best." Then he added. "Remember that they were allies of the Soviets and probably still are. We don't even know for sure whether the Americans recognize the Baltic republics any more.

"The Americans don't know much about the Russians," Harry continued. "They haven't had our kind of experience with them. So there are two reasons for not using our own flag. The first is that it might embarrass the United States government; the other is that we have women and children aboard and, therefore, we must be very careful. Our women and children probably wouldn't be able to stand another trip—to South America, Australia, Argentina, or wherever we might have to go if the United States should turn us down."

A certain finality in Harry's tone made our three shipmates drop the argument, but they were far from satisfied. Coming down the companionway Paul grunted, "We'll see. I'll *never* land under the Swedish flag."

Early the next morning when the decks were clear of witnesses, Paul and Lembit talked with Maia. She too was passionately in favour of using the Estonian flag. But when Lembit asked her if she could make a flag, she didn't know where she could find the material. Down in the after cabin she started a frantic search for blue, black, and white cloth to make the Estonian tricolour. For a while the quest looked hopeless, until Heino had an idea.

"My coat has a solid black satin lining. How about cutting a piece out of that?"

The idea was greeted with enthusiasm. Besides, it gave a new trend to the search; everyone went over his belongings once more. Rommy discovered that his unused trunks were the proper sky blue. It was harder to find material for the remaining white. There were many white pieces of garments, but they were either too small, too crumpled, too thin, or not white enough. Paul offered his two shirts, but Maia refused them because they would need lots of soap, fresh water, soda, time and patience before they would be white again.

"We can't use them," Lembit agreed. "Don't affront our flag."

At last Heino, going over his scanty belongings for the third time, came upon a small package wrapped in brown paper.

"I wonder what I tucked away here," he muttered. Out rolled a brand-new white bed sheet. After a moment of astonished silence, Heino exclaimed, "Why, I forgot all about that sheet. It seemed foolish to throw it away so I brought it along."

"Handsome Heino certainly likes nice things," grinned Rommy.

With a sweeping gesture Heino handed Maia the sheet.

"There's enough here for ten flags," she said.

Soon the flag was ready. We eyed it with awe and patriotic fervour. Then Paul folded it and placed it in the bottom of his suitcase.

"What next?" Maia asked, "and when do you expect to use it?"

Paul stared gloomily at her. We all stared at him.

He had become the head of the revolt, and everybody waited for what he had to say. He shook his head slowly.

"I don't know exactly. I think it's best to have another talk with Harry. If he hasn't changed his mind after a couple of days, well, we'll still have some time left and can decide what to do. All I know is that I won't land under a foreign flag."

That was the last we heard of the subject until the next morning. It was sun-up, a light breeze was blowing over the scintillating sea, Heino held the wheel and Paul, restless as ever, walked up and down the deck, peering over the rail for fish. But the ocean seemed to be empty. Because the *Erma* no longer needed an engineer, Paul had been appointed our third officer soon after our departure from Madeira, and ever since, he had shared in watch duty.

Suddenly Paul stopped at the starboard railing. He squinted his eyes, looking into the glowing sun just above the horizon.

"There's a ship going north," he said. "On the horizon, just out of the glare of the sun."

Heino stood up and soon spotted it.

"Kind of unusual looking. Maybe some sort of man-of-war," he guessed.

They watched as the ship moved ahead and became recognizable.

"An aircraft carrier," Paul decided. "Look at the long, flat deck with the tower behind."

"Do you think they can see us?" Heino asked.

"Probably. We are much smaller, but they are higher and can see farther. And our white sail might attract their attention."

Then Heino had an idea.

"How do you like being taken for a Swedish boat?"

192

he asked. "Wouldn't it be better if we had our own flag astern . . . or atop?" He looked up toward the mast.

Paul didn't say anything, he just stared at Heino, then at the warship. Suddenly he rushed down to the after cabin and reappeared with the newly sewn Estonian flag and a roll of thin white line.

Heino raised his brows and watched silently as Paul hurried to the mast.

"Need any help?"

"No, you just keep the course."

Paul freed the halyard and quietly lowered the jib, then he led the thin cord through the block of the jib top until the flag ran against it, and hoisted the sail. The wind caught the small tricolour and waved it serenely above the tip of the jib. By now the greyish hull of the aircraft carrier was distinctly visible on the horizon.

Paul glanced at his wrist watch.

"At five twenty-five a.m. of 26 November, the flag of a small country, after more than five years of humiliation, waves freely in front of another free flag," he said.

Heino did not answer. Mutely he pointed to the slide of the main cabin. It moved back slowly, worked open from the inside. Ellen's yellow head appeared in the hatchway.

"Good morning," she said.

Sleep still in her eyes, she glanced around at the sea. The next moment she looked directly up at the flag. For a second she remained stiffly immobile, then a bewildered "Oh" broke from her lips.

If Heino and Paul were expecting to hear Ellen, as the captain's wife, take issue with them, they showed scant knowledge of women. When Ellen had collected herself sufficiently, she said, "It's a poor job. Whoever sewed it should have done better." With that she went below and shut the slide.

After a moment Paul said, "She didn't notice the warship." It was ahead of us, disappearing behind the horizon. "Harry'll come out any time now, but just the same, I hope the Americans saw us and the flag."

"Yes." Paul and Heino looked up at the flag, then back at the main cabin. But the cabin stayed closed, and Harry did not appear. A full half-hour passed and still Harry did not come. At last Paul left and went to the mast. Slowly, hand over hand, he lowered the flag, pulled the line out of the block, folded the flag, coiled the line, and left for the after cabin.

Harry did not appear until eight o'clock, when he took over the watch. Just as Paul was leaving, Harry said in his slow, calm voice, "Paul, I think one flag is about enough for the *Erma*. We've already decided this flag question and there has been no reason to reconsider our decision. On this ship we're trying to work together on a purely voluntary basis, without paying too much attention to the niceties of the maritime code." Harry's face bore the trace of a smile. "But according to the traditional law of the sea this morning's incident was a mutinous act."

Paul did not answer a word; still his face had softened a bit as he passed me on his way below.

22

DURING THE forenoon watch of 27 November, Harry and Arvid sat on top of the forward cabin trying to decide our future course. It was a clear, warm morning, so warm that Arvid had removed his shirt and was sitting in only his shorts. He watched the low, blue swell rolling by and his eyes narrowed as if the glittering sea made them smart. He asked Harry if he still expected to make for New York.

"I guess I do," Harry said slowly.

"Well," Arvid looked down at the toes of his worn tennis shoes, "during the last few days I've been thinking it might be difficult to go that far. It's so late in the season that we may run into contrary winds. And we've almost no fuel. On the other hand, we're not too far from Florida. Miami can't be more than three hundred and fifty or three hundred and seventy-five miles away."

"I've thought of that, too," Harry said. He touched the canvas of the jib absent-mindedly, then went to the cleat and slackened the line a mite. When he came back his face was set in deep thought.

"New York is still close to eight hundred miles away," Arvid continued. "That's quite a difference, especially in our condition. As far as I can see, the only reasonable thing to do is to set our course due west and make for Miami. Don't you think so?"

"You forget the Gulf Stream. When we get into it, and we'll be there any time now, it will give us an extra push of say, two miles an hour, and that'll help our northward sailing considerably."

"The Gulf Stream is mighty changeable and uneven," Arvid replied. "I wouldn't put too much faith in it. And our supplies are already too low. Yesterday we ate our last potatoes. The water's near the bottom of the tanks. Rice is practically our only food left, and there isn't too much of it."

"Right," said Harry. "But living on rice for four days to get to Miami or eight days to get to New York doesn't make a big difference."

"Eight days?"

"Or even if it takes ten or eleven. We may not be able to reach New York, we may have to land somewhere along the way, but we'll be that much closer to our original goal."

"And why the heck do you want to get closer to that original goal?" Arvid was becoming irritated, his eyes were flashing under his black brows.

"Well," Harry answered with a question of his own, "why *don't* you want to get there?"

This display of quiet stubbornness was too much for Arvid.

"Why," he said, "because it's senseless. I don't see why you want to take such chances, especially since you're always so concerned about the women and children."

By now Harry, too, was losing his composure. His ears flushed and he swept his unruly hair back nervously from his forehead.

"I don't think the route north will be too dangerous. The *Erma* has shown that she can take a beating, and, as I said, I don't expect to get there for sure, but I'd like to try."

"But why, for God's sake?"

"Because it's our plan, and we haven't got a good reason for changing it."

"We haven't!" Arvid looked flabbergasted.

After a painful silence Harry continued, "Besides, my father is in New York. He's a United States citizen; he knows about visas and the immigration laws. He's an influential man and he has many good friends up there. He might be a great help to all of us."

Arvid did not answer for a long time. Finally he looked up at Harry and said, "That's a good reason all right, but frankly, I don't think it's good enough. However, if you insist, we'll make a try for it." He laughed a sudden dry laugh. "The only other way to settle the matter would be to fight it out with fists or Finnish knives."

Harry attempted a smile. "It wouldn't be worth it." He sounded apologetic. "You may be right, but our way north parallels the coast, and if we can't make New York, we can land somewhere else."

"Let's hope so," Arvid said, flashing his old grin.

So the *Erma's* course, instead of being to the southwest, was put to north-north-west. The wind, however, which had been a nice moderate north-easterly, began to grow and veer. By the time we had finished our dinner (our second rice meal) it was east to east-south-east. The faces of Harry, Arvid, and Grandma P. showed that they did not like this development, but when Maia asked Grandma the reason, she only shook her head.

"Nothing special. We're now in the zone of the variables and can't expect to have steady winds any more."

During the day the wind kept veering and increasing. The barometer was falling, we did not need to ask the captains or Grandma P. what it meant, we knew that rough weather was ahead. That same afternoon Aunt Juliana appeared in the companionway, her face pale, and said with a trembling voice, "The water is almost gone." A moment later Ellen thrust up her head and said, "My God! What'll we do now!"

Then Harry too came up from the cabin.

"Don't pay any attention to what the women just said. They misunderstood me. The water isn't all gone. Just the same, it's quite low, and we'll have to reduce the ration."

Arvid came from the peak. He and Harry stepped into the cabin and talked there. When they returned Harry announced that the water ration would be reduced to one pint daily, beginning with to-morrow.

Harry said this casually, with his usual slow calmness, but our hearts sank.

"One pint!" Maia exclaimed. "That's nothing— just one mugful. Even a quart was far too little. I can't imagine how we can get by with that little."

"We have to," Harry said shortly.

"The children will suffer," Aunt Juliana reminded him.

"How can we cook with so little water?" Nora asked.

"Cook?" Arvid smiled patiently. "To cook half a cup of rice doesn't take more than a cup of water, does it?"

We did not mention water again that day, but our mood had changed, there was less talk about the nearing landfall. We were preoccupied now with the coming gale. The wind had veered to west and was growing stronger, the western and northern skies were covered with cloud racks, and the setting sun spread an orange and green glow over a big thundercloud. The seas were becoming agitated, and froth swirled over their twisted crests. Spray in showers and seas slammed over the *Erma's* port bow and sides. For extra strength we had eaten our emergency rations, opening

198

one of the last Stockholm tins of hash or fish cakes.

Paul steered with his left hand from the leeward seat, his back against the after cabin, his bare feet braced against the seat. Ellen and Maia watched gloomily from the main companionway.

"The barometer is still falling," Ellen said.

The thunder shower struck with a heavy downpour, and an angry wind sent us quickly to reefing the mainsail. Thunder showers kept coming continuously until past midnight, churning the seas. The *Erma* felt the rage of both. We had not experienced this kind of weather for a long while, not since we left the waters opposite Biscay, and we did not like it. The pump was manned most of the time. Once, just before midnight, it got clogged, and we couldn't start it again until Heino fished a potato out of the pump can.

After midnight the skies cleared, and by four o'clock, when Paul and I relieved Harry and Lembit, a fresh to strong westerly was blowing, stabilizing the seas so that our by-the-wind sailing was smooth as compared with the recent tumult. Paul, wrapped in his top coat, settled comfortably on the leeward seat, and I took the helm. The waning half moon was reaching down into the west and it cast a leaden sheen over the billows. Occasionally spray tickled my cheek, and the breeze was curiously invigorating. I almost believed that I smelled the tang of earth and woods mixed with the salty breath of the sea. Paul said America was only two or three hundred miles away and that with west winds land scents might be carried far out to sea.

"A plagued wind sack is coming against us," he said as the mainsail's luff suddenly began to flap.

I had to let her go twenty degrees eastward. A thin strip of cloud was sailing against and over us, and it had turned the wind north-west. The sea became livelier again, the spray flew denser. Soon the little cloud sailed past, but the wind remained north-west and strong. This seemed to annoy Paul.

"Sail as close to the wind as you can," he commanded curtly. "Don't let her fall off the course."

This was a big order, but with the *Erma's* good pointing qualities it was possible to steer her north, only forty-five degrees off the wind, and as it vacillated a little, she occasionally almost approximated our NNW course, sailing 350 deg. to 345 deg.

But the prospect looked discouraging to me. The seas broke higher and higher, and the wind grew stronger by the minute. Forced to sail close-hauled against a strong wind, the *Erma* buried her nose under the seas and ploughed straight ahead, half inclined to the starboard, foamy layers of water rushing over her decks. In a minute water was sloshing in the cockpit above my bare ankles. Never during our voyage had I seen her plough forward in this fashion, and I could not help thinking about certain timbers in her port bow, up to now carefully protected from the full impact of the seas. The stays whined and the luff of the main was rattling like a machine gun. I looked up and, to my horror, saw the top of the mast bending like a bow under the pull of the sail.

"Look at that," I called hastily and pointed upward. "Don't you think we should reef?"

Paul looked up at the mast cutting elaborate patterns against the dawn-grey skies, and for a while did not answer. Then he said, "No, no reefing."

"But think of those ant-infested timbers in her bow. Won't she fall apart?"

"Nonsense," Paul said. "The old lady can take it. Let's have a nice run just for a few minutes."

So we had a nice run! The *Erma* shook and

shivered, jumped and jerked, but kept going straight ahead, her canvas taut to bursting, and water sloshing over her. She heeled to starboard like a yacht—we had never seen her do that before. Paul sat up and appeared to enjoy the race tremendously. Soon, to my surprise, I found that I did too. It was an exciting sensation, this rushing forward, and there was the additional pleasure of holding the wheel and feeling her respond to my steering. Soon I forgot about the bending mast above us and the little black ants in her port bow. The water ran over her now in a steady, thick stream, and occasionally only the mast and cabin tops showed above the foam.

"Like a submarine, eh?" Paul shouted ecstatically.

This yachting spree did not last long. I thought I heard wailing voices and excited talk below, but in the pandemonium around us I was not sure. Now suddenly, the slide of the fore cabin opened and Arvid's bare head appeared. "Have you gone crazy?" he shouted in a voice that sharply cut through the rumble of the elements. The next moment he was out and shouting, "Let her fall off." I obeyed instantly, while Arvid grabbed the crank and started to reef the mainsail. He brushed aside Paul's help and finished the reefing single-handed, then turned back to the cabin. Before going down he frowned at us and said, "You lunatics were lucky not to drive her under. You spoiled our clothes below."

The weather deteriorated rapidly. By eight o'clock low clouds had almost covered the skies, and a little later the first cold shower rattled on the deck. The mainsail was lowered to repair four slides that had torn loose—the result of our yachting spree. After re-serving the slides it was decided not to hoist the main—the wind already had reached gale force. Before noon Arvid and Harry changed the big white jib for the smaller russet one.

The seas had stabilized into tremendous water mountains. Under the low, showery skies they rolled by, dark, ominous, rumbling deep and hoarse. They were very long, the interval between them appearing to be at least a quarter of a mile, and to us, used to the sunny Trades seascapes, the *Erma* seemed to be sailing in a sea of bad dreams.

In the afternoon Harry, clad in his overcoat and old oil coat, took over the wheel. He stood in the cockpit with his feet widespread, watching the billows coming nearer, turning stern to when they roared by, letting her get closer in the troughs. Ellen had come up from the cabin wearing Harry's coat with the sleeves dangling over her hands and the collar up. Supported against the main cabin, she watched the seas with half-frightened, half-fascinated eyes. For more than two hours, until dusk, she stood there in the wet cockpit beside Harry. Before she left she asked, "We are driven back into the ocean, aren't we? Away from America?"

"Yes, temporarily. The best we can do now is to head north-east."

"How long do you think the gale will last?"

Harry shrugged his shoulders. Ellen did not ask any more questions. Soon she left the deck.

23

THE GALE did not grow worse during the night but neither did it ease. In a wordless, gloomy mood we sat, slept, and fought through it. The pump was manned again much of the time. It clogged once, and Heino fingered out another potato from the pump can. Lembit said that at this rate the bilge might keep us provided with food, but nobody thought him funny.

Outside, Paul constructed for the helmsman a shelter against rain and spray by fastening one end of the idle white jib to the boom while the other end of canvas was to be held by the back and shoulders of the helmsman.

When I left my watch at midnight, Paul spotted a steamer's green starboard and mast lights to our port. The lights kept disappearing every now and then, which meant that the waves were higher than her mast lights. In the early morning the wind rose again. It increased, slowly but steadily, and during the forenoon watch reached full gale strength. The spume-filled wind rushed over us, angrily howling, and the *Erma's* steel rigging trembled and cried. In particularly wild gusts, it screamed as though in anguish. Enormous seas rolled by, their crests wrapped in froth and thunder. Above them dark clouds raced, spouting cold showers; jagged fragments from their lower edges, torn by the gale, hung down like ugly rags trying to sweep the seas.

I stooped over the pump handle, straining to keep my balance. Warm water flowed over my bare feet; the *Erma* was taking water through the bottom, the deck, and the cabins. Up and down went the pump.

"How many strokes?" Harry asked.

I leaned against the roof of the after cabin and inhaled deeply a couple of times before answering.

"Five hundred and fifty."

This had been the second pumping during the watch and there was at least one more long one to come.

Harry said something that I could not hear in the shrieking wind. He was steering as he had yesterday, standing with feet widespread before the wheel, looking back to port where the water mountains came rolling; keeping the *Erma* in the trough, but turning her before the seas when they swooped towards her.

Another rumbling sea. Harry worked the wheel and we were carried over the boiling top of the crest, then slid down the back slope that was darkly opaque like molten glass, striped with long branching streams of snow-white foam. Harry put up the helm, and the *Erma* slung herself forward again as we dropped towards the half-becalmed bottom of the trough.

The next sea looked more than a quarter of a mile away, but it approached very fast. It grew larger and larger, like a solidified mass of thundercloud. We were carried higher and higher along its long forward slope, then, suddenly, were flung ahead on its top where, the horizon widening, we could see endless rows of similar ridges. Before we knew it we were sliding down into the next deep valley. All in all, the time of getting from one trough to another might have been not more than half a minute.

As I gave another stroke of the pump I saw Arvid's head rise under the water-blackened jib. He came up from the cabin and shut the slide. The wind, blowing across from the port side, brought spray and the words of the captains with it.

"Yes, to north-east," Harry was saying. "Or, more exactly, to north-east by east."

"We have headed this way about thirty hours now," Arvid said, "blown away from the land."

"Yes."

"At about five knots . . . and it looks like only the beginning."

A roar split our ears. I looked up from the pump and saw Harry stooped over the wheel partly hidden behind Arvid's lean, leather-jacketed figure. Then something gripped us, wrenching us, and the *Erma* shot forward amidst a cloud of spray. A layer of warm water flowed over my feet. Then we slid down. I rose to my feet and resumed pumping.

"Our provisions are so low that they won't last much more than a week, even eating only once a day," Arvid continued. "And you know the water. . . ."

"Yes, it's bad."

A sudden burst of rain hit us, rattling loudly on the bottom of Rommy's tarpaulin which I was wearing, then ended as suddenly as it had started.

"And it looks like it's going to blow a couple more days. That means it'll be six or seven hundred miles to shore instead of the four or five hundred that we are now. To try to come back from so far, in this late season—and without supplies!"

Harry shook the rain from his face and looked at Arvid balancing beside him.

"How about trying the sea anchor? It's too darned small for the *Erma's* size, so it won't check her drift much but it's better than nothing."

I reached the four hundredth stroke and knelt down once more to rest a little, thinking about the sea anchor. Funny, I'd been on the *Erma* for almost four months and never had seen it. I had no idea what it looked like.

As I resumed pumping I noticed that Arvid had taken over the wheel. Harry was rapping on the window of the after cabin, shouting to Paul to bring the sea anchor. So we were going to try it. I pulled hard on the pump handle just as the *Erma* slanted downhill and the bilge water flowed to the port side. The pump bolted up empty so suddenly that I lost balance and fell on all fours. Struggling up, I looked to port. From the tilted level of the downward sliding boat, the onrushing sea appeared to be rolling down upon us from an overturned world.

Astern, Heino loomed up to relieve me at the pump. He had rolled his pants to his knees and wrapped his blue bandanna tightly about his hair. As he slid over the shining wet deck and landed in the cockpit he looked almost like an Arab pirate. Before I managed to give him Rommy's tarpaulin and weather coat, the rain had drenched him and was dripping from his beard.

At that moment Paul appeared, supporting himself against the heeling cabin top and carrying a bundle in his right armpit.

"Here," he said, giving it to Harry. Together, they rolled out what seemed to be a green canvas bag.

"Why, it's only a sack," I said wonderingly to Heino.

"Sure. What did you think it was?"

I clutched the after-cabin top and strained for a closer look. After all I had heard about sea anchors I had expected to see an intricate contrivance that by some shrewd trick would cut down a boat's drift. Now as it dangled from Harry's hands, and Paul, shivering in his dungarees, straightened out the lines on its upper end, its simplicity startled me.

Our sea anchor resembled a funnel whose wider end was fastened around an iron hoop about eighteen inches in diameter. The opening on its narrow end measured only an inch. On the wider end a three-branched bridle was attached for fastening it to a streaming line. It was self-evident that the bag would be launched with its wide mouth towards the boat so that the resistance of the water against its inside surface would slow the boat's drift. I couldn't figure out why the smaller end was open and asked Heino about it.

"Why, to prevent the canvas from bursting under the pressure of the water," he told me. For a moment I had a vague feeling that I was not yet a full-fledged sailor.

"Bring the line," Harry shouted.

Lembit was already in the after cockpit lifting the ninety-foot coil of rope that had been presented to us in Fraserburgh. In a matter of seconds Harry tied one end of it to the bridle of the canvas bag. Paul took hold of the coil and walked forward, Harry following with the sea anchor. They stooped over the forward cabin as a toppling crest shot across the deck, then continued forward and tied the line to the windlass. At the same time Arvid put the helm up.

"Go to the halyard," he said to Heino, "and when she swings into the wind, lower the jib."

The *Erma* pivoted on her broad stern and slung her bow closer to the wind just as the next sea hit us. Luckily, its crest did not break over us. The *Erma's* bows pointed upward and she was hurled astern as the big seas rushed by, then she was wrenched violently to starboard by the rearguard of the attacking waters. But by that time she had topped the hump and was slipping down over the back slope.

As soon as the jib started to slat, Harry cast the sea anchor overboard. Like an elongated serpent with an evil green head, the canvas bag dashed away with its long, yellow line trailing. The next wave snatched it and carried it towards us for a moment, then left it behind. The line yanked taut, jerking the *Erma's* bows down so that a gurgling thin layer rushed over her decks. However small, the sea anchor was strong enough to make itself felt.

Arvid left the cockpit and joined the others around the mast.

"Not so bad, after all," he said. Harry did not say anything. He just kept looking forward, following the small, scarcely perceptible green spot ahead, and then staring at the bow of the *Erma*. Another sea snapped the line taut, and the *Erma*, tearing at it like a frenzied animal, ducked her bow. She shook from side to side as a stream of water spouted over her bows, but she kept level with the water.

"If she only stays hove-to," Harry said. "With her shallow . . ." He did not get farther. A vicious sea, a bubbling part of an overhanging breaker, hit the *Erma* on her port bow with a high, almost metallic sound, hurling us broadside. Instead of swinging back into the wind, she immediately started to veer away to port in a wide circle, the sea anchor being the centre of it and the lines its radius, until she floated length-wise in the bottom of the trough.

We fell into frantic action.

"Hoist the jib," Arvid shouted, as he leaped to the helm. Heino and Lembit pulled on the jib with desperate yanks. Harry and Paul were up in the bow, working hand over hand on the stubborn sea anchor.

We knew well enough that getting swamped when being broadside-to meant danger. And there it came, another huge hill, dark as night, streaked with a creamy net of froth, thundering and swishing.

"Watch out," Arvid cried. Harry and Paul gripped the windlass. Frightened, I cast a quick glance at the crest above and noticed that it was not toppling over us. But anyway . . . We sidled up its steep side, the spray flew about us, the *Erma* heeled to starboard, whirled herself this way and that, and I hung on to the cabin top. Then it was gone, and we coasted down the slope.

"It didn't break," Lembit said with a sigh that sounded almost like a prayer. "We're lucky."

The jib was up and the boat under control again. The four men forward heaved on the last feet of the dripping rope and lifted aboard the sea anchor. So once again the *Erma* was sailing on her reverse course. Soaking wet, the five men stood in the cockpit eyeing the seas and clouds uneasily.

"It just didn't work this way," Harry said at last.

I looked at the big swell with something like relief. It didn't seem half so perilous as it had before.

"I wonder how it would work from the stern," Harry continued thoughtfully. "Although she's a double-ender, her stern is not as shallow as her bow. The keel has a depth of twelve inches right behind the rudder."

"But there is even less overhang than under her bow," Arvid said. "The swamping might be more disastrous." Both men were silent. Finally Arvid concluded, "We might as well try it."

Harry tied the pointer to the middle of the main traveller, Arvid took the helm and steered the *Erma* before the wind, then Heino lowered the jib and Harry launched the sea anchor. This way was simpler and easier. The sack went dancing off over the wash of the waters. The line straightened out; every sea pulled the *Erma* deeper into the water, but the seas rushed by and did not come aboard. She stayed steadier on the line, she did not go off broadside with every sideways push.

For some time we watched the tug and tear between the boat and the sea anchor. After a while Harry said, "Seems all right." He sounded rather surprised.

Arvid nodded. He turned slowly away from the port railing.

"I think I'll go below."

"I don't know any particular reason why we shouldn't all turn in," Harry told us. We were soaked and cold, and as the *Erma*, secured by her sea anchor, needed no one at the wheel, we were glad to go. Harry cast one more look behind, then we all trooped down, and for the first time during the voyage the *Erma's* decks were left alone.

24

NO SOONER had we left the *Erma* unattended, with her rigging howling and her small green anchor hidden behind a screen of showers than a huge sea hit us. For a moment we felt the *Erma* drop deeper into the water, then the rushing floods rolled over her with a deafening roar. Although both the slide and the doors of the companionway were shut, the cabin at once half filled with water which spurted in through the cracks. In a flash we were out of our bunks, stooping, soaking wet, under the low ceiling, Rommy eyeing the wet book in his hand and I still clutching the diary in which I had been trying to write. The next moment we had torn open the slide and were scrambling out.

Harry was already on deck, and forward. Arvid was stepping out of his cabin. From below came the wails of the children. Ellen thrust a frightened face out of the companionway.

"We all fell on to the floor," she said. "Stoves, shoes, clothes, everything is awash." Behind her Grandma P. was peering about grimly trying to assess the damage. To our relief, everything aboard looked unharmed, although the after cockpit was filled with water.

Harry bent over the traveller and grasped the end of the line.

"Lend a hand, will you?" he called.

Rommy and Paul jumped to the slippery stern. There, on the narrow segment of bare deck, flush with the sea and in a cloud of spray, the three men commenced to haul in the taut line.

Arvid, now in the cockpit, ordered Heino and me to

hoist the jib—and fast. We ran to the mast and as we pulled on the wet canvas, Arvid put the helm down. The *Erma* caught steerageway and turned slowly to port.

Then I went aft to lend a hand. There was some free space left on the very end of the stern, so I passed the others and grabbed the line beside the rudderhead. It was hard work, but most of the line was already on board. Finally we heaved the sea anchor aboard, emptied it of water and set it in the after cockpit.

Thus our second attempt to curtail the *Erma's* offshore drift had failed. As we stood in a puzzled, discouraged group, trying to think what to do next, the main hatch opened and Grandma P. stood in the companionway, her hair flying in the wind and spray. She viewed the seas with a determined face, her usually calm eyes flickering.

"There must be some way we can use the sea anchor," she said, looking at Harry. "How about launching it from the stern, but instead of dead astern, streaming it from one corner of the traveller so that she'll ride before quartering seas?"

"Hell, she wouldn't stay that way," Arvid said.

"Why not, if you hoist the jib and steer her on the right course?"

"Yes, you're right," Arvid acknowledged slowly, "but we'd still make fast headway."

"It would be slower, though, than now," Grandma P. persisted.

"Hey, wait a minute." Arvid suddenly looked up. "What your mother says makes sense, Harry. But we'd still run at three or four knots. We'll have to make the sea anchor heavier, too. The only question is, how."

Harry suggested the big, six-foot beam that was

I can think of. We can use half of it. That'll give us sixty feet of heavy chain."

Paul, Lembit, Rommy, and I went forward with Harry. Paul and I worked the windlass, rotating the first sixty feet of the chain around the drum. The second half was joined to the first by a thinner chain wrapped through the connecting links of the halves. Harry unfastened it, and as he let the chain out of the pit, we dragged it to the stern, distributing ourselves at even intervals along the deck to prevent the heavy chain from beating against cabin houses or railing.

The chain safely in the after cockpit, Harry fastened one end of it around the traveller, then directed us to pull in the line for a couple of feet so he could untie it and connect it with the chain. We fell on it, all five of us, and slowly it began to come in. Suddenly Harry called, "Let it back. You can't hold it. I'll douse the jib."

He ran to the mast and let the canvas down. Before that Arvid had held her stern-to in the wind. As the *Erma* floated free, the tension eased considerably, and we pulled the line inboard for some feet. Harry loosened the line from the traveller and tied it to the last link of the free end of the chain.

While we still held the end of the line inboard, Harry and Arvid let out the chain, slowly and carefully, hand over hand. We eyed the ocean warily. Seas did sweep over us, soaking us, but no killers came along. As we let the line go, the bag and beam danced away for a hundred and fifty feet. Heino hoisted the jib, Arvid took the helm and the *Erma* resumed her course.

"Well, at last that's the job." Arvid watched the slowly heaving chain. Intermittently it rapped at the traveller which clanged with a gong-like ring, but the pulls were not so strong.

"We're making only two knots now—or two and a half at most," Harry estimated. We felt an inner satisfaction with our achievement and would have been more pleased with ourselves if it hadn't been for the storm which howled on with undiminished strength. The *Erma's* deck resounded under the barrage of the sweeping seas; every blow sounded as though it were the last the boat could take.

We had gone below, everybody except the captains and Heino, when a toppling sea hit us again, a moment after the anchor had drawn the *Erma* deeply to port and slackened suddenly so that she rolled over to starboard. With a noise like a shell burst the comber fell on her exposed side, pouring a cascade of water over her. Possibly she would have capsized but for the pull of the sea anchor.

We opened the slides and looked out. Everything was in order except that both cockpits were filled with water. Heino was pumping. Harry's face was expressionless as usual, but Arvid looked annoyed.

"I don't like it. It alarms the women and children. They aren't accustomed to it yet."

He was looking at Nora's white face in the companionway. When he made a reassuring gesture, she disappeared.

"If we had an oil bag we could try oiling the surface." Grandma P., who was standing in the main companionway, suggested some sugar bags we had bought in Madeira. She dived down, and after a while reappeared with a small linen sack. Paul took it below and filled it with the old Swedish "tar." It dripped like a sieve.

After a short debate Arvid hung it out from the same port corner of the traveller to which the sea anchor was attached. The effect was almost instantaneous; the water behind took on soft, curved lines, and even the wildest seas, although they still rolled over, were not so sharp.

"It's magic," said Lembit.

But Arvid was not entirely satisfied.

"The oiled area won't be large enough to keep occasional seas from hitting us."

At that Grandma P. smiled.

"Better half an egg than an empty shell."

It was past four o'clock. Our battle with the sea and the sea anchor had lasted for three hours. Presently it seemed that we had won; we had fettered the *Erma* and cut down the drift as much as possible. Now, after the strain of action had passed, we suddenly felt very hungry—it was more than twenty-four hours since we had eaten our last rice. We cast one more look over the long seas and went down, all of us except Rommy who stayed at the helm. We were wet, tired, cold and hungry, but deep inside we felt satisfied.

A little after five o'clock Rommy called down to Harry, asking if he could leave the deck for a moment to use the stove before we let it go out. Harry, just about to eat himself, said he thought it would be all right to leave the helm alone for that short time; the *Erma* wouldn't swing away so soon.

But she did. Rommy was helping himself to the last spoonfuls of his oily flour mess when Heino exclaimed "Hell, it almost shot my eye out!" A jet of water that had burst through some crack in the timbers had hit him neatly on the eye-ball. How was it that the seas were coming from the starboard quarter?

We all ran on deck. The boat had swung over, the seas had beaten her out of her east to east-south-east course and carried her about in a quarter circle so that she headed now south by west. Harry looked from the compass to the thundering crests rolling toward us from our starboard quarter. Then he shrugged.

"This doesn't make much difference. Maybe south by west is even a little better. We won't be carried so far away from the coast."

Arvid who had appeared to rinse his soup pot, asked, "Can you see the sea anchor? I can't."

We stared behind. Snow-white mops of the blackish rollers gleamed in the early twilight. It was not raining but we could see neither the green bag nor the log.

"It's because it's too dark," said Rommy.

"Nonsense, it isn't that dark," protested Paul. "We should see it."

The old bow line on the timber might have broken and thus account for the loss of the sea anchor. Paul hurried aft and put his hand on the chain.

"The pull is still terrific. I can't feel any difference by touch."

"Well," Harry reminded him, "you'd certainly feel sixty feet of heavy chain."

Paul started to curse. After all our fuss and toil it would be rotten luck to be riding freely once more in the open sea.

Silently, one by one, we left the deck with heavy feet. I crawled into the wet bunk and tried not to think about the long, black night that was descending on us.

And it was miserable; we thought it would never end. The inside of the boat echoed eerily with the pounding of waves, and several times they crashed so violently that even the children woke. I thought about the oil bag. Probably it was already empty. Yuta and Ulla started to cry. Nora soothed Ulla with a song, her mellow soprano rising above the noise in a sad Estonian folk tune. It made a melancholy accompaniment to our troubled thoughts.

Towards dawn the gale seemed to be abating, but at what ought to have been sun-up it was blowing again as strongly as yesterday. The storm seemed to be going on for ever. There was, however, one bit of good news; the morning light revealed that our sea anchor was still hanging on, as sound as it had been when we launched it eighteen hours earlier. Rommy brought this glad message when he returned from the early morning watch. We rushed to the companion to get the proof with our own eyes, and there it danced on the white froth of the seas.

Lembit, at the helm, laughed at us. We were able to laugh too. After two days of hell, it was wonderful to feel so good.

25

FOR ANOTHER day big frothy seas swept away our hopes of resuming the westward course. The next night was nearly as miserable as the previous one; the same dampness in the cabins, the same wetness outside, although there was only a little rain, the same toiling at the pump and pump priming. The difference was in ourselves—we had become more accustomed to the racket, particularly the children, who slept without waking. By the morning of 2 December the waves were already stabilizing and at eleven o'clock, when the sun broke through the clouds, the talk of getting under way popped up openly.

At noon Harry took the sextant out of its worn mahogany case, checked its screws and mirrors, then muttered, "Hell! Salt water has got into the case. The mirrors are ruined."

Arvid looked at the two tiny pieces of glass. They were coated with a solid white layer of dried salt, as was practically the whole sextant. Arvid began to rub off the salt which came away rather easily from the metal parts and the faces of the mirrors, but on their backs it had partially ruined the thin silver film.

"The horizon glass is all right," Harry decided after a while, "but the index glass looks bad."

He stepped on top of the cabin and steadied himself against the mast while Arvid held up his wrist to give the right time. In spite of the bad mirror Harry managed to "take the sun." The computation of the data was put off temporarily because it was time to swing the *Erma's* bow towards America once again.

Anxious to get started I asked if it would be long before we could take in the sea anchor.

"No, my lad, not long. We'll start right now," Harry decided. "Call out the boys."

Soon all the men were out, laughing and joking.

"Get set on the stern and haul on the chain," commanded Arvid. "Don't pull it inboard, let it run back into the water as you work it nearer, hand over hand. Now, look alive."

There was no need for urging, we fell on the chain, braced ourselves against the traveller and the stern deck as best we could and pulled with a will.

"One-two, one-two," we chanted, and the sea anchor neared slowly as the gathering slack of the chain sank deeper beside the boat.

"Hold fast now!"

Arvid yelled the warning when a crest overtook us and the line yanked taut. We managed to hold our own although it felt as though our arms had snapped out of joint. The pull threatened to drag us overboard. The boat continued to swing around and ended by heading north-east, lengthwise into the trough. We moved alongside to the port quarter, thus gaining more space and a firmer hold behind the gunwale and the corner of the railing. The accumulating sag of the sea anchor caused the *Erma* to cant deeply to port so that she had only eight or twelve inches of freeboard. Consequently, the water lapped over us most of the time, but this did not quench our eagerness.

"Watch out for that log." Harry indicated the heavy beam that floated alongside, only a dozen feet away. "It may land aboard by itself."

The next big sea dropped the black timber barely an arm's length away from the *Erma's* side. This was dangerous.

"Heino, Lembit, pull it just a little closer and hold the line fast," Arvid shouted, the water dripping from his hair. "Paul, Rommy, grab the back end and pull it over the corner of the railing the moment you can reach it. Hold it until Harry and I get the other end. Then we'll heave it aboard."

But this didn't work. As Rommy and Paul grasped their end of the beam the *Erma* sidled uphill, and an eddying stream kicked the slippery beam from their hands. The next moment the swaying crest took hold of it and threw it back towards us. It landed against the *Erma's* exposed port side, then sprang off and was swung away. Carried by the rush of the wave, it hurled another whacking blow at her side.

"Hell, don't let it knock us cold," cried Arvid angrily. "Pull it closer and grab it."

Paul and Rommy, who had crawled through the railing in their eagerness to reach the dancing log, almost fell overboard. Heino and Lembit automatically had slackened the line for some feet. Just as it seemed that Rommy had grabbed the end of it, a cross-wave swirled the beam halfway around, then gave it a sudden lift. With a violent upward wrenching of his body, Rommy escaped being hit with the forward end of the log as it bounced on to the edge of the gunwale. In an instant it sprang off again like a skittish stallion. It turned broadside, and now Rommy and Paul got their fingers behind it. Before the next sea could reach it, four pairs of hands lifted it aboard. Then Harry pulled in the sea anchor.

"Well, those two blows will mean a lot more pumping." Lembit kicked at the beam sullenly.

"You can bet your life they do." Arvid climbed over the railing, knelt on the outer edge of the coaming, holding on to an upright of the railing, and bent over to take a look. We held to the belt of his leather jacket and his feet, as a wave swept clean over his body. When Arvid climbed back on to the deck, dripping and shining like a seal, there was a thoughtful look in his eyes.

"These nineteenth-century boats are *really* stout."

"So the planking is all right?" we asked.

"Yes, as far as I could see. I spotted only two small nicks on the edges of two planks. But it sounded as if she was broken clean through."

The dripping line was soon coiled on deck; but handling the heavy and slippery chain was more complicated. It almost pulled me overboard and lacerated my index finger when it surged back several feet.

"Easy now, easy," Harry warned time after time, whenever the seas washed over. At last when about half the chain was in, Rommy lost patience.

"Damn it, I don't like this fooling around. Let me handle it alone." He stooped over the railing, grabbed the chain with his spread hands and with a great swing, rattled it aboard; then, within three seconds, coiled the rest out of the sea. The last few feet came in so easily that Rommy lost his balance and landed flat on the wet deck, still clutching the chain to his breast.

For a moment we were breathless with awe and amazement; after all, our anchor chain was no ordinary sailboat affair but solid, three-inch linked big-ship stuff. Rommy looked at his hands, threw down the chain and walked away. Paul stared after him in bewilderment. At last he shook his head.

"The man must have some extra food stored away."

Next Arvid replaced the wet and beaten Irish-reefed jib with the bigger white jib. Then Harry hoisted the mainsail, Heino set the jib, the sails filled and Arvid steered her slowly over south-east to south. Round she turned, closer and closer to the wind, then as Harry hauled the main sheet as close as possible, she reached west. After three and a half days the *Erma* was heading towards America again.

certain direction. At first we could not believe it but
soon we had to recognize with a heavy heart that it blew
again from the north-west, the same wind that had
brought us the gale.

"A dead calm would be better than this," Rommy

26

IN THE night the wind died completely and by the
sunrise of 3 December the *Erma* floated lazily in the
noiseless ground swell. The air was mild, almost warm,
and the all-embracing stillness was such a contrast to
the riot of the last few days that it seemed unreal. We
slept longer than usual and our rested bodies felt more
keenly than ever the inadequacy of the one-meal and
one-pint diet.

Lembit complained of a sharp nipping in his
stomach. Ulla kept asking her mother, "Haven't we
any sandwiches left?" but was satisfied when Nora
promised her bread crumbs and a whole spoonful of
jelly with her rice meal.

The children were gay and laughing as usual, but
their Trade Wind tan had grown bleaker, more wax
coloured. Yuta, who was rather fragile and of lighter
complexion, actually looked pale. Heino, watching
them, suddenly remembered the condensed milk he
had bought in Stockholm and was saving for a special
occasion. He went below, dug out the small tin and
gave it to Ellen for Yuta.

The shooting of the three o'clock longitude, together with our morning latitude, showed that we had
done seventy-four miles westing and eight miles south-
ing during the last twenty-four hours. We were still
three hundred and fifty miles from the nearest point
on the Florida coast, and the present dead calm did
not quiet our uneasiness.

The air began to stir soon after the longitude shooting, although it took some time to settle down in a

certain direction. At first we could not believe it but soon we had to recognize with a heavy heart that it blew again from the north-west, the same wind that had brought us the gale.

"A dead calm would be better than this," Rommy said.

"It's all right," comforted Harry. "The barometer is the same. We can make a little headway directly towards the nearest coast."

Actually we made very little. It was only a light breeze, and under close-hauled sails the advance was slower than it would have been on a reach, with a quartering wind, so very soon Arvid slacked the sheets a little and steered her west-south-west.

After two hours, the puny north-westerly collapsed, and we felt something like relief.

"The chances are that we'll get a different wind when the calm ends," Harry said cheerily. "The wind seldom starts from the same quarter."

During these two hours of sailing we probably had not made more than three miles. However, it was better than nothing, and better than floating help-lessly on a glassy, dying swell. After a while the uneasy restlessness sneaked back into us. The children were the only ones who did not worry. They played with dolls, dog-eared picture books, pieces of paper, already dry from the moisture of the last gale, and a few broken pencils and crayons. The nipping in our stomachs, always sharpest after meal-times, had subsided by this pre-sunset hour.

It was a warm, mild and peaceful evening, but the adults could not enjoy it. Harry and Arvid sat on the main cabin discussing the new situation. Harry spread between them our small general chart of the North Atlantic and set a pair of callipers on it. Then they took a pencil and marked the *Erma's* present position with a little dot, in addition to the long string of dots that traced her route.

"Now that our chances of making New York aren't too good," Arvid said, "don't you think we ought to land as soon as possible?" He pointed to the north-eastern curve of the coastline between North Florida and Cape Hatteras. "This is the only logical place to aim for. See: Jacksonville, Savannah, Charleston, Wilmington. If we keep sailing north-west in a general direction we could enter any of them, whichever turns out to be nearest."

"Only if we get favourable winds," Harry reminded him. "And we can't expect them in this season. In case of another north-westerly we could try to sail close-hauled directly west." Harry was thinking aloud. "But there's the Gulf Stream to be taken into account. We're almost on its eastern border already. It would cancel whatever westing we could make—unless the wind is strong enough. But with strong winds, close-hauled sailing is out of the question with the *Erma.*"

"Nevertheless, if we get a north-westerly of just the right strength—a fresh breeze—we could make it," Arvid insisted. "Yes, we could reach Jacksonville in seven or eight days."

Harry shook his head.

"Too long. Our supplies won't hold out."

Arvid nodded.

"For the same reason taking a south-westerly course is no good. Only a gale could push us through against the Gulf Stream fast enough. That leaves us Savannah, Charleston, and Wilmington to choose from. We've got to get into one of them, north-westerlies or not."

Harry took callipers and measured the distances on the chart. Jacksonville was farthest away—almost three

227

hundred and fifty miles. Wilmington was about forty or fifty miles nearer.

"Under good conditions we could reach Wilmington in four or even three days without experiencing real hunger. All we need now is a breeze, any breeze except a north-westerly."

But there was no breeze. Still feeling the battering of the last gale, some of us tried to get extra sleep; others tried to kill the time with reading or talking, but our minds were restless and our nerves taut.

Everything seemed to be wrong. Relatively small things loomed big. Heino came down from the afternoon watch and said, "We'll soon need life belts. Five hundred pump strokes in a watch, although it's dead calm!" Lembit drawled "Yes?" and we all remembered that we had no life belts. Then somebody from the main cabin, Ellen or Grandma P., informed us that the barometer had fallen one mm. during the day. This was the tiniest fall possible and did not mean much. However, the southerly skies had grown hazy; down on the horizon a cirro-stratus web was forming. This did not mean too much either, for we were now out of the clear skies of the Trades, but somebody said, "We're going to get another wallop."

Then there was the incident of the clay bottle. In one of these five-gallon demijohns that we had taken on in Fraserburgh and which were lashed to the starboard railing there had been a little water left. At least, we had thought so a week ago when the one-pint ration had gone into effect. We had planned to save it for a while and then dole it out in half-pint portions. Paul hurried down the ladder.

"The water bottle is empty. Only a few drops left."

"Who did it?" Words were tossed back and forth. Heino asked how much was left before. Paul did not know exactly; not too much, he thought, but surely much more than now. Rommy, belligerent as ever, doubted him. This aroused Paul's suspicions and prompted a direct accusation. Rommy shot back, "And why were you nosing around the bottle?"

So it went. I tried to explain the disappearance as caused by the leaky cork and evaporation, pointing out that the salty taste of the remainder proved that the cork had not been tight. After a while the heat of the argument lessened, then quite suddenly, the subject was dropped altogether. Nobody really cared.

Finally, that night the wind came, a gentle southeasterly, but this did not matter, the main thing was that it had come—and not from the north-west. It grew stronger all the time. Once when I awoke towards morning, I heard the swishing sound behind the planks and felt the gentle pitching of the boat. This meant that we were making nice headway.

The next morning the wind had veered to south-south-east. It was a strong breeze, the sea was full of foaming whitecaps, though not yet very large, and we made a fast run, as fast as any the *Erma* had done. Even Grandma P. estimated that we had made more than twenty miles that morning while the after cabin insisted that it was twenty-five. The *Erma* leaped from one crest to another, her canvas taut as a drum. The wind blew taut our sagging spirits, too. Gone were yesterday's tensions. Everybody looked around for something to do.

In our bachelor quarters Lembit lifted the floorboards to search the bilge water once more. Paul stepped out of his way so he did not see what Lembit fished up before our unbelieving eyes. A tin of beans! A whole day's provisions for five men, to supplement our rice bag and a dozen spoonfuls of sugar. Rommy had a little flour left, even less than our portion. And then there was a tin of peas, the last remnant of our first Stockholm provisions.

In the forward cabin Nora was making a frantic inventory. Ellen, Grandma P., and Maia in the middle cabin felt around in the half-empty lockers, checking every nook and corner along the sides, under the bunks, slopping in the bilges. Their supplies were a little more diversified than ours, one half-empty tin of jelly, a few tins of fish, half the tin of condensed milk that Heino had given to Yuta, and a small bagful of hard bread crumbs, stale or salt-water-soaked remnants of Swedish bread. The Kuuns had a tin of vegetable soup in addition to their rice. Maia estimated that at best it was enough for six or seven days.

For some time Harry stood on the main-cabin roof and tried to shoot the sun. The skies were hazy now all over, and in the south and west were long stratus belts, yet the sun shone at its noontime high, only slightly dimmed by the overcast.

"The index mirror is entirely out of order," Harry said at last as he stepped down. "The sea water has ruined the silver on its back. I can't make a reliable observation with that thing."

"Let me see it," Paul asked. "Can't we replace it? I mean, make a new one?"

"Only if we can find a thin mirror of a better quality," Harry answered.

"Lembit, bring our pocket mirror," Paul called. "Although I think it's too thick."

Lembit appeared with it and simultaneously I brought mine, a broken splinter that Heino and I had used for shaving.

Paul gave the mirror back to Lembit.

"Too thick. And yours, Val—I wouldn't call that

a mirror. I was frightened when I saw myself in it."

"The women should have some better ones." Harry stuck his head into the companionway. "Hey, bring out your purse mirrors for a moment, please," he called. "We want a new mirror for our sextant, and Paul will cut it if we can find a good clear one." As a silence followed, Harry added, "Without a sextant we can't land. You know that. We just have to do it."

"Oh," came from below. Maia handed up her mirror to Paul, a pretty horn-inlaid and silver-monogrammed piece, but rather thick.

"If we don't find a thinner one we might use it," Harry said and gave it back.

Maia sighed, relieved.

Ellen's was a small round mirror, quite a fine one, and it took only a moment for Paul to check on its thickness and say, "This is it."

Harry unscrewed the old glass from the top of the sextant. It was small, about a half-inch square. He asked Paul how he planned to cut the new one as we had no diamond cutter with us.

"I'll try to do it with the sharp edge of our smaller file. I'll wet the glass and hope it won't crack."

Anxiously we watched Paul wet the surface of the glass, set the sextant's mirror on top of it and scratch the outline of the small square. Then he filed cautiously along the four lines, always keeping the glass wet. After a while he called, "Bring me one of our metal soup plates. I won't take any chances." He put the mirror in it and poured a little water over it, just enough to cover it, then continued to file. Soon the first side broke off, smooth enough and without a crack, then the second, third, and finally the fourth, each of them without mishap.

"Well done, big brother." Lembit slapped Paul's shoulder. "You'll make a living in America."

Harry fastened the new mirror on the sextant with a satisfied expression.

"Fits all right."

But he could not try it out because the hazy cirrus cover over the skies was thickening all the time. We could still see the outline of the sun behind the foggy layer occasionally; still it was too dim and it vanished too fast to get a sight. Soon low scuds caught us and started to race over us. The weather certainly did not look good. The barometer had fallen almost a quarter of an inch during the last three hours. The *Erma* lurched through the following seas.

"We can't go on this way," Arvid said. "We can't do the impossible." He went to the boom and shortened the mainsail a round or two. Instantly her speed fell off, but, even so, it was a fast ride.

"Couldn't she run full a little longer?" Rommy asked rather sullenly, but Arvid gave him no satisfaction.

"No sense in letting her pound her seams open."

Rommy was not the only one who would have preferred to sail full; the reefing was a bitter blow to all of us in the after cabin. Paul came down and blurted, "Damn these captains. I think they're scared. The *Erma* can take more than a cruiser. Why don't they use this wind for what it's worth?" All of us were seized with something like anger or despair at not being able to grasp fully this wonderful opportunity to push the *Erma* to the limit. But the women did not share our resentment. For them "our Harry" and "my Arvid" were the wisest seafarers in the world.

To make matters worse, Arvid turned in another reef at four o'clock. It was fully justified because the wind really was a young gale. This time Paul did not say a word; he just came down and climbed into the bunk. Rommy, always taking issue with Paul, pointed out philosophically, "We can't ask too much. We've had perhaps our best sailing day and, what's more, our stomachs are full—almost full at least—of beans that we did not even know existed. What more do you want?" To which Paul answered nothing, just gave him a contemptuous stare.

Although our quartering was a trifle too much west, we were still running before the wind. When Grandma P. came out at sunset she looked into the darkening sky, sniffed the breeze and said, "It's good. We are going in the right direction and at a very fine rate at that."

"We could land in forty-eight hours if we keep this up," Harry told us. Then, seeing our surprised delight, he added, "But don't count on it, southerlies don't last that long in this season."

Harry's warning turned out to be right. A storm was coming. At eight o'clock, when I relieved Lembit, the wind was whistling in the rigging.

"You are going to get it," he said, and he did not sound very compassionate. "It smells like rain."

For a minute we stood wordless, Harry at the wheel, Arvid and I on either side. Then Arvid said, "A rain sack is chasing us." A moment later Harry called to me, "Look behind." I looked and what I saw was not comforting. It was a dark night, one could not tell the sky from the sea, but the cloud that was approaching was such an intense black that it stood out against the night as if it were in a sunlit sky. This ink-deep blackness had an ominous quality about it, and its warm, heavy breath made me shiver. I did not want to look at the cloud, but even without looking, I could feel it advancing, and waited for it to reach us, charged with high-voltage tension.

Curiously, the wind abated, but there was a threat in its stillness.

"It takes a breath before blowing full," Harry said. "A tropical squall. Won't last long."

It started as though a big door had been pulled open before a wild draught, and the next moment the skies fell in and solid water squashed us, so that our shoulders hurt and our knees bent under the weight of the onslaught. In a moment the cockpit was half filled, the water swiftly rising up our shins. Through the roar of the downpour, Harry tugged my sleeve and cried, "Go astern and halfway haul in the mainsheet."

I jumped out of the cockpit and lunged astern, toward the unprotected after deck. The only thing to hold on to was the iron bar of the traveller across the stern, and there, happily, I landed. Kneeling down behind it and bracing my thighs against its starboard corner, I reached overboard to catch the main sheet's tackle and started to pull. Lightning lit the sky here and there, dimmed by the rain. Spray whipped across my back, and with every lurch my knees slipped a little on the edge of the deck, but, luckily, the opposite side of the stern was taking the seas.

Having pulled the sheet halfway in, I quickly sneaked back into the haven of the helm cockpit which was full of water. Without looking at me, Harry said, "Put the jib back on the forestay if you can. It's flapping to pieces."

If I could! I never had done it before, even in daylight and calm weather. But I went. One of the jib's uppermost spring hooks kept catching the shroud, threatening to tear the canvas. Whenever I loosened it, it caught again, sometimes even before I got down to unloosen the clew of the sail. So I returned and reported the situation.

Harry pounded against the after-cabin's window and called Paul, who appeared in his dungarees and held the wheel while we went forward, took the canvas and set it on the forestay above the wildly pitching bow, a job nine-parts Harry's and one-part mine. When we returned, Paul went below in anything but a good mood.

After that there was a brief pause during which the rain ceased and the wind momentarily died away. Then a new and even stronger squall hit us. Harry sent me forward again: "Reef the mainsail as much as you can," he said, "and quick, or we'll lose it."

Usually the reefing was done by two or three men. Only Arvid occasionally did it alone—and in daytime —I thought bitterly as I crawled on all fours towards the mast, elbow deep in the foaming water. When I found the mast, I embraced it with both arms, trying to concentrate on how to do the job.

Seeing was out, I could not see beyond a few inches. So was hearing, as far as asking questions of Harry was concerned; even a lion's lungs would not have sufficed for that. So the sense of touch and whatever I remembered about the handling of the gear was all I had to rely on.

At first it worked out all right. I had wrapped up two short turns of the sail and started the third when I discovered that the wrapping had sneaked forward and pressed on the crank to such an extent that I could not turn it.

Well! I said to myself work it back. Unwrap the thing and start over again.

So I did. But the second time it came out the same way. Try once more and look alive. Don't waste time.

It was a wonder that the sail had not been torn to pieces. It yelped like an angry anti-aircraft battery.

I was getting fidgety. Once, after having let the sail down a bit, I threw the halyard over the pin to fasten it and failed to keep it taut enough. The line surged away for a stretch, but I stopped it before the sail dropped altogether. Another time I accidentally loosened the jib halyard and, worse yet, did it at the moment of a particularly strong gust that tore the line through my hands and doused the jib almost completely. My God, what a blunder! A sloop without its jib—especially in a storm!

I fell on to the line with all my weight, pulling with whatever strength despair gave me. Sudden lurches of the boat repeatedly robbed me of foothold, tossed me out of balance and threw me off deck. I was flung high up into the air, whirled dizzily against the mainsail and around the mast, and landed again, not very tenderly. At last, with the use of the belaying pin I worked the jib back and got on with the reefing.

Back and forth I struggled for what seemed endless time. Finally I decided that this was about all I could do, and that the sail actually was somewhat shortened. Sliding back, I landed in the cockpit, a very tired, but self-satisfied man. However, in Harry's voice there was no trace of satisfaction when he called to me with unusual harshness, "What the heck were you doing there for so long? I shouted myself hoarse calling to you. I thought you'd been swept overboard."

There I was, beaten to a pulp! Slumping on the bench, I wanted only one thing in the world—to rest a minute. But almost at once I was yanked up again by Harry's voice rasping the one word, *"Pump."*

27

AGAIN THE storm was followed by a dead calm. For six long hours the *Erma* rattled her boom and shook her bare pole in the stirless air, but in the morning a gay, fresh breeze from the south-west blew away our gloom and Lembit and Arvid set her port side towards the wind. She was on her good old north-west course.

Soon Nora appeared in the companionway dragging an armful of blankets and clothing which she began to spread on the top of the main and fore cabins. Ulla's small, round face rose in the opening.

"Linda, Leida, and Karen are all wet," she said. "Is Karunass wet too?" she asked Yuta, who was sitting in the cockpit with her grandmother.

"No," Yuta said. "I put him under my blanket and we all slept together, he and I and Margit and Mall." She indicated her dolls spread on the main cabin. "Aunt Juliana and Aunt Maia got wet and water dropped on the head of my mother and into her eyes and ears. Isn't that funny?" Yuta and Ulla burst into gales of laughter.

Aimi and Inga were now on deck. Although their faces were thinner and their cheekbones higher than they used to be, they were as gay and mercurial as ever. Inga had a thin pile of old newspapers under her arm which she began to spread on the main-cabin roof, uncoiling the end of the main halyard and laying the line on the papers to prevent them from blowing away.

"We're going to cut out all kinds of things," Inga explained, "fish, houses, boats, ships, flowers, everything."

"And whales," Aimi added, "and sharks. But first we have to dry the paper."

"I see smoke on the horizon," Lembit called from the helm, " a little forward of the port beam."

We looked. There it was, a dirty brown streak of smoke, low and drawn out northward before the wind. We followed the smoke for some minutes.

"Going south," Grandma P. said. "I can see funnel and bridge."

Harry was looking through his binoculars.

"Yes, a Liberty ship. We're still outside the Gulf Stream; low-powered steamers keep out of it when sailing south."

A little later as Maia stepped out of the cabin she was wearing a black well-fitting dress that we had not seen since we left Ireland, and what's more, a pair of good black shoes!

"It's a couple of hours too early," Lembit remarked. "The Statue of Liberty isn't in sight yet."

"This is in your honour, peacock Lembit."

"Me?"

"Yes, my boy. Let me be the first to congratulate you on your twenty-fifth birthday. It's nice you grew up." She shook Lembit's hand.

We all had forgotten his birthday except Maia and, it seemed, the other women of the main cabin. They shook Lembit's hand, one by one.

"That's what I call typically female, to remember such things in times like this," said Paul, and shook his head.

"Here, peacock Lembit, is something for you—a birthday present from the main cabin." Maia produced a small package wrapped in an old newspaper.

"Oh, thank you. . . . Thank you all." Lembit, quite

238

taken by surprise, slowly unwrapped the package. "Look at that!" he exclaimed. "Genuine Portuguese sardines! Wonderful! How did you manage to save them, Maia? Thanks again."

As we scrambled to get nearer, Lembit showed us the shining tin.

"Look at that, boys! The finest present I ever had in my life."

We stared at the little thing with bulging, unbelieving eyes. Heino suddenly left for the after cabin and returned a moment later with one of our metal plates. Paul had taken out his army jack-knife. Then after a strained silence Lembit said, "Paul, give me the knife."

While Paul took over the wheel, Lembit opened the can and poured its contents into Heino's plate.

"One, two, three . . . seven, eight, nine," Heino counted. "Nine large sardines!"

Lembit thought a minute, his forehead wrinkled under his curly hair.

"Cut each one into three pieces."

Heino did so.

"Now, let's see," Lembit said. "We have twenty-seven pieces. Aimi, Inga, Yuta, Ulla, come here and take two pieces each. That's fine, blondie," he said as each child passed by the plate, took her pieces and thanked him with a curtsy. "Every lady come and take your two pieces. No protests, please. No, no, Mrs. Paalberg, you must have your share, every one of you. That's my birthday wish. Take it, please.

"Still nine pieces left," Lembit counted. "Every male gets one piece. . . . But what will we do with the two extra pieces? . . . Me? No, ma'am, not me,' Lembit protested when Nora said that the birthday child should have them. "No, no, I refuse. . . . No—or . . .

239

Well, one, if you insist. But Maia, you have to take the last piece. . . . Well, they were your sardines, weren't they?"

Finally it was decided that Maia's mother should take the last one. Heino drained the oil from the tin on to the plate. "For future use," and so the festive birthday ended in peace and contentment.

However, this bit of fish soon made us madly hungry.

"My insides are all stirred up," Rommy complained. "I can hardly stand it."

Lembit proposed that we open our tin of peas. Everybody agreed, so he brought them up from the space behind the bunk. Unfortunately they proved to be not cooked but dried peas. Paul tasted them with his teeth.

"Hard as quartz," he said.

"We must soak them first," Heino decided. "We must soak them for twenty-four hours before we cook them."

"I'll pour my water ration over them," Lembit offered. He went for the water with his sheet-metal mug and when he returned, he said, "The water is almost gone. It'll last only two or three days if we keep using it at the present rate. Harry's going to cut our daily rations to half a mug."

He poured the water glumly over the peas in the aluminium soup pot. It did not cover them entirely. He looked up.

"Not enough!"

"Well, we can't use up all our water just for soaking peas, and we can't cook them to-day anyway, because we have to save our water for cooking rice. That one piece of fish just didn't do the trick," Heino said.

"How about soaking the peas with sea water?" suggested Rommy.

"Are you crazy? That would spoil them," Lembit shuddered.

"Well, don't use much of it. Just enough to cover them. That will save our salt. We haven't much left."

After further arguing, Rommy's proposal was accepted, and Heino added a little salt water to cover them, then he set the pot under the ladder.

Life did not stir again on the *Erma* until that evening. Heino sighted a steamer's lights on our port beam and called, "Look, the lights are green. She's going north." He knelt and touched the water. "It's warm as consommé. We're in the Gulf Stream at last." In his elation he gave Arvid a short butt of a cigarette, his last one, saying, "I've given up smoking."

"Thanks." Arvid reached for the glowing point in the darkness. "Yours lasted well. Mine were gone a week ago." He finished the butt in three puffs.

We were now moving along at a smart clip. The wind kept up all night and the next morning when the captains made their dead reckonings we were less than eighty miles off the nearest stretch of land at Cape Hatteras. But before we could shout, "Hurrah," Harry warned us that we couldn't land there. It was too dangerous—all shoals and tides.

"So what *do* we do? Not land at all?" Maia protested bitterly.

"We have to go to the nearest port. Wilmington, North Carolina, is only a hundred and twenty-five miles away."

"That would take about twenty-four hours if we get a good breeze," Grandma P. reassured her.

But at this moment we were suddenly becalmed. How could anybody be glad about anything under such circumstances!

The morning wore on. Nora opened her last tin of

241

soup. Rommy and Lembit started to cook our sea-watered pea soup, but the peas were still a little hard. Heino estimated that it would be at least an hour and a half before they were soft and ready to eat.

A little before one o'clock, when Nora came out to wash her empty pot, she glanced to port, stopped suddenly, then called out, "For Heaven's sake, what's that?"

Her call brought out every one of us, except pot-tender Rommy, and we saw something most of us had never seen before. About a mile away the eastern skies were covered with a thick but rather small blue-black cumulus cloud. Under its heavy outer edge there was a broad, dark column, widening funnel-like at its upper end. The surface of the sea under it was agitated, boiling with foam and spray. Its forward motion was scarcely perceptible, probably because it was moving in a direct line towards us. There was something actually monstrous and frightening about this strange apparition.

"A water spout," Harry called. "Stand by for trimming. You women better go below."

The women obeyed immediately—nobody spoke a word. A faint groaning sound reached us. As it grew steadily louder, the water spout advanced towards us, its cloudy head appearing wider and somewhat lower, a few smoky cloud fringes swirling around its mushrooming top and a ring of white spray flying around its slender foot.

Ellen and Maia crouched in the main companionway, anguish plain on their faces. Ellen asked Harry, "Is it very dangerous?"

Harry hesitated a moment.

"Not exactly. If it hit us it would be pretty bad, but I think we are out of its course by now."

242

He did not sound very convincing. The water spout was so close that the edge of the cloud was almost overhead. The pillar suddenly bent its upper end to the right. Simultaneously the funnel broadened, then reached down as if drawn by a monstrous draught. And while it kept widening like an opening fan, its foot separated from the sea level and dangled for a second, then the widening head stretched lower and the whole thing collapsed into a murky screen of rain. Only a few drops fell; the squall sailed across to the east just in front of us and did not change our wind which still blew from the west.

While we were talking about the water spout the skies closed in and looked to us now like those of a typical northern gale. The wind kept rising, and white caps streaked the water. Within five minutes the wind reached gale strength.

Once again Arvid leaped to the mast and reefed the sail single-handed.

"Don't keep her too close," he shouted to Lembit. "Keep the wind abeam."

Lembit obeyed and let her fall off the wind until she ran exactly north-east.

"Good-bye, Wilmington." Lembit waved sadly to the west. "It was nice being so close to you."

In our cabin we bachelors sat in sullen resignation. Rommy had finished cooking when the gale set in. He pulled the soup pot out from under the ladder, set it in the centre of the floor and laid out our plates and spoons. We all took a bite.

"This is poison," Paul spat out in disgust. Rommy tried a second spoonful and said, "It's a little salty but it's edible."

"It may be edible, but will our stomachs take it? It's not only salty; it's got a repulsive after-taste."

243

"There's nothing repulsive about it," Rommy persisted. "That's just the regular taste of sea water."

"How witty," snapped Paul, trying to swallow another bite.

Fighting back reluctance, we attacked our small portions of the soup, but, hungry as we were, it was hard to take. After a while Paul proposed, "Let's put some rice in it and cook it over again. Maybe rice will make it less salty."

His proposition was accepted unanimously and Rommy took charge of the re-cooking. When we tried the peas again we discovered that the new meal was scarcely better than the first. We ate a little of the bitter stuff but left some of it for "to-morrow." It had been a long time since we had failed to polish off the pot.

"After this tasty dinner, we need a longer smoke to-day," Paul said to Lembit, reaching under what he called his mattress (consisting of Lembit's and Paul's suits and underwear spread over the bunk) and pulling out a small paper bag of tea and an old newspaper. He tore off a piece of paper, poured a heap of the black, dry tea leaves on it, and then rolled it into a cigarette with the dimensions of a giant Havana. Then he lighted it and started to enjoy his after-dinner smoke.

For more than a week now, since his last Madeira cigarettes ran out, Paul had been puffing two big tea cigarettes daily: an after-dinner one and an evening smoke. After finishing the latter, Paul said, "It makes you feel cosy and drowsy, just ready for bed." Rommy smirked and said that it had knocked out Paul. Lembit, somewhat hesitantly, had joined his brother's experiment some days later, but nobody else did. "Better suffer a lack of tobacco than risk suicide," was Heino's opinion, and Arvid seconded him, saying that for him there was enough trouble in gales and calms. Why add new dangers?

Even now, after two or three days' practice, Lembit's attempts seemed a bit half-hearted. He coughed and complained that the stuff was a little rough on the chest. "Weakling," scoffed Paul. "It's good for your lungs. It clears them up. And it has good flavour, this Portaferry tea. God bless the good Irish for giving us tea."

Lembit did not answer. He puffed bravely and stared with bleary eyes through the smoke of the good Irish tea.

All the while the wind kept increasing. The *Erma* made wallowing progress as the billows carried her lengthwise and sidewise, bending and heeling her on their slopes, roughing her on their crests. No mountain mule could have had a harder time.

A little before midnight when Arvid came out he and Harry held a council.

"It's too damned much to eastward," Arvid said after looking into the binnacle. "Seventy-five degrees. We're going straight east. Hell, we can't afford that."

"Yes, but what'll we do? We can't put out the sea anchor in the dark."

Arvid did not answer immediately. When he did his voice was firm as if he finally had made up his mind.

"Let's sail close-hauled again, as close to the north as possible. She can take it."

He put the helm down. Slowly the *Erma* began to swing towards the north, closer and closer to the wind, weltering desperately.

"We can't quite make north-north-east," Arvid said

Harry nodded.

"Good enough under the circumstances."

In the morning the whole crew gathered round the binnacle and clung to the after-cabin roof as the *Erma* stumbled and bobbled along, and watched the compass with almost unbelieving eyes.

"We're nearing the shore again," Lembit exclaimed.

Throughout that day we held her parallel to the shore in spite of the gale.

28

FOR TWO days and two nights the *Erma* battled the gale. Towards the third morning while the women huddled desperately in their wet bunks, trying to keep the children warm, a strange new sound rose above the wail of the wind, feebly at first, but growing until it penetrated the barrier of the surrounding din. It sounded like a far-away melody eerily echoing the lament of the wind.

"What's that?" Grandma P. asked sharply.

Between gusts she could recognize clear human voices chanting, "A better land you cannot find than Saaremaa in summer time."

"My word," Maia exclaimed. "Arvid and Lembit are singing!"

Incredulously Ellen crawled out of her bunk and pressed her ear against the companion doors. The women were bewildered and fascinated. Somehow, this lively song, contrasted with the violence of the storm, seemed about as fitting as drinking at a funeral or playing cards under artillery fire. But it was good to hear.

> *"Come to our saun and look at our maids.*
> *See if they have their hair in braids . . ."*

Arvid and Lembit shouted the rollicking old song of their seaman forefathers, throwing it defiantly into the teeth of the storm.

*　　*　　*

At sun-up the next morning the barometer had

risen and everything looked brighter except that the wind blew the same full gale. Harry was at the wheel. Not long after it had become light his eyes detected something strange about the *Erma's* stern. He looked again, sprang up and almost threw the boat off her course.

"What's happened to our flag?" he demanded of Rommy, who was crouching opposite him on the starboard seat of the cockpit. Over the wet and shining stern the flagpole stood bare and slender, and drew circles in the flying spray. There was no flag on it.

"Who did it, do you know?"

Rommy shook his head.

"I don't know. Honestly, I haven't an idea." His eyes were wide with surprise and he sounded sincere.

Suddenly Harry burst into a quiet guffaw.

"You know," he said, still grinning, "I just can't get over it. While we're fighting the gale, he, whoever it is, feels so sure of our happy arrival that in the pitch dark, during the worst wash we've had, he fights his way to the slippery stern and takes down the Swedish flag. What a man!"

Rommy laughed too. After a minute he added, "Maybe he just hated to go down under a foreign flag."

All that morning we were pushed by the gale farther north and east, but by mid-afternoon the wind began to drop and soon the captains decided to set a new course to the west.

"It's not exactly west," Harry explained to the elated people looking out of the companionways. "Probably closer to the north-west, and that's just about the right course for sailing straight into the port of Norfolk."

In the growing twilight we counted once more the hours that separated us from the nearest port, but there was a difference; high spirited though we were, there was no open talk about our hopes. We had grown cautious, even superstitious, about saying anything lest we spoil our luck.

Later that evening, as the wind died to a light breeze, our spirits slumped, and by midnight when we were in a dead calm, a dull resignation took hold of us. Those who were lying in their bunks pressed their backs against each other to keep warm and tried to sleep, but their sleep was restless and uneasy.

At four o'clock Paul got up, mumbling that he did not want to sleep any more, and left the cabin.

"Hey, Lembit, have you noticed the wind?" he called to his brother, who had the watch duty. A few minutes later they both felt a light puff and then still another that lasted considerably longer. The brothers ran to the mast and grabbed the main halyard. The first rattle of the line on the sheaves awoke the people below, and the mutter of excitement and relief passed from cabin to cabin; "The sail is being hoisted. The wind is blowing again."

At daybreak it was blowing a full fresh south-westerly, lustily pushing the *Erma* before it. Harry ordered us to hoist the white sail. As it filled, the *Erma* regained her speed. Fighting through the crests, her slacked-out boom swinging threateningly with every pitch, she yawed considerably, but she was rushing on.

After Harry took a meridian altitude sight, the captains sat in the cockpit with their worn old chart spread on the seat between them and held another council.

"We're already past Norfolk," Arvid said, "so we'll have to head for the next inlet—Delaware Bay. If we could get behind the headland of Cape May we'd be safe."

"But from there it's a long ride to Philadelphia." Harry scratched his head. "We have no river charts and no fuel." He looked again at the chart, then put his finger a little farther up, just above Cape May on the curving shore line of New Jersey. "How about Atlantic City? Although it's not an important port, we can't be too choosy now."

They calculated the distances and found that it was about one hundred and eighty miles either way. Atlantic City appeared to be even a little nearer, so they decided to head for it.

"Now let's see about our food situation. December 9 is the day when we thought our supplies might run out. As to our cabin," Harry reported, "there still are bread crumbs and rice for one more meal—enough for to-morrow. Lembit, how's the after cabin?"

"Still rice for two more meals, I think, if we squeeze the portions to less than a half-cupful a head as we have for the last two days."

"I happen to know that Rommy finished his last flour yesterday," Heino said.

Harry looked back at Rommy's gaunt face staring out of the companionway. "Is that right?"

"Well . . . yes, but it's not so bad. It doesn't feel half as bad as I thought it would."

"Nonsense," Paul cut him short. "Naturally, we'll pool our rice. This means that the whole after cabin is O.K., Cap'n."

Arvid answered with a smile on his leathery face. "The fore cabin to-day made a final clean-up. It's all right, though. Aimi and Inga have decided that they can take three foodless days without even feeling it. And that goes for Ulla, Nora, and me."

A storm of protest rose. We offered our rice, of course, but Arvid didn't like it.

"A half-cup of rice won't make any difference," he said firmly, "and we won't miss the coast this time, so it doesn't matter."

"I don't give a damn if you start to starve a little earlier than I do," Lembit insisted, "but none of us would eat a mouthful knowing that the children are starving. I'm not asking to help you but I do ask you to keep us from throwing the last rice overboard. Because that's just what we'll do."

Arvid laughed.

"You certainly make it sound pathetic, but if you feel that way, I accept, and with thanks."

"That settles the food. As to the drinking water," Harry continued, "it only trickles from the spigot so to-morrow we'll probably have our last water. But it doesn't matter." Harry looked around at us with his shy smile. "We'll soon cast our mooring lines and, I hope, without even one foodless day."

That was bold talk from Harry, but it seemed justified and it clicked with our mood which, as always, fluctuated with the weather.

During the afternoon we saw ships again—it had been four days since we had spotted the last one—all headed south, far away on our port side. Another new sight was flocks of sea birds around us, terns, Arvid said. Their soaring and crying made us feel that the coast was just out of sight.

That evening the captains estimated that we had made about sixty miles during the last nine hours, our fastest sailing ever. Harry and I had the midnight watch. I stared out at the towering waves, feeling the hypnotic power of the wind and seas. Harry must have felt it too.

"If this wind holds," he said, "we'll tie her up about sundown."

I let the meaning of his words sink in; landing after fourteen or fifteen hours! I tried to imagine what it would be like. Would we have somewhere to sleep and food? What kind of reception would we get?

However, our hopes were dashed again, for the next morning the *Erma* was floating helplessly in a dead calm. Gales, calms—blown to the east, inching hopefully towards the west, up the coast and down again, but never able to get into port! It was as though we were bewitched.

As we were only about seventy miles from the coast, Arvid suggested that we start the engine. We had five gallons of oil left, enough for eight hours, even one or two more if we kept the motor running slowly. Harry conceded that it was better than nothing; so after several weeks of rest the old one-lunger breathed again. Paul set it low; at this rate the *Erma* made only three and a half knots and it would take us nineteen hours to reach Atlantic City, but at least we were making headway.

The day passed in a half-sullen, half-hopeful expectancy. The engine's dogged chugging was the only sound in the lifeless sea.

At about three o'clock we had our last meal. Everyone ate quietly his half-cupful of thick rice pudding, dallying over it, chewing it more thoroughly than usual. The barometer was 29.64 and falling.

By late afternoon the clouds had condensed to a uniform grey-blue cover and the *Erma* with her sails slack and useless plodded through the dusky gloom. Harry called both crew members of the watch to duty.

"I hope it won't be a strong blast," he said, "but it's better to be ready for everything." Then he ordered us to fill and light the compass lamp although it was not yet dark.

A few minutes later the gale struck us. The heavy masonite engine cover that Paul had lifted temporarily to the after-cabin roof was blown away in a flash. It fluttered high in the air like a small brown butterfly.

Harry had thrown himself on the wheel and called, "Reef the sail," then in the same breath to Paul, "Shut off the engine." I ran to the mast and grabbed the crank when Harry called again in a hoarse voice, "Douse the mainsail, quick!"

As I saw the reason, terror seized me. The *Erma's* port side was sinking under the water, her handrail covered with small, angry seas, Harry, at the halyard, whipped the line from behind the cleat. The canvas dropped with the suddenness of a released bow. It knocked me over, but the *Erma* slowly steadied herself and was saved from capsizing.

Then rain came, a cold, hard-hitting rain that poured in sheets. It was a savage, mean north-westerly, worse than all the previous ones. Harry, Arvid, Rommy and I stood in the helm cockpit, held fast to the cabin roofs and felt how the *Erma* was driven through the black, thick darkness—away from America. The consciousness of disaster was so concrete and close that we could almost touch it, a sticky, repulsive thought slowly rolling over and over in our minds.

After midnight a big breaker pooped us, covering the *Erma* completely. Arvid ducked behind the after cabin and held on while the waters cascaded over him, but Heino was thrown on the main cabin and only by sheer luck managed to grasp the edge of the skylight and thus escape being swept overboard. Below we lay in our bunks staring petrified at the ceiling that gleamed in the dim light of our single electric bulb, thinking, "This is the end. She can't right herself."

Hundreds of thin streams spouted down, pressing through every tiny crack. After a minute that seemed like eternity, she rose, however, and the rumble of seas returned. But the danger stayed with us. We lay awake, tense, drenched, nobody speaking, for this was the most instant peril the sea had flung at us. The *Erma* would be swallowed by this sea or the next, and we with her. For a long time—how long we did not know—we waited, and then, finally, we knew that she would pull through. Our muscles relaxed a little and we began to breathe normally. Presently we heard a buzzing that came from the port bunk and topped the din of the gale. It was the most reassuring sound we could have heard . . . Paul's snore.

29

WHEN DAWN broke we got our first sight of the tremendous seas, higher than we ever had seen them. And they were only four or five hundred feet apart as compared with their quarter-mile intervals when we were lying at sea anchor. Our horizon was limited whenever we slid down into a trough. From the murky bottom of one of these canyons I watched fascinated as a roller swiftly neared its crest.

"These seas are much higher than the *Erma's* mast. At least fifty feet, wouldn't you say?"

"Probably," Harry answered curtly. Something in his manner made me stare at him. The drawn face was the same, cheekbones projecting in the frame of his Finnish winter cap tied under his bristling chin, but his eyes were restless, and that was not like Harry. I sensed that for the first time he had lost his confidence.

Desperately I tried to think of something good to say about our situation.

"We can't be too much out from the coast. After all, we couldn't have been pushed very far last night—not more than fifty or sixty miles."

"Don't fool yourself," Harry answered between tight lips. "With this wind we would have made four knots even under a bare pole. We're at least a hundred and fifty miles from the nearest coast—somewhat north of Cape Hatteras."

I pulled my hand from my coat pocket and stuck it in the water that streamed over the deck. To my half-frozen fingers it felt warm. Harry was right, we were back in the Gulf Stream.

"Don't you think we ought to ask help of a passing ship?" I asked cautiously.

"Yes, it's the only thing we can do now, but we aren't likely to meet one in these waters. They are west of us. Maybe we'll soon be able to change our course." Then he smiled and his face didn't look so pinched. "After all, we did get through last night and it was pretty close."

When Arvid appeared in his winter overcoat, with his woollen seaman's cap pulled down over his ears, he seemed surprisingly cheerful. Instantly we felt less hopeless.

"Well, my lads," he said, "it's nice to be alive after our big night."

As he took over the wheel he looked astern towards the leaden wall of the nearing roller.

"We have to pull out of this place. The seas are more or less stabilizing, and I'll soon put her to the west."

And he did. It seemed to me something like a miracle. About fifteen minutes after he took over he started to "play" the *Erma* westward, degree by degree, point by point. Occasionally a roaring sea tossed her back, but Arvid cuddled and coaxed her.

"You have to say the right words at the right moment and make her turn when she feels like it." Our co-captain was enjoying himself; his eyes were shining.

The wind howled more fiercely as we steered closer to it, and the *Erma* danced more madly. I looked exultantly at the flying spray, feeling all of a sudden that this stormy sea was the most beautiful thing in the world.

Ducking into the cabin, I shouted, "We're going west." Immediately Rommy, Paul, and Lembit jumped out of the bunks and pressed beside me into the companionway. We smiled at each other and in a fourfold, hoarse-voiced chorus that we hoped sounded like an Indian war whoop, roared, "We're going west."

At this moment a sudden rattle sounded above, followed by a series of scraping noises.

"They're hoisting the mainsail," Paul exclaimed triumphantly. "Now we'll make headway."

When Heino came back from his watch he groaned as he wriggled out of his overcoat.

"Lumbago. I haven't felt it for a couple of years, but this cold and wet brings it back."

I made way for him to crawl to the inner side of the bunk. He groaned again.

"I must find something to wrap up my feet and knees—and my back."

"I don't see why the sea should cure Aunt Juliana's arthritis and at the same time give you lumbago," Lembit commented. "It doesn't make sense. How did you manage to become rheumatic so early in your life?"

"By courtesy of the Soviet Union," Heino answered shortly. "It made me live underground. You may not believe it, but a cave has more moisture in it than our *Erma*."

"In the summer of 1941?" I asked. "I didn't know you were one of the cave dwellers."

"Yes, during the siege of Tallin. And if you think a cave is a cosy spot with artillery shells popping over your head, you can have it."

Paul was re-living this period too; he glared at us as though we were a squad of Russians, and you could almost imagine him grinding his teeth. So Lembit tried to strike a lighter note.

"Don't you think that a slight rheumatism is a cheap

price to pay for being alive—or escaping deportation which means about the same as being dead?"

"Yes, I certainly do." Then as Heino's shoulder gave another twinge, he added, "But I wouldn't call it slight."

Presently, when our dinner hour approached and our stomachs began to nag us, Lembit burst out, "I could eat eighteen pork chops now and after that I probably could eat several more."

"It's just a question of getting used to hunger," Paul comforted him. "To-morrow it'll be better. In Norway I went without food for five days, and after three or four I didn't feel bad at all."

Lembit tried to crack a lugubrious joke.

"If we keep it up for two or three more weeks we won't need food then. We can abandon the habit of eating entirely."

This talk reminded us that we hadn't carried the last of the rice to the children, so I took the sack from the space behind the companion ladder—there couldn't have been more than a cupful or so in it—and climbed out. A biting wind hit my face but there was less spray flying, and the mainsail was a heartening sight.

Rommy was alone in the cockpit.

"New rules," he said. "From now on, we'll have only one man on watch at a time. We change every two hours so we can preserve our strength in this cold weather."

"They'll let us sail her single-handed in seas like these!" I was astonished.

"And why not?" Rommy was belligerent. "What's complicated about it?"

Going down the ladder to the main cabin I almost stepped on Harry who crouched before the port-side watertank, holding a mug under its cock.

"That's all the water I was able to drain out." He pointed to the mug that was partly filled with a brackish liquid. "About two cups; one and a half for the fore cabin, the rest for Yuta." He poured the larger part into another mug. Then we measured the rice. Yuta got a little less than half a cup; the remainder was poured back into the bag for Arvid's girls. I took the bag and the mug, climbed out and succeeded in reaching the fore cabin without spilling the water.

Nora started the stove at once. Inga and Ulla sat in the port bunk in their winter overcoats and Aimi knelt before it. They were busy cutting out figures. Inga, who held the scissors, did not seem hampered by her woollen mittens.

"They have used up all the paper so now they are recutting the old figures," Nora said.

The miracle of it! These children had forgotten their hunger and with a pair of scissors and some old papers they were building for themselves a dream world full of whales and ducks and fish.

Before I returned to the after cabin I stopped at the helm-cockpit. Shivering with cold I grabbed the pump handle.

"You don't mind if I take a few pulls, Rommy?" I asked.

Without awaiting his answer, I started to pull. The pump caught at once, and a flow of warm water streamed from the opening. It was good to give the half-frozen body a workout, to put the blood into circulation, even if it made your heart pound and your lungs gasp. Slowly I began to feel something like warmth inside.

At my fortieth pull Rommy interrupted me.

"Don't you think that's about enough for you?"

Not understanding, I stopped and sat on the edge of the after cabin.

"What do you mean?" I asked. He looked at me, surprised.

"It's not your watch, is it? It's not your turn to pump, so why do you interfere?"

Then it dawned on me. Pumping, the once-hated slave labour, had become a valuable way to help preserve one's life! I glanced at Rommy's shrunken face. During this last week the atmosphere in our cabin had become more tense. The feud between Paul and Rommy that had been at first half joking, half earnest, had now settled down into a sullen truce but it was there all the time beneath the surface. Somehow, without being conscious of it, Heino and I had drifted into Paul's camp and left Rommy isolated. Brooding, half-starved, he began to give way to morbid fancies. And according to Lembit, Rommy distrusted us all so thoroughly that he was afraid to be on deck alone at night.

In the after cabin an open suitcase covered the floor and another lay open on the starboard bunk. Lembit bent over them. There was scarcely room to step.

"How about this *Time* magazine?" Lembit held up a copy that had been given to us by the Scandinavian consul in Madeira.

"Not bad," Heino answered, "but it's too slick. Soft, unglazed paper is better."

"Well, I'm afraid we'll have to use our souvenirs and clippings." Lembit sounded resigned. "It's the only soft paper we have."

"What do you need paper for?" I asked, puzzled.

Without speaking Lembit pulled his shoes from his feet. They were low street shoes, new and brown when we left Sweden, now almost white with salt. Then he took a handful of papers out of his suitcase; pages of Stockholm's *Dagens Nyheter* covered with news pictures of Estonian refugee boats, and pages of Stockholm's Estonian newspaper with stories about the arrival of refugees. We had saved them for sentimental reasons; they showed the vessels in which we had escaped and the camps in which we lived; they were pictures of our friends on their arrival, tired but thankful to be alive. Among them was a half-page story with a picture of the "Estonian Armada" after Sweden agreed in 1945 to give back to the Soviet Union all the Estonian boats (for which they paid the refugee owners). There they were, more than six hundred boats gathered in Fridtorp Bay, from small rowing boats to two-masted schooners.

Lembit looked a bit apologetic as he wrapped the pages around his feet and stuffed them into his shoes. Then he rolled up his trousers, wrapped sheets around his knees and tied them with pieces of string.

"Time to go," Lembit rolled down his trousers and went out to take over his trick.

Heino began to stuff paper under the back of his coat.

"I hate to use this copy of *Paevaleht*. Do you remember it?"

I looked over Heino's shoulder. The sheet was dated 28 August, 1941. It was a half-triumphant, half-defiant editorial on the day the Russians left Tallin that had reflected and strengthened our mood, building up our hope that freedom would return—and our independence in its old democratic form.

"I wouldn't take it if I had anything else." Heino sighed, then he stuck the editorial into the toe of his right shoe.

30

A SNOW SQUALL whirled around us, cold gusts howled screeching through the *Erma's* standing rigging and left their trails filled with bewildering snow that melted instantly upon hitting the warm, bubbling water on her deck. Occasionally it blanketed out the mast and the luff of the sail from my eyes, but I tried to keep her as close to the wind as possible.

It was cold. For thirty hours we had been in a state of perpetual palsy. Every time I looked at my mittens, I felt rather sick. They were knitted in a pattern of black and white squares and stripes, just like the peasants' mittens in our museums, old-fashioned, solid work, rugged but warm. Mother had knitted them. Every time I wore them, something more painful than hunger stabbed me, and I didn't care whether I froze or starved or ever landed at all.

When Harry ascended from the companionway, there was a ghost of a smile in his eyes. "He certainly feels better than he did yesterday," I thought.

"We should sight land any time within the next eight hours," Harry said. "We shouldn't miss America this time."

At his words joy surged through me and made me suddenly quite warm.

"Yesterday morning you thought we were a hundred and fifty miles from shore, so if it weren't for the Gulf Stream we would be landing right now, wouldn't we?"

"Yes, if the calculations were right."

Just then the main cabin's slide opened, and

Grandma P.'s head rose from the opening. Now that hunger had drawn the skin tight to her skull she looked much more like Harry. She scanned the murk with impatient eyes.

"Are we still in the Gulf Stream?"

"Yes, we are." Harry took the mitten from his left hand and stuck his fingers in the water that occasionally came over the deck.

"I can't make it out," his mother said. "Maybe your dead reckoning isn't right. It's three days since you've had a chance to make observations. In any case, let's keep a sharp lookout to-night."

As Grandma P. descended and closed the slide, I suddenly felt cold again.

That night the cold was bitter. While Rommy was on deck keeping a fruitless watch, we shivered in our bunks. Suddenly Paul rolled off the port bunk, got down on his knees and pulled a bottle from under the after cockpit.

"My God! You're not going to light the alcohol," Lembit asked incredulously. "You'll set us afire!"

"We'll see." Paul sounded confident, and at the same time curious. I heard the cork pop, then the bubbling of the liquid being poured out. Then Paul struck a match and touched it to the alcohol on the floor. Instantly, and with an audible puff, the little cabin was full of glaring fire. I snatched a blanket to throw over it, but Paul held me back.

"The floor and bunks are so soaked, they won't catch fire."

He was right. The first flare-up died immediately and only a foot-high flame was left dancing above a spot of alcohol. We crouched around it as close as possible, absorbing the warmth. Our faces glowed, the blood stirred in our veins. Our shivering did not cease instantly, it even increased, but it was a warm enjoyable shudder.

When the flame burned down, Paul poured more alcohol, and after this too had burned, he did it again. Then he put the bottle away under the cockpit. It was almost empty and it was our last alcohol.

After a while I managed to go to sleep. When I awoke it was eight o'clock and Lembit was climbing out for his watch. In the port bunk Paul was lying on his side, his bent knees jutting over the edge, and the blankets grasped firmly under his chin. His beret had fallen off and his hair hung over his forehead. With every breath a cloud of vapour blew out of his open mouth. Behind him Rommy lay with his head buried under the blanket. It occurred to me that one of them had sat on the floor for two hours, because when Arvid had his trick all five of us had been free of duty.

When I went on deck the skies were covered with patches of low fog, but at ten o'clock the sun shone long enough for Harry to get a time sight, and again at noon. Then all stood around tensely like a party of defendants waiting for the jury's verdict. As Harry and Arvid came out of the main cabin I looked at the captain's face for a sign. It had been shaved that morning and looked smaller than ever, but there was no smile, no gleam in his eyes.

"We are about eighty miles from the North Carolina coast," he said. "The Gulf Stream probably is so strong here that it has held us back."

"Eighty miles!" exclaimed Maia. "Why not eight hundred?" She looked at Harry with wide-eyed alarm. Nora suddenly turned white. She said with bitter finality, "We won't be able to land at all."

For a moment we were silent, struck with consternation. Grandma P. snapped us back.

"What's the nearest port now?" she asked in a matter-of-fact voice.

"Norfolk again."

"How far?"

"About a hundred miles north-west."

"A hundred miles!" Maia rose and started for the forward cabin. Grandma P. ducked to let her pass.

"It seems to me that there's a special zone surrounding America," Rommy said, "and that it's very difficult to penetrate. Perhaps the most reasonable solution would be to stay in this *cordon sanitaire*. Only the supply problem is complicated." His droning, ironical voice enraged Paul who growled, "Does he think he's witty?"

Quietly we scattered, not looking at each other. A half-hour later I sat alone in the *Erma's* cockpit trying to keep awake. I was so weak that it was hard to keep my eyelids open. Suddenly I was hit on my left ear; the boom almost bounced me over the wheel. Hastily I looked around; the sea was the same grey, everything was the same except that my ear was aching and we were twenty degrees off course.

A strong, high-pitched voice shook me awake. Half dazed, I saw Ellen's yellow head in the companionway.

"My God!" she cried. "A ship, right here!"

I sprang to my feet, stooped and looked under the mainsail to port. There she was, a small dark ship not much more than a quarter of a mile away. She carried an American flag. Where had she come from so suddenly? Risen out of the sea? All at once the decks were astir. We were like a covey of twittering birds.

"A motor ship," Arvid said, "and about a thousand tons."

"Look, she's loaded with soldiers."

"No, they're Navy men. See their little white caps."

"They've seen us. They're coming nearer."

Despite our excitement our talk was curiously subdued. We were waiting for what came next. Then a booming voice megaphoned from the ship.

"Are you all right?"

The voice expanded like rolling thunder; it seemed to lift to the clouds and fill the universe. Arvid leaped to the rail, set his hands around his mouth and shouted, "No, we need food, water, and fuel."

"Come alee," the voice thundered.

Arvid took the wheel from me and as the *Erma* slowly turned towards the ship, Harry was busy tearing off his frayed, half-melted rubber coat that had become glued to his overcoat during these last few weeks. Ellen and Grandma P. were helping him. Meanwhile the ship—we could see no name, just the number 74—manœuvred herself into a west-east direction waiting for us. As we approached slowly, we made out her name painted across her stern, *John P. Gray*.

Heino lowered the mainsail and the little *Erma* slid in the lee of the steamer. The ship, that had appeared so small, now at close range looked high; her steel side, hovering over us, reached halfway up the *Erma's* mast. When we were close enough two lines were thrown from the ship which Arvid and I fastened to the main traveller and the windlass. Paul and Lembit arranged the rope fenders that had been lowered over the rail of the *John P. Gray* to lessen the impact. The rails of the vessel were lined with young men in navy jackets, wind jackets, working togs, and they were bending over the handrail shooting us with cameras.

"Got a bad thrashing, didn't you?"

"Quite crowded, aren't you?"

"Look, they have kids with them!" A bearded man directed his camera upon Aimi, Inga and Ulla, who had just come up with their mother. Yuta in her coat and tight hood held on to her grandmother and examined the strange ship gravely.

"That man has a genuine German Leica," Paul pointed to the man with the full beard. The questions continued to pour down.

"Where you from? Norfolk?"

"North Carolina?"

By now Arvid had made everything ready and ship-shape. "We're from Stockholm," he answered.

"Stockholm, what?"

"Stockholm, Sweden."

"Sweden! My God, that's impossible!"

"Look, these people say they're from Sweden!"

Arvid's statement caused quite a stir among the sailors. They were still firing questions at us when Harry stepped out of the cabin with the *Erma's* papers in his hand. I noticed that he had been applying a comb to his unruly hair. It hadn't done much good, but they wouldn't expect him to have it waved and set. He climbed up the rope ladder, was greeted by a young officer and disappeared behind the wall of men.

The sailors concentrated on us again.

"When did you leave?" "Why did you risk your lives in such a small boat?"

Arvid tried to explain the state of the refugees of eastern Europe, and I added a few words, but found my English inadequate. Often I couldn't understand a word the sailors said. As for making them understand that we came from Sweden but were not Swedes; that we were Estonians and that Estonia was . . . well, you can imagine what a mess we made of it. Lembit nudged me.

"Look how they smoke. See those butts. They practically throw away whole cigarettes!"

267

Just then two thick hoses were lowered to the *Erma*. "Diesel oil," called a squat man in oil-spotted overalls. "Where's your chief engineer?"

Paul was there already and with Lembit he dragged the hose into the cockpit.

"Hold it tight," called the swarthy man. "It comes under pressure." It did; in less than a minute after Paul had opened the cock of the hose nozzle, the tank was full and running over. The other hose was for fresh water. As soon as the starboard tank was full, Aunt Juliana and Ellen filled mugs with water and reached them up to us. We drank long draughts. Never in my life had anything tasted so good. Grandma P. sipped it appraisingly.

"Very good water," she decided.

Then cigarettes began to fall from the *John P. Gray*, whole packages of them. We tore away the wrappings. After a first drag Lembit smacked his lips voluptuously. Paul had no words at all, he just inhaled, looked at the cigarette in his hand, then exhaled with a long, half-whistling sound.

When Harry returned he handed to Arvid a pile of charts.

"Our position was right to the minute. We are a hundred miles from Norfolk."

"Hey, boys, hey." Loud calls sounded from the *John P. Gray* as a burlap bag was eased over the railing.

"Potatoes," shouted a man in a white Navy cap. Heino spread his legs wide and held out his arms waiting for the bag. He must have been a bewildering sight to the Americans with his hair sticking out from under his cap like a clinging vine and his trousers thrust into Harry's boots Cossack fashion.

After the bag of potatoes the sailors lowered a wooden box containing a ten-pound ham, the same

268

amount of bacon and pork, three dozen eggs, a bag of flour, bags of coffee and cocoa, twelve loaves of bread, twelve tins of condensed milk, a sack of sugar and another of salt. Harry tried to protest that it was much more than enough for one day, but the young man in the officer's cap called back, "You may need it. You can't tell how long you'll be making port."

But this wasn't all. One more box came down, filled with several cartons of cigarettes, a bottle of pure alcohol, several tiny bottles of brandy, a dozen pairs of woollen gloves, a dozen woollen winter caps and a pile of American magazines. Last came a can of kerosene for our primuses. The generosity of the Americans was so sweeping that we were stunned and at first we didn't know exactly what to do. Then Arvid clenched his fists together and shook them to the men above as a gesture of "thank you." The men shook back and cheered.

"Don't miss America this time," they bellowed.

It was time to part. Harry looked towards Paul in the companionway; he flourished the glowing blowlamp and answered, "Already heated." He climbed behind the engine, the old engine sneezed and spat a few times, then thought better of it and burst into a low steady rumble; the mooring lines flew back to the ship, and the *Erma* started to move. As slowly she turned around and set her nose to the north-west, the first heavy snow-flakes fell. We bared our heads and waved our caps towards the *John P. Gray*. Ellen and Nora took off their bandannas and waved them from atop the cabins.

"Goodbye," Nora called in her strong, clear voice.

The ship grew dim behind the curtain of snow and then, all at once, she wasn't there at all. If it hadn't been for the boxes piled about the deck we would have thought she was a dream.

31

WITH FUEL, water, food, not to mention shore charts, the *Erma* was a floating paradise. Even the snow seemed warm and comfortable now.

At our first meal we were cautious—a little ham and bread with coffee. Then we slept, and before midnight we ate again—eggs, ham and bread, and more coffee. And a pint of water! The engine warmed up the after cabin. In the morning we would land; nothing could stop us now.

"But suppose another north-westerly gale comes up. Our engines wouldn't help us then and we'd have to run out to sea again." Lembit spoke in mock seriousness, as if in our beatific state it was fun to conjure up fresh mishaps.

"And it's dead calm again outside," I added, playing the game.

"And the barometer has fallen a fourth of an inch during the last eight hours," Rommy piled it on.

"Cut out this foolishness." Paul was not amused. "If we have to claw off the shore, we'll come back after the gale. We have everything to last it out. Nothing can happen now."

"Theoretically, anything can happen to an old, leaky boat in a gale," Lembit said.

"The *Erma* can beat every theory, and you know it," Paul replied.

"Yes, but let's suppose . . ."

"No sense to it. Go to sleep." Paul was bored by this game.

We were so well fed and contented that none of us—not even Rommy—could keep awake to bait Paul. When I awoke at a little before seven and looked out, we were crossing a shipping lane, alive with heavy traffic. Harry thought they were boats plying between Norfolk and Baltimore. At one time we counted as many as nine side lights around us. The coast could not be very far away.

When I went down again, my cabin-mates were still asleep. It was pleasant to hear Paul's snores mingling with the gentle rumble of the engine. He was sleeping in his dungarees and beret, his left arm hanging over the bunk and resting on the clutch lever of the engine, his ears cocked to its voice even in his sleep. In spite of his devil-may-care attitude, he was one of those sensitive men who are always alert when on duty, whether waking or sleeping. Perhaps it was a heritage of the War. Suddenly he sprang to his feet, his stubbled face taut, and listened with such intensity that I sat up too although I did not hear anything peculiar.

"The engine, listen to the engine," he said in a hoarse voice. Now I heard. The engine's steady, low purr had changed to a louder rattle.

"It's the propeller. The screw is gone."

Paul thrust open the slide and ran out. I followed him to the companionway. He was kneeling on the stern leaning over the edge. Harry was watching him anxiously. Finally Paul straightened up and repeated, "the screw is gone."

Harry raised his eyebrows in bewildered unbelief.

"Yes, it's true." Paul jumped down into the cabin, kicked out the clutch and shut off the engine. Coming back up, he reported to Harry, "It's the shaft, the rusty old shaft. When we put on a new screw in Stockholm we didn't replace the old shaft. It's broken clean through."

Harry, apparently, was at a loss for words. At last, he said, "That's too bad."

Paul winced at this understatement, but all he said was. "It's a shame. And just when we had a tankful of good oil!"

Harry looked up at the skies. They were covered with uniform, low clouds that had no snow or rain in them. The wind was light to moderate, blowing from north-north-west, and there was only a low, gentle swell rolling on the sea. He patted the boom with his mittened hand.

"We'll do all right," he said.

But Paul would not be solaced. He came down and sat on his bunk a beaten man. He was not even interested in the fact that we were still making headway.

* * *

"Land!" We sighted it the same morning, 14 December, at thirteen minutes before nine o'clock. Nobody knew exactly who had been the first to see it. Arvid and Lembit were on duty, Nora and Ellen were outside and Grandma P. and Aunt Juliana were watching from the companionway. Suddenly the chorus of their voices sang out, "Land! America!"

Through the dim light of the cloudy morning we saw a narrow, yellowish-white strip, quite low on the western horizon.

"It's the low, sandy beach of North Carolina," Arvid said, "or maybe Virginia." He tried to be matter-of-fact, but I noticed that his hands were trembling.

We moved restlessly. Aunt Juliana still could not make up her mind that the shore was a reality. She stared and stared, then said, "At last . . ." Her voice broke, and she hastily retired from the companionway. Like most northern people she did not like to show her feelings.

Grandma P. did not move. During the next hour as we neared the shore she kept her eyes fixed on it.

"One hundred and twenty-seven days since we left Stockholm; fifty-six days since Madeira," Rommy counted.

"Fifty-six days! I feel as if it had been fifty-six years." Maia's voice was exultant. "I hardly remember Madeira."

Lembit could not restrain his high spirits. It did not happen often, but when he did break out of his reserve he acted like a delirious schoolboy. Now he slapped the backs of Paul, Rommy, and Heino, gestured towards the shore and kept repeating. "There she is. There she is. The land of liberty, gold, and honey."

Then after waltzing Maia around the deck to the delight of the children, he tried to climb the mast. He made only a few feet and slid back, but this was good enough for the children, who laughed at Uncle Lembit's antics. He, himself, was disgusted at his weakness.

"Still short of fuel," he said, breathing hard and thumping his chest. "Let's eat."

Soon the smell of ham, pork, and coffee spread through the *Erma*. It was probably the heaviest breakfast any of us ever had eaten. But before we fell upon the food we opened the tiny bottles of brandy. Arvid came into the helm cockpit, lifted his mug and said, "Let's toast America." He paused a moment, then added, "And let's drink to something more—let's hope America will clean up the messy world and put order

273

in it, her own kind of order, so freedom will not be lost."

We fell silent. Arvid's simple and halting words made us gulp. He had never been like this before.

"And let's drink to our friends and relatives who are worse off than we are. Maybe, some day, some of them will be saved."

"Amen," we said. For many minutes we ate and drank slowly and reluctantly, but, growing hungrier and hungrier with the taste of food, we finished every bit of the rich breakfast. When we came on deck again, the yellowish strip extended all along the western horizon. We could make out trees and patches of undergrowth, even cars no bigger than cockroaches running along the sandy flats.

About a mile offshore we tacked up along the coast towards Norfolk. Our progress was painfully slow; except for the exciting knowledge that we were skirting America, the low desolate beach did not offer anything of interest. For hours we zigzagged back and forth, a short half-mile stretch offshore on our port tack, then back again. There were no ships in sight. All this lonesomeness seemed strange. Where were the people and the buildings?

At noon when I came on duty, Harry gave me the task of cleaning up the deck and putting everything shipshape. During the last hectic weeks small things had been neglected. The chain that we had used with the sea anchor had been left lying in the bottom of the after cockpit. I dragged it back and slid it into the chain pit. A piece of old rope on the windlass post, soaked and full of kinks, had to be straightened out and the whole coiled down. Harry saw to it that not even a foot was left over.

Everybody was making a quick check-up on what

274

was left of his clothing. It was not much. Our aim had been to have one more or less clean set of clothes for our arrival, but only the women and children were that lucky. With purely female ingenuity the women had saved for themselves and their children dresses that were not spotted with salt and mould. But clothes were not very important any more; all this inspection went on only as a necessary part of putting the boat in order.

The weather did not change. At four o'clock, when the daylight started to fade, Ellen asked Harry, "Where's Norfolk? Shouldn't we have sighted it by now?"

"About twenty-five more miles to go," he told her. "It will be sixteen or seventeen hours."

"So we have to spend another night on the boat." Ellen was surprised. She shivered. "It's cold."

We all felt it; surely it was the coldest night of the whole trip. The spray on the deck froze to a thin layer of ice. In the darkness we slipped and fell as we handled the sheets. Luckily we were able to keep the primuses burning and every little while those of us who were in the cabins reached out mugs of hot tea to the shivering watchmen.

To make matters worse, many of us began to feel ill. Up to this time one or another occasionally had been bothered with a sore throat, but it had cured itself. Now, all of a sudden, half of our party couldn't swallow. Arvid said this was because of our closeness to the shore. On the open sea, he added, you don't catch cold.

Slowly we skirted the coast in the pitch-dark. The frequent red mast lights of airfields served us as markers. After midnight a vague, flashing light started to show ahead.

"It's the beacon of Cape Henry," Arvid told us. "After we round this, it won't be much farther to Norfolk." Presently he said, "There it is." He pointed to a faint, reddish glow in the northern sky.

It was not yet quite daylight when we rounded Cape Henry and, following the twisting coastline, set our course to the west. The wind had risen with the dawn, and as it now blew abeam, there was no need for tacking, and our progress was much faster. Closer to the shore we began to feel the shaking of the tidal currents and the dirty grey swell raised by an on-shore breeze.

We sailed now in lively traffic; Liberty ships, Victory ships, long-bodied oil tankers, big and small transport ships, and almost all of them packed with troops. They still wore war paint and carried guns. We noticed two modern Swedish cargo steamers, the yellow cross and blue background painted large in the middle of their hulls. Not one of them took any notice of us; none of them guessed that this worn, turtle-bodied sloop of ours that flew no flag was from the other side of the ocean.

Towards nine o'clock snow began to fall. It came with a strong wind, and so thickly that it cut down the visibility to a mere hundred yards. Arvid took over the wheel and Harry held the chart on the cabin top, alternately staring at it and looking about us to spot the markers. It would not be so good to run aground or have a collision at the very entrance of the port.

Suddenly, Arvid asked, "Do you have any wrecks or sunken ships marked on the chart?" There was a sharp edge to his voice.

"No, not here. Why?"

"Look at the darned compass. Magnetic trouble."

We rushed to the binnacle and saw that the compass

was indeed crazy; it fluttered, jumped back and forth, sometimes made a full circle but did not rest for a moment.

Harry shook his head.

"Maybe we're sailing over an old and unmarked pile of junk."

"Well, we can't sail this way." Arvid asked if we were near a small port, a cove or inlet.

Harry ran his finger over the snow-blotched chart.

"Here's one called Little Creek. It should be just about abreast of us and it looks pretty wide." We stared in the direction of the coast, but all we could see was a blurred wall of whirling snow. "Pretty soupy," Harry drawled.

Arvid shrugged.

"All right," Harry said. "Rommy, go to the bow and keep a sharp lookout." He himself went astern and paid out the main sheet as Arvid bore her away. "I hope it *is* the direction of the shore."

To our surprise we had our answer in about five or ten minutes. Suddenly a low object rose to starboard; it emerged as a streak of bush and rapidly grew larger. Arvid put the helm up hard, spinning the steering wheel. Rommy grabbed the boat-hook from the railing and ran to the bow. The bushes ahead receded. We pursued them as they slowly curved inward. The swell was dying until it was scarcely noticeable. The shore slowly moved by to starboard; vegetation, stretches of low, snow-covered flat land, then a barn-like building that appeared and disappeared in the blizzard. The silence of the inlet was disquieting after the howl of the wind.

Grandma P. who had been watching us sail into the harbour, called from the companionway. "We may run aground." But her voice was eager.

"So what!" Arvid laughed. "We can let her sink now, can't we? It's only a short way to wade."

Grandma P. laughed too—I had never heard her laugh so heartily. "But we might just as well let down the mainsail. It's pretty shallow water."

Arvid nodded to Lembit, who went to the mast. Then, above the flapping of the mainsail we heard Rommy's voice.

"Ship ahead."

A small, slowly chugging vessel came out of the snow, bearing straight down towards our port bow. Paul, standing beside me in the companionway said, "A small mine-sweeper."

The boat slowed down and came alongside. A young man in an oilskin coat and an officer's cap with ear flaps, looked down from the camouflaged bridge and called, "Mine planter *Schofield* from Little Creek Army Mine Base. Who are you?"

"Sloop *Erma* from Stockholm," Arvid answered.

"Oh, you're the one the *John P. Gray* reported." He said something to Arvid that I couldn't understand—something about a plane. Then he spoke into his engine-room speaking tube and with a low roar the *Schofield* began to bear off. "Follow me," the captain called to us. She moved ahead in low speed, and we sailed close in her wake.

"Arvid," I asked, "what was the captain telling you about a plane?"

"He said a plane had been sent out yesterday to search for us but couldn't locate us. They thought we might be in distress again."

"Really!" Grandma P. was very much surprised, and so was I.

"They sent out a plane to look for a refugee boat!" Rommy couldn't believe it.

278

Soon the dim outline of piers, buildings, and boats rose ahead. The stream broadened and turned, and a quay with many jutting wooden piers stuck out before us. The captain of the *Schofield* motioned us to come along to the piers. As his boat turned away, he called something to a small band of men ashore who started to run towards the pier for which we were heading. These young men in Army work clothes caught our lines and secured them to the high mooring piles. One of them asked us something, but the others just kept watching us with silent curiosity.

All this and what followed seemed to us like a sequence in a motion picture, as if our minds suddenly had been caught unprepared and could not understand that it was real.

Soon the piers and the quay were crowded with men in uniform. A ruddy-cheeked officer, a Captain Russell, introduced himself to Harry and Arvid and appeared to be inviting our party ashore.

And there we were, leaving the boat in our motley, salt-spotted outfits, only half-believing it. The four little girls went first, hanging on to the hands of their parents, looking wide-eyed at the almost silent crowd of men. Aunt Juliana clung to Maia's arm, feeling the ground swaying under her, then came Heino in his damp and wrinkled monk's cape, with Maia's shawl wrapped around his sore throat.

We entered a long building. The warm air and the long-forgotten atmosphere of a human living place nearly overwhelmed us. In the glow of the coals in the fireplace our cheeks smarted. Friendly men offered us hot coffee. This was an American Army Base officers' mess, and our voyage was at an end. Captain Russell, friendly and courteous, said something to Harry which he repeated to us.

"The immigration officials of Norfolk will be here in half an hour."

Despite the imminence of the fateful meeting we did not feel much suspense. I think we understood that, whatever the decision, we would not be forced to leave immediately, we would have time to sit and rest. For the moment that was what mattered most.

As for the children, they did not care to sit or rest; already they were romping around. Young officers gave them candy until their hands were full of it, but this did not keep them from running back and forth, chasing friendly "uncles." Their laughter rose high to the cross beams of the ceiling. Already they felt at home.

★ 32 ★

AMERICA WITH its strange ways and friendly people excited and dazed us. The long peaceful nights, three plentiful meals, and, above all, the new feeling of safety, were in their way as bracing as the presence of danger.

During the first two days ashore we gradually returned to the likeness of human beings. The immigration doctor gave us a clean bill of health—there was nothing wrong with us except loss of weight; the barber of the Base trimmed our monstrous growths of hair; the commander distributed to us men Army sweaters, woollen caps and mittens—our women, as we said before, had somehow managed to save clothes for themselves and the children. We revelled in hot showers. It was wonderful!

On the third day we were told at the Norfolk Immigration office that since we had no visas we could not hope for permission to stay, but that we had a right to appeal to the Attorney General. So we signed our applications and were released on parole to await the final decision.

On the same day Captain Paalberg arrived from Lakewood, N.J. It was a joyful meeting between the old sea king, his wife, and the son he had not seen for almost six years. He gave his daughter-in-law a quick once-over and a hearty handshake that meant acceptance, then threw Yuta into the air and caught her in his Herculean arms. Yuta, surprisingly, accepted this vigorous treatment with complete calm.

The captain took his family, Maia and her mother

281

to Lakewood for the duration of the parole, Arvid and his family were quartered in a small apartment, and the rest of us moved into the Norfolk Navy Y.M.C.A. The help of the Travellers' Aid and contributions from the Estonian Relief Society tided us over these first weeks while we were waiting for the decision of Washington and could not look for work.

We struggled to adapt ourselves to America, and to its freedom of thought and speech which struck us as astonishing, although we ourselves had enjoyed the same freedoms only six years earlier. It was difficult to straighten out the kinks that years of suppression, suspicion and tension had wound in our minds. Now and then we discovered subtle remnants of irritations and jealousies of each other for which there was no reason, and occasionally our relations with the outer world were coloured by our tense attitudes.

For example, there was the episode with a Navy Air Force sergeant who was quartered on our floor. Soon we discovered him furtively trailing us wherever we went. This instantly aroused our suspicions—undoubtedly the man was a Soviet spy.

We planned to catch him. It was not very clear what we intended to do with him when caught, but catch him we must. So one day, when Paul, Lembit, and I were walking down the stairs and spotted our man peeping down at us from the next floor, we went into action. Lembit and I ran upstairs after the fleeing sergeant while Paul stormed to the other end of the floor to cut off his escape by the opposite stairs. We met Paul midway on the next floor, but the sergeant had disappeared. I bounced up to a Navy M.P., a giant three-hundred-pounder, excitedly explained to him that a Soviet agent was roaming around, and asked him to help us in our search. It is doubtful that he understood a word I said. He looked very bewildered and finally laughed and walked away.

The next day one of Paul's Navy acquaintances told him that the sergeant was mentally defective. It was an obvious explanation but none of us had considered that possibility, so sure were we that we had discovered a spy.

After five weeks of suspense, we were notified by Washington that we had been granted visitors' visas for six months. This did not solve our problem permanently, but it was better than being turned down, and it did show us that there was sympathy for us in the United States. It seems that Captain Russell of the Army Mine Base, who in civilian life was a Washington lawyer, had interested one of the capital's foremost law firms in our case and that the firm had represented us without charge. Then too, Captain Paalberg's friends and the Estonian Consul General said a word on our behalf; the latter guaranteeing our political reliability.

It was understood that we could get a six-month extension of our temporary quota. We all submitted our applications. The Estonian quota was so small and so heavily oversubscribed that there was not much hope, but momentarily we were not worried. Each of us started to look around for work.

Arvid got a job in the Norfolk shipyard, Rommy found something with the local Lutheran church and Paul and Lembit worked in an auto repair shop. Heino obtained permission to go to New York to a childhood friend. Two weeks later he wrote me that— true to his tradition—he had visited the local Y.M.C.A. and had been given work in the checkroom of one of the branches. Why didn't I come to New York too? Why not, indeed!

Stubbornly, almost resentfully I dismissed the warning of our kind guardian at the Travellers' Aid. She told me that the big city would be a tough place for a stranger and that it took money to move about in the United States. But I had a bus ticket and nearly a whole dollar in cash. Why should I worry?

On the way I stopped off in Philadelphia to visit an Estonian engineer, a friend of one of my friends in Sweden. He lived in Ridley Park, a remote suburb, and it was almost ten o'clock in the evening before I succeeded in finding his house. But nobody answered the door bell, a possibility that I had completely overlooked.

Until well past midnight I walked about in the vicinity of the house, but the engineer did not come home. It was a cold night, particularly for a man without an overcoat. Shivering and clutching my last sixty cents, I began to understand what the agent of the Travellers' Aid had meant. At last I made up my mind to stop a patrolling police car and ask for help. This was a desperate step, conditioned as I was to fear of the police and without proper knowledge of the language or any papers whatsoever. But the policeman with the big Boy Scout hat turned out to be a friendly fellow.

"Sorry," he told me, "our station house is cold, the heating system has broken down." He thought for a minute. "Why not stay here in my car? It's warm. Come on in."

So I stepped in and throughout that night we circled around his district. Every half-hour he stopped by a police phone box and called the Estonian's number, but nobody answered. Several times we checked on the parked cars in the streets and lanes, turning the searchlights on them. The flustered occupants—the policeman taught me that they were called "necking couples" —hastily drove away. Once he apologized to an embarrassed young couple and later said, "I know them both, they are very nice people." All of which puzzled and interested me. This was seeing America in an entirely new light.

Towards morning I was awakened from a doze by the wailing of the siren. We were chasing wildly after a speeding car. We caught up with it, and the driver, obviously intoxicated, was duly presented with a ticket. At last, at six-thirty in the morning, the engineer arrived home, and I left my new friend the American policeman.

        *   *   *

During the past six years since landing we have been working and learning to know and like American customs. Somehow our visa difficulties have been overcome, although in different ways. Harry and his family were lucky because their applications had been made by the old captain before we left Sweden. They will become citizens any time now. Nora, fortunately, was born in Moscow and was admitted under the Russian quota, practically unused since 1917, and with her also, Aimi, Inga, and Ulla. Arvid followed them with a simple Estonian visa, almost four years later.

Maia, Aunt Juliana, Heino, and I, tired of waiting for our turn under the Estonian quota, made new applications under the D.P. law of 1948. I have had my final hearing and at the moment am waiting for the papers to arrive. In New York Heino went through much the same procedure, but with Maia and her mother complications arose. The immigration office, no doubt after the unpredictable fashion of all immigration offices, sent them deportation orders. Poor Aunt

Juliana was frightened no end. But now she and Maia believe they will find a solution.

As for Paul, Lembit, and Rommy, they had a fantastic bit of luck. In the spring of 1946, while they were peacefully at work on their various jobs, they received greetings from the United States government and an invitation to visit the Norfolk Draft Board. This was a mistake, they knew, but a mistake that tremendously appealed to them, so they went and were drafted. After eighteen months of military training all were given their honourable discharges. Rommy entered Springfield University in Massachusetts, and the brothers found jobs in Miami. Then, out of the blue, Paul and Lembit received another letter, this time a deportation order from the immigration office.

"This must be a mistake," Paul said. "Let's get a lawyer."

They found one who pointed out their service in the United States Army, and ten days later in the same courtroom Paul and Lembit were solemnly sworn in as United States citizens.

Rommy, hearing of this, decided that he had been tardy in letting Paul get ahead of him, and soon followed suit. During his training in the Army he had suffered from his old war wounds and had been taken apart and put together again by service doctors. A year later he made both the soccer and track teams of his university. He graduated in two years, in sociology, and is now a social worker in Boston.

While Lembit in Miami was collecting money for the city's parking meters and cleaning the guns and rifles of the city police force, he was planning how to learn more about plastics, with which he had worked in the Army. He married an American girl, moved to California, graduated from a plastics school in Los

286

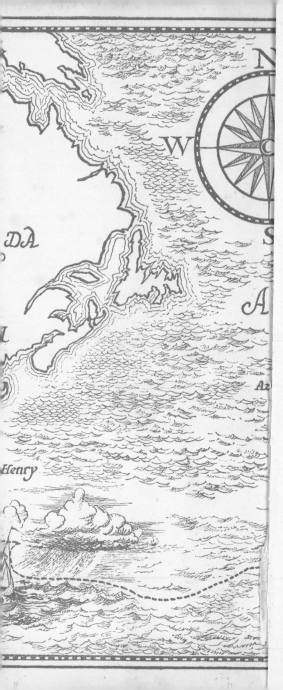

Angeles and now is working in his chosen field.

Angeles and now is working in his chosen field. Paul's life in the New World has been a little less stormy than in the Old, but not without its adventures. After a series of jobs ashore, he went back to the sea and worked as engineer or captain on several motor yachts. He married, was divorced and married again. For the last few months nothing extraordinary has happened. Could it be that Paul is settling down?

Heino, after being connected for more than a year with the Y.M.C.A., worked in New York drugstores for a while, and is presently employed as a technician in a therapeutic research laboratory. He is studying at night and will soon be getting his chemistry degree from Upsala College.

Harry was a mate on his father's ships until the grand old captain died. Now he and a partner sail a new fifty-eight-foot fishing boat. She has a 275-h.p. diesel engine and is quite an improvement on the *Erma*. Yuta is growing into a lovely blonde like Ellen and now has a little brother who, at the age of four, is so mechanically minded that he can tell the difference between a Chevrolet and a Cadillac.

As to Grandma P., neither the years nor the death of the captain have been able to break her. She looks considerably younger than her age. The same is true of Aunt Juliana. The miracle of the voyage has stayed with her; not a trace of arthritis is left in her, and she says she feels better than ever before in her life. She lives near the Paalbergs, not too far from New York where Maia is doing social work in a Lutheran Mission and studying at night at Hunter College.

Arvid is still living in Norfolk and recently moved into his own house. Aimi and Inga have grown into attractive young ladies. Ulla, who was in New York with her mother in the autumn of 1946, entered a

"Tiny Tots" parade of the International Women's Exhibition and with her naturalness, lovely blonde curls and native costume, she stole the show. She won top honours and a picture in the *New York Times*.

As for myself, I have been a janitor, millinery clerk, messenger, painter, translator, farm hand, labourer, factory worker, florist, sales clerk, in New York, Ithaca, and Vermont. There were hard days, and jobless days, but altogether it has been an interesting time. I discovered, as so many before me have discovered, that one meets the greatest friendliness and kindness among people who work with their hands.

And finally I must tell you the fate of our beloved old *Erma*. When we landed she was in poor shape, as you can imagine. She leaked at every seam, and during the first bitter cold days that immediately followed our landing, her bilges froze. In March of 1946 we sold her to a Baltimore shipyard owner for five hundred dollars, which price we thought was not too low, considering her condition. The new owner repaired and refitted her completely and sold her to a Washington lawyer for a family pleasure boat. The last we heard of her she was doing fine. Harry still believes she is indestructible.